DAILY GUIDEPOSTS

2015

Guideposts

New York

Daily Guideposts 2015

Regular print ISBN-13: 978-0-8249-0467-8
Large print ISBN-13: 978-0-8249-0468-5
Faux leather half-jacket ISBN-13: 978-0-8249-0469-2
Faux leather O-ring ISBN-13: 978-0-8249-0470-8
E-pub ISBN-13: 978-0-8249-0471-5
E-pdf ISBN-13: 978-0-8249-0472-2

Published by Guideposts Books & Inspirational Media
110 William Street
New York, New York 10038
Guideposts.org

Distributed by Ideals Publications, a Guideposts Company
2630 Elm Hill Pike, Suite 100
Nashville, Tennessee 37214

Guideposts, Ideals, and *Daily Guideposts* are registered trademarks of Guideposts.

Acknowledgments

Every attempt has been made to credit the sources of copyrighted material used in this book. If any such acknowledgment has been inadvertently omitted or miscredited, receipt of such information would be appreciated.

Scripture quotations marked (AMP) are from *Amplified Bible.* Copyright © 1954, 1958, 1962, 1964, 1965, 1987 by the Lockman Foundation. Used by permission.

Scripture quotations marked (ASV) are taken from *American Standard Version of the Bible.*

Scripture quotations marked (CEB) are taken from *Common English Bible.* Copyright © 2011 by Common English Bible.

Scripture quotations marked (CEV) are taken from *Holy Bible: Contemporary English Version.* Copyright © 1991, 1992, 1995 American Bible Society. Used by permission.

Scripture quotations marked (ESV) are taken from *Holy Bible, English Standard Version.* Copyright © 2001 by Crossway Bibles, a division of Good News Publishers. Used by permission. All rights reserved.

Scripture quotations marked (GNT) are taken from *Good News Translation.* Copyright © 1992 by American Bible Society. All rights reserved.

Scripture quotations marked (JPS) are taken from the 1917 or 1985 edition of *Tanakh: A New Translation of the Holy Scriptures according to the Traditional Hebrew Text.* Copyright © 1985 by the Jewish Publication Society. All rights reserved.

Scripture quotations marked (KJV) are taken from *The King James Version of the Bible.*

Scripture quotations marked (MSG) are taken from *The Message.* Copyright © 1993, 1994, 1995, 1996, 2000, 2001, 2002 by Eugene H. Peterson. Used by permission of Tyndale House Publishers, Inc.

Scripture quotations marked (NAS) are taken from *New American Standard Bible.* Copyright © 1960, 1962, 1963, 1968, 1971, 1972, 1973, 1975, 1977, 1995 by the Lockman Foundation. Used by permission.

Scripture quotations marked (NET) are taken from *New English Translation Bible.* Copyright © 1996–2006 by Biblical Studies Press, LLC. http://netbible.com. All rights reserved.

Scripture quotations marked (NIRV) are taken from *New International Reader's Version.* Copyright © 1996, 1998 by Biblica.

Scripture quotations marked (NIV) are taken from *The Holy Bible, New International Version.* Copyright © 1973, 1978, 1984, 2011 by Biblica, Inc. Used by permission of Zondervan. All rights reserved worldwide. www.zondervan.com.

Scripture quotations marked (NKJV) are taken from *The Holy Bible, New King James Version.* Copyright © 1982 by Thomas Nelson, Inc. Used by permission. All rights reserved.

Scripture quotations marked (NLT) are from *Holy Bible, New Living Translation.* Copyright © 1996, 2004, 2007, 2013 by Tyndale House Foundation. Used by permission of Tyndale House Publishers, Inc., Carol Stream, Illinois 60188. All rights reserved.

Scripture quotations marked (NRSV) are taken from *New Revised Standard Version Bible.* Copyright © 1989 by the Division of Christian Education of the National Council of the Churches of Christ in the United States of America. Used by permission. All rights reserved.

Scripture quotations marked (RSV) are taken from *Revised Standard Version of the Bible.* Copyright © 1946, 1952, 1971 by Division of Christian Education of the National Council of Churches of Christ in the United States of America. Used by permission.

Scripture quotations marked (TIB) are taken from *The Inclusive Bible: The First Egalitarian Translation.* Copyright © 2007 by Priests for Equality. All rights reserved.

Scripture quotations marked (TLB) are taken from *The Living Bible.* Copyright © 1971. Used by permission of Tyndale House Publishers, Inc., Carol Stream, Illinois 60188. All rights reserved.

Andrew Attaway photo by Doug Snyder; Evelyn Bence photo by David Singer; Brian Doyle photo by Jerry Hart; Edward Grinnan photo by Jane Wexler; Rick Hamlin photo by Nina Subin; Roberta Messner photo by Jan D. Witter/Camelot Photography; Elizabeth Sherrill photo by LifeTouch.

Cover and monthly page opening design by Müllerhaus
Cover and monthly page opener photos by Shutterstock

Interior design by Lorie Pagnozzi
Indexed by Patricia Woodruff
Typeset by Aptara

Printed and bound in the United States of America
10 9 8 7 6 5 4 3 2 1

Hello, my friend.

Imagine the year ahead filled with love and goodness each dawn, all day long, and at dusk. Fifty-two companions from *Daily Guideposts 2015* will share their triumphs and struggles and walk with you through the year. Their collective offerings reflect this year's theme, "Filled with Joy."

"May the God of hope fill you with all joy and peace in believing, so that by the power of the Holy Spirit you may abound in hope" (Romans 15:13, ESV). This Scripture offers the promise that God's great love is sustaining you. Begin each day with gratitude and praise: the blessings are already here!

Welcome newcomers Shawnelle Eliasen, Carla Hendricks, Kim Henry, and Stephanie Thompson.

We said good-bye to beloved *Daily Guideposts* contributor Marilyn Morgan King, who passed away peacefully at home. And Isabel Wolseley, Gina Bridgeman, Oscar Greene, and Dolphus Weary stepped down after years of inspired writing.

During Holy Week and Easter, in the series "A Turkish Lent," Gail Thorell Schilling embarks on a trip to the land where Jesus walked. During Advent, Mark Collins finds peace that surpasses understanding in "Gifts of Joy." Every month Elizabeth Sherrill is thrilled by the "God of Joyful Surprises," Marci Alborghetti finds rest in the weeklong series "Making Marriage Work," and Julie Garmon learns to say to God, "I Surrender All."

Many more snapshot-blessings await you inside *Daily Guideposts 2015.* You'll come to experience that infinite, all-knowing, all-loving connection with God, whose greatest delight is filling you with hope so that you may abound in it all the days of the coming year.

Faithfully yours,
Keren Baltzer, *Daily Guideposts* Editor

CONNECT WITH US ONLINE

Whether you use Facebook, Twitter, or send hand-written letters, we want to connect with you.

Find us at DailyGuideposts.org and Facebook.com/DailyGuideposts. Or follow us on Twitter@DailyGuideposts.

Write to us: DailyGPEditors@guideposts.org or *Daily Guideposts* Editor, Guideposts Books & Inspirational Media, 110 William Street, New York, NY 10038.

DAILY GUIDEPOSTS IN YOUR IN-BOX

Enjoy the faith-building inspiration of *Daily Guideposts* wherever you are! Receive each day's devotion on your computer, tablet, or smartphone. This is a valuable benefit Guideposts offers only to members of the *Daily Guideposts* family. Visit DailyGuideposts.org/DGP2015 and enter this code: joy.

JANUARY

You make known to me the path of life;
in your presence there is fullness of joy;
at your right hand are pleasures forevermore.

—PSALM 16:11 (ESV)

Thu 1

What is your life? You are a mist that appears for a little while and then vanishes. —JAMES 4:14 (NIV)

Most of my life has been spent waiting. Whether I'm on the phone with the phone company (oh, the irony!), pondering whether my boyfriend would ever propose (He did and we married in 2009!), or just sitting at a red light, wait I must.

This year has been a trial in waiting. I waited to learn if my job would evaporate. I waited to hear from God if now was the time to expand our family. I waited three weeks for a piece of mail that finally arrived with no apparent reason for its delay.

Each time I'm forced to wait, I remind myself of a quote that I read online: "In Spanish, the verbs 'to wait' and 'to hope' are the same: *esperar.* Waiting is negative; hoping is positive. So try to wait with hope. This will help you remember that you're on your way to something worth waiting for."

How often do I wait with my arms crossed, foot tapping, an eye-roll cued up and ready to go? How many hours have I wasted with my eyes narrowed on the clock? A life of frustration is not what God wants for me. God calls me to share love, to seek others, and to rejoice in creation.

Our moments here are not promised, but they are precious—and I plan to embrace each one.

Lord, I praise You in Your great wisdom.
Even across languages, Your Word speaks
volumes and brings light unto my path,
teaching me to wait hopefully.
—ASHLEY KAPPEL

Digging Deeper: JOB 5:16, 11:18; PSALM 25:21

Fri 2 *Being confident of this, that he who began a good work in you will carry it on to completion until the day of Christ Jesus.* —PHILIPPIANS 1:6 (NIV)

My family was set to move from Virginia to Florida. Dad was leaving his job as an accountant to go to seminary. Afterward, we would return to Virginia and he would become the assistant pastor at our church. Then the unexpected happened: I got cancer. Seminary plans were scrapped as my life hung in the balance for a year, and those plans were never recovered even after I did.

I did not get the feeling Dad blamed me for his lost dream; he is a man of deeper faith than that. He was just confused as to why God would place such a burden on his heart if ministry was not meant to be part of his career.

It's been nineteen years since my family took that detour. I now live in the Washington, DC, metro area about two hours from where I grew up. Dad recently accepted a job as an accounting manager for the very church I attend, and he is elated. He thought he needed seminary to do God's work, but it turns out God had a different plan.

I'm not naive enough to think God is in the business of fulfilling all of our dreams in this lifetime, but sometimes He lays an idea in our hearts for a reason. And seeing His faithfulness in my dad's career reminds me that there are times when what seems like a door shutting is actually a message that we need to wait patiently until God opens a different door in His own time.

Lord, please give me patience and faith to wait for Your perfect timing. —JOSHUA SUNDQUIST

Digging Deeper: PROVERBS 3:5–6, ISAIAH 40:31

I SURRENDER ALL

Sat 3   *Take every thought captive to obey Christ.* —2 CORINTHIANS 10:5 (ESV)

DISCOVERY

It was time to choose a new one-word theme for the next year. Usually, a word slips easily into my heart. Not this time. *Surrender* kept circling in my mind, but I didn't want that word, didn't think I needed it.

Yes, I'd become a workaholic. Sometimes I even skipped meals, exercise, and my quiet time—whatever it took to get the job done.

Desperate for another word, I plodded to my prayer chair and opened *My Utmost for His Highest* by Oswald Chambers. I wanted something fun like *joy* or *freedom*. Instead, *surrender* leaped off the page... twice! Suddenly, the words I'd learned while attending Al-Anon years earlier came back to me: *there must be a surrender of the will... I must surrender myself completely to God.*

I got the book with the Twelve Steps down from the shelf and skimmed them again. Step Three jumped off the page: "Made a decision to turn our will and our lives over to the care of God as we understood Him."

Thoughts came quickly. Using a red pen, I didn't stop to edit myself: "My relationships. My plans. My goals. My fear."

God's spirit squeezed my heart: *There's more, Julie. Go deeper.*

I wanted to hide under my prayer chair. I hated the truth. "Putting my job ahead of You, Lord. I've cared more about pleasing people than pleasing You. Forgive my pride."

Finally, I admitted the difficult truth: my priorities were a mess.

Father, I see now why You've given me this word
for the year. What's on the other side of it?
Please help me get there.
—JULIE GARMON

Digging Deeper: PROVERBS 4:23

Sun 4   *I have learned to be content whatever*
the circumstances.
—PHILIPPIANS 4:11 (NIV)

My pity party was in full swing when my two-year-old sidled up to me in the kitchen and asked, "Mommy, where is your happy heart?"

Prisca's intuition nailed me. My heart was happy for so many reasons, even as my face betrayed my stress. It was happy because I was well loved and well sheltered, because I had food to eat every single day. It was happy because I lived in freedom in a free country, free to worship a good God. For all the big, important reasons, my heart was as happy as could be.

And yet... for all the small, less important reasons, I was totally down in the dumps. I could confide in my child, but really now, how do you explain deadlines and angst to someone who's not even three? I took the conundrum to heart. If I wanted to train my beloved daughter to keep the important things in life as the main things, then she needed to witness my doing the same.

I rolled back my shoulders, exhaled my immediate frustration, and hugged little Prisca tight to my leg. Attitude adjustment accomplished; the half-pint's intervention had worked.

Thank You, Father, for making the way for happy-heartedness to be within reach.
—Ashley Wiersma

Digging Deeper: 1 Thessalonians 5:11

Mon 5

The Lord your God is going ahead of you....
—Deuteronomy 1:30 (NLT)

When I sat down to write my resolutions for the new year, I looked back through my journal to resolutions I'd made over the last twenty years. "*Hmm,*" I said to my friend who'd met with me so that we could write our resolutions together, "it seems that each year my resolutions are basically the same. Eat better, exercise more, and read my Bible daily." I shut my journal. "I don't want to write a laundry list of things to do this year."

"I have an idea," my friend said. "How about we write our resolutions based not on things to *do* but based on how to *be*?" She opened her journal. "A friend shared some ideas with me the other day. I think they are just what we are looking for." She read, "Be prayerful. Be trustful. Be obedient. Be forgiving. Be faithful. And, finally, be a follower of Jesus."

"Wow, these are great resolutions!" I said. "I must admit, though, they seem like a pretty tall order. I mean, without even knowing what will happen, we are resolving to handle everything this year as true followers of Christ. I love the idea, but it's a bit daunting."

"Let's remember this thought then," she said. "What's important about this new year is not *what* is ahead of us but *Who* is ahead of us."

Jesus, I know You will never lead me into
anything You won't lead me through.
Help me to be a prayerful, trustful, obedient,
forgiving, faithful follower of
You this year. Amen.
—MELODY BONNETTE SWANG

Digging Deeper: JOSHUA 1:9, JEREMIAH 29:11

GOD OF JOYFUL SURPRISES

Tue 6   *They were amazed and filled with joy....* —LUKE 24:41 (NIRV)

STEP-BY-STEP

I used to hate the month of January. Christmas was over, spring so far away, nights so long. Then I began attending church and discovered a very different calendar. Christians call this darkest time of year the season when we see the light. They named it *Epiphany,* focusing on four different times when God "shows forth" who Jesus is: the coming of the wise men; the baptism in the Jordan; the wedding feast at Cana; the Transfiguration on the mountaintop. And each epiphany is a total surprise.

The wise men were certainly surprised to find the newborn "King of the Jews" housed in a stable in a backwater town. John the Baptist must have been amazed to discover that the Christ whose coming he'd been proclaiming so forcefully was none other than his own cousin Jesus, a carpenter from Nazareth.

The Messiah's first miracle would surely be something spectacular, like feeding a multitude or raising the dead. Instead, it was an ordinary domestic crisis. The wine had run out at a party, and only the servants knew the best wine they were now pouring came from the water jar.

His three closest friends were with Jesus on the mountaintop when, radiant in light, He conversed with Moses and Elijah. Surely, the three disciples thought, this was the glorious climax to the story, but of course the story was only beginning. They had to take the journey step-by-step, and each January, I can join them on this surprising journey of faith. It's a wonderful month!

God of joyful surprises, show me Yourself as I walk step-by-step through this new year.
—ELIZABETH SHERRILL

Digging Deeper: JOHN 10:9–10

Wed 7

". . . Though He is not far from each one of us." —ACTS 17:27 (NKJV)

I was cramming my Christmas decorations into a closet and daydreaming about my "secret storage room." You see, our house is built on a steep hill, leaving a potential space under the garage for storage. But no matter who I asked, everyone insisted that the area, which was completely blocked in, would have been filled with concrete from the building site. Still, I dreamed.

This overflowing closet sure isn't my only problem, I thought, as a jumble of commitments filled my head. *Can I raise enough money to keep our Zimbabwe projects going? Can I meet the requests of a friend who needs my care? How am I going to come up with a year's worth of meaningful programs for an organization I head and fulfill my family and work obligations as well?*

A box tumbled from the top shelf and bounced off my head. "There's no room for all this stuff!" I wailed out loud.

Later that night, I woke to the sound of rushing water. I ran downstairs to investigate and found water everywhere. My husband called the insurance company, and the next morning I started pulling stuff out of my Christmas closet and moving it to a dry location.

David looked at the water-soaked drywall. "If we're ever going to solve your fantasy room mystery, this is the perfect time." He began drilling a hole in the concrete wall. Next, he inserted a long pipe through the hole. "Wow," he said, "it's hollow." Within a day David had cut a door into the mysterious room below the garage. All it needed was a plywood floor, a string of lights, and some storage shelves.

As I organized my new miracle space, I had a clear sense that God was swinging the door open and inviting me to store all of my worries with Him. Calmed by this expanse, I inventoried my duties, made a checklist, and did just that.

Father, I anticipate Your good gifts, Your secret rooms, Your opportunities for expansion. —PAM KIDD

Digging Deeper: PSALMS 34:10, 107:9; JEREMIAH 23:24

Thu 8

Those who are wise understand these things; those who are discerning know them.... —HOSEA 14:9 (NRSV)

My friend Kelly and I have pessimism in our DNA. It is such a relief to have someone to talk to who understands! Our conversations are a dark comedy that only we can see the humor in. "Who are you going to vote for?" one of us will ask. "*Phhsh*," the other will answer, "why not just flip a coin?" On the sunniest day of the year, we're scanning the forecast for the next storm. Our discussions often begin with "Don't you just hate it when...?"

But there is one difference that we've come to accept: I have a deep faith and attend church regularly; Kelly doesn't.

One night we were talking in the usual vein when Kelly hesitated. "Um, I'm on a new kick," she said. "I'm trying not to be negative."

What? I almost demanded in outrage, but there was something in her tone, so I waited.

"I don't want to get older and be angry and bitter," she explained. "But it's not easy to change."

She was right. Earlier in the year, I had tried to avoid saying one negative thing every day. It hadn't been easy, and I'd since let the practice slip. "Maybe I'll try again," I told Kelly.

She was pleased. "It should be easier for you, with your faith."

Though she'd meant it to be encouraging, it hit me full force. True faith does not indulge negativity, and neither should I.

Lord, help me to remember: if you can't say something good, don't say anything at all.
—MARCI ALBORGHETTI

Digging Deeper: MICAH 7:19

Fri 9

So I commend the enjoyment of life, because there is nothing better for a person under the sun than to eat and drink and be glad....
—ECCLESIASTES 8:15 (NIV)

"Can we have popcorn?" Solomon asks.
"And pull the couch out to a bed?" Henry chimes in.

"Sure," I answer.

"Yes!" Solomon clasps one hand into a fist and pulls it toward his chest as if he's just caught a wish.

Every Friday after dinner, we get in our pajamas and nestle under comfy blankets to watch a movie. Years ago when movie night first started, although my eyes were on the screen, my thoughts were worlds away on work or worries. But one Friday, in the midst of an animated feature, Solomon said, "Mom, you're not paying attention." So I made an effort to focus.

In *Up!* I sobbed as an old man grieved the loss of his wife. I sat on the edge of my seat as a little fish braved the ocean to find his dad. Last year my favorite movie was an animated feature about taming a dragon. "Yup, Mom's crying again," Solomon said, looking over at me as the boy put his hand on a fierce yet fragile dragon. "Henry's crying too," Solomon reported.

"I am not!" Henry answered. "I'm just tired."

Most Fridays Solomon and Henry don't ask what movie we'll watch. I guess they know what I've come to realize: it's not the movie that makes movie night special. It's our shared attention, laughing, crying, or even complaining that it's not the greatest film, cuddled together on our lumpy pull-out couch.

Dear Lord, thank You for these joyful everyday moments that bring my family closer together.
—SABRA CIANCANELLI

Digging Deeper: PROVERBS 17:22, ROMANS 15:32

Sat 10

Would not God have discovered it, since he knows the secrets of the heart?
—PSALM 44:21 (NIV)

My wife, Carol, is a dyed-in-the-wool Anglophile and so, naturally, we began watching *Downton Abbey,* a TV series about a British earl, his American heiress wife, and his family in early twentieth-century England. The series was catnip for Carol because years ago she coauthored a book called *To Marry an English Lord,* an anecdotal history of that phenomenon when American heiresses trolled English waters for British aristocrats to wed.

At the launch of the second season, an article appeared in a newspaper profiling the show's screenwriter, Julian Fellowes. As it turned out, Carol's book was his inspiration. She was thrilled.

"You should write to him," I said. "Tell him how grateful you are."

"I would love to," she replied, "but how can I find his address?"

There was the prayer or, at least, the unspoken prayer. The very next day, on my way home from work, I ran into two friends, one of whom happened to work for a British charity. The two women brought up Carol's six-degrees-of-separation connection to *Downton Abbey.* Without any prompting, the woman who works for the British charity said, "You know, I actually have Julian Fellowes's address."

The connection came from a prayer that neither Carol nor I felt bold enough to say out loud. It mattered not. God knows the secrets of our hearts anyway.

Lord, You know what we need and want better than we know it ourselves. —RICK HAMLIN

Digging Deeper: HEBREWS 11:1

Sun 11

"When they said, 'Let's go to the house of God,' my heart leaped for joy." —PSALM 122:1 (MSG)

I was traveling with a friend in France, doing research for a book I was writing about Gothic architecture. We were driving to every village and city within a hundred-mile radius of Paris with a significant church to see. Not a bad way to spend a week in the summertime!

I will always remember several of those magnificent churches, their buttresses and naves. But I will also remember an old man in one of them, late in the afternoon, all by himself.

I saw him fasten his bicycle to a lamppost in the courtyard outside the church just as we were strolling around. He gave us a quick glance and hustled inside. I followed. He was clearly the warden, responsible for maintenance and upkeep—everything from rearranging chairs after a service to picking flowers for the altar. He dusted the lightbulbs of the simple chandelier above the altar as if he were washing a baby's body.

My traveling companion spoke perfect French. He stopped the man and asked, "Sir, is it your job—to care for this church?"

"It is not my occupation," he responded. "It is my love. I am cleaning the courts of the Lord."

God, I am like a man hungry and thirsty today,
needing to be in Your holy presence.
—Jon Sweeney

Digging Deeper: Psalm 84:4, 10

Mon 12

Hear my cry for help, my King and my God, for to you I pray.
—Psalm 5:2 (NIV)

I feel that terrible Monday-morning surge of angst and adrenaline. I have to get started on my pile of work! No time for office pleasantries or chitchat. Suddenly, a ding sounds on my computer, an e-mail from a colleague: "Prayer Fellowship at 9:45 AM in the conference room. Everyone welcome."

Prayer Fellowship is a decades-long tradition at Guideposts. We sit together around the conference-room table at 9:45 every Monday morning, reading prayer requests sent in by our readers. Then we each choose one or two requests to read out loud. Someone leads us in a final prayer, and we get to work at our desks. Prayer Fellowship is completely voluntary, but at least a handful of editors always show up.

"No time for Prayer Fellowship this morning," I mutter, until I realize what I have just said. *No time for prayer? Really? Is there such a thing as a prayer-free zone in my life? Especially when I'm feeling stressed? No time for God?*

I look at the stack of manuscripts and the computer screen full of unopened e-mails. They can wait. Not because they are unimportant. Quite the opposite. They are very important.

I join my colleagues at the table. I read some letters that make my problems look like blessings by comparison. I thank God for the opportunity to work. And I do what I should have done first thing that morning: I ask for His help.

Father, there are times when my anxiety comes between You and me, when I am more concerned with worry than prayer. Let me never forget that prayer is the best way to prepare to meet my day every day.
—EDWARD GRINNAN

Digging Deeper: PSALMS 59:16, 88:13, 90:14

Tue 13

As we have therefore opportunity, let us do good unto all men....
—GALATIANS 6:10 (KJV)

The way I see it, these people just want handouts."

My heart sank deeper with each word the man said because I was responsible for his being here. For years I had worked at Nashville, Tennessee's oldest nonprofit mission. I had seen the center make life better for countless individuals. This was a meeting to attract volunteers, and the last thing we needed was negativity.

The room went still. Enthusiasm leaked like a deflating balloon. I looked at Marsha, the center's director, and was astonished to see her smiling. "Let me tell you a story about one of 'these people,'" she said. "One woman's children attend our Early Learning Center, and we're helping her continue her education. One day, she asked me, completely out of the blue, 'Why are you here, Miss Marsha?'

"Too busy to visit, I gave her some generic answer.

"She stopped me. 'No, that's not right,' she said. 'I know why you are here. God sent you.'

"Taken aback, I answered with a question: 'Why are *you* here, Rochelle?'"

We all waited while Marsha reached into a file and pulled out an envelope. "I got this note the next day."

"Dear Ms. Marsha," she read, "the center is here for anyone who wants to better themselves. I am living proof. God knows what I have had to overcome since moving into the projects. I asked God why this has happened to me, and He gave me the answer: I am here to help others. That's why I'm here. Sincerely, Rochelle."

Immediately, the earlier cynic raised his hand and said, "How can I sign up?"

Father, let me never lose sight of the gift of giving.
—BROCK KIDD

Digging Deeper: PROVERBS 14:21, MATTHEW 10:8

Wed 14

We are given no signs from God; no prophets are left, and none of us knows how long this will be.
—PSALM 74:9 (NIV)

Maggie is not well. I wish I could say what is wrong with my eleven-year-old, but it's not simple. "I am broken," she says. She is clinically depressed, anxious, fearful, erratic, suicidal. She has a good therapist, a social worker who comes to our home, medication, a supportive family, but things are not getting better. My heart bleeds as I watch my beautiful, bright, creative child suffer and shrink and suffer some more.

I am afraid. I am afraid for her and for us and for me. "Will she recover?" I ask God.

God replies quietly, *I am with you.* And that is all. God gives me no answers, hands me no solutions.

I watch my child suffer and pull the feelings from my heart to offer to God one by one: grief, sadness, love, hope, longing, determination, and what seems like either resignation or acceptance.

I say to my Lord, "I love You, even in all this. I will serve You, whatever happens." It's all I can do. It's all I can give. It's everything.

Christ Jesus, let every drop of suffering unite me with You more. —JULIA ATTAWAY

Digging Deeper: MATTHEW 6:10, 1 THESSALONIANS 5:18

Thu 15

How does a man become wise? The first step is to trust and reverence the Lord! —PROVERBS 1:7 (TLB)

Every day as my old computer got slower and slower, I'd moan and groan as I sat there waiting and waiting. I prayed that God was a computer genius who could ramp up my rams or gigabytes or whatever it is you need for speed.

One day someone sent me one of those forwarded e-mails that had the secret to growing older with grace, in six words: *Do not fear. Do not regret.* For some reason, those six words struck a chord with me. *Do not fear. Do not regret.*

I'd been fearing the idea of getting a new computer because I'd already spent eight years getting to know my old one and figured I'd just begun to master the beast. I didn't want to start over. I rationalized, *Maybe my old one will last me another eight years if I just learn some patience.*

But those six words kept flying through my brain until one day I leaped off the platform without a parachute, bought a new computer, and within two days was jumping out of my skin with joy. Talk about fast! Talk about easier to use! Talk about a gazillion more things I can do with it!

I started to think of other things I should stop fearing and just do without regret: apologize to a friend for a careless remark I'd made; let go of some of my hard-earned savings to pay for a trip for my husband and me; buy and wrap a dozen gifts and deposit them at the doors of a dozen strangers at the local nursing home.

Do not fear. Do not regret. I'm going to live by those words for the rest of my life.

Father, hold my hand and help me to step out, do the unusual, try new things, and know that You are there to help me through. —PATRICIA LORENZ

Digging Deeper: PROVERBS 1:29, 14:27;
2 CORINTHIANS 11:3

Fri 16   *And pray one for another. . . .*
—JAMES 5:16 (KJV)

As I stood waiting impatiently to be helped at a store, I became aware of the woman standing beside me. She appeared troubled, but no way did I have time to become involved.

A longtime friend named John came in. He and I hugged, and with a smile as wide as the Grand Canyon, he said, "As bad as things get in our lives, when we trust God, He will make every bit as good as the good things."

The woman standing near us said softly, "I hope so."

"Are you needing God for something?" John inquired, looking right at her.

She nodded. "My son's in jail and . . ."

"Well, this woman right here," he looked toward me, "is the one who can encourage you today." Despite my earlier intention, I had become involved.

"Well, yes," I said. "I'm sort of the queen of mothers with sons in jail. The thing I've learned is that God can work wonders in these confined places. And I've experienced some big-time trust. Right now things are . . . well . . . beautiful."

"Tell me your name and your son's," John asked as he draped an arm around the woman. He prayed for her and her son and for God's perfect will.

Business came to a standstill. I didn't hear any movement, voices, or machines humming—only John's intercession for the stranger. After his amen, she murmured to us, blinking away tears, "Oh, thank you so much."

Father, thank You for people like John who make outreach seem so natural. —MARION BOND WEST

Digging Deeper: MATTHEW 5:44, COLOSSIANS 1:9

Sat 17

That is why, for Christ's sake, I delight in weaknesses, in insults, in hardships, in persecutions, in difficulties. For when I am weak, then I am strong.
—2 CORINTHIANS 12:10 (NIV)

We were invited to a Saturday evening gathering and were asked to bring something for the dinner. I groaned when I saw that only salad remained on the e-mail list.

I don't do salads because mine always turn into limp lumps of wilted lettuce with too much dressing. So I avoid the inevitable flop by bringing my safe standbys of mushroom rice or chicken casserole—anything but salad!

I rechecked the list, looking for someone who might trade with me, when I saw a sticky note on my desk: "When you do hard things, your brain grows." I had written it down a few days earlier after hearing a talk about exercising our brains to make them stronger. The speaker explained the difference between people who avoid hard challenges and give up easily and people who embrace them with a desire to learn. "If you want to grow your brain, tackle challenges," the speaker summarized. So I'd been looking for doable ways to grow my brain.

Surely that doesn't mean signing up for salad, I rationalized as I did some easy tasks: putting wet clothes in the dryer, watering plants, taking the dog for a walk.

Several hours later I signed up to bring a salad and then started searching the Internet for recipes.

Lord, You nudged me toward this small challenge, probably not because You care much about unsoggy salads but about making choices to grow and change and be more fully alive in every season of life.
—CAROL KUYKENDALL

Digging Deeper: JAMES 1:4

Sun 18   *I call on you, my God, for you will answer me; turn your ear to me and hear my prayer.*
—PSALM 17:6 (NIV)

Have you ever heard of the Fly Lady? She runs a Web site that encourages folks to tackle one cleaning project every day: laundry one day, the baseboards the following day, vacuuming the next. The idea is, if you clean a little every day, your house will never get dirty.

One problem: I don't think the Fly Lady has kids. If she did, she'd know that even if I was to clean my baseboards on Monday and do laundry on Tuesday, come Wednesday there would still be a giant explosion of toys littering my living room floor and a pile of laundry waiting for me to find time to put away.

My spiritual life feels like that sometimes. I may spend a half hour on my knees on Monday and an hour in the Word on Tuesday, but on Wednesday, hopelessness, envy, and bitterness seep in. My tendency to rely on myself instead of God sneaks its way in the backdoor, leaving muddy footprints across my heart.

Half an hour here and ten minutes there with God just isn't enough. God asks us to rely on Him, to stay alert—not a little bit every day but every moment of every day.

Lord, I want my first instinct in every situation to be to turn to You in prayer. Amen.
—ERIN MACPHERSON

Digging Deeper: 1 CORINTHIANS 14:15, EPHESIANS 6:18

Mon 19

Rejoice in the Lord always: and again I say, Rejoice.
—Philippians 4:4 (KJV)

During my childhood, I remember twirling around in my tutu, pretending to be a member of the Dance Theatre of Harlem. Later I would stand in front of the mirror, reciting lines from *Porgy and Bess*. And still later I'd cry through Alex Haley's TV series *Roots*, thinking of how difficult the lives of my ancestors had been during slavery.

My parents didn't shield my sisters and me from our history. They made sure we knew it, understood it, felt it. They also quizzed us from time to time. *Who led the civil rights movement of the 1960s?* Dr. Martin Luther King Jr. *Who refused to give up her seat on the bus in Montgomery, Alabama, so a white man could sit down?* Rosa Parks. *What was the name given to the nine Black children in Arkansas who faced an angry mob on the first day of school, all for the right to attend the high school of their choice?* The Little Rock Nine.

These quizzes also included how I perceived and identified myself. *Carla, what color are you?* I dropped my eyes and looked at my fingers, my hands, my arms. After a thorough inspection, I declared, "I'm golden." My parents erupted into laughter.

It wasn't until I was a parent with four children of my own that I understood my parents' delight at my answer. My response displayed the simplistic thinking of a child full of innocence and wonder, and they loved that.

Today I'm taking a page from my parents' lesson book. Amid the chaos of endless housework, piles of laundry, and after-school activities, I'm learning to embrace the innocence and wonder of my own "golden" children.

Lord, help me find joy in the everyday responsibilities and duties of life and motherhood.
—CARLA HENDRICKS

Digging Deeper: PSALMS 5:11, 16:11; JOHN 15:9–11

Tue 20 *Teach me your way, Lord....*
—PSALM 27:11 (NIV)

A crowded Los Angeles freeway, twenty lanes of cars crawling in both directions, an orange sun squatting on a smoggy horizon—I couldn't have been happier. I was back in my favorite city, where I grew up and where I still feel most at home.

This visit was for a newspaper I once worked for, the *Orange County Register.* They asked me to write a column on religion. I live in San Jose now, so I make periodic trips south for business.

When I last worked for the *Register*, before I was married or had kids, I drove this same freeway every day to and from work, often late at night when deadlines kept me at the office. Now I watched the sun sink below the horizon and thought about how much has changed since that time. Kate. Frances and Benjamin. Moving to New York, then back to California.

I'd become someone who made a point of never staying at the office late because I think family is more important than work. Back then I dreamed of having a family. But, really, I had no idea what that meant. And yet then, as now, God knew what I didn't. He was leading me. He knew about Kate. He knew Frances's and Benjamin's names. He knows what will happen to them after they're grown and I'm gone.

I gazed at LA's endless horizon and suddenly saw it cupped in God's hands. I breathed in the cool, humid air and thanked God for every breath, now and to come.

> *God, You are with me always.*
> *Help me to follow Your lead.*
> —JIM HINCH

Digging Deeper: LUKE 12:6–7

Wed 21

You have turned for me my mourning into dancing....
—PSALM 30:11 (NKJV)

Unable to sleep, I pace the kitchen floor, staring out the window at the blinding white landscape. This has been a hard winter with one blizzard on top of another. The shrubs and trees are hanging low from the weight of snow. The house lights flicker, warning of yet another power outage. "Lord, give us relief from this snow. I feel imprisoned in my own house."

The next day there is a short break in the weather. Quickly I pull on my boots and head outdoors, where I begin to build a snowman. Soon I am so involved in my creation that I don't even notice the cold. I am packing snow with my bare hands and singing "Sleigh Ride."

I can see my wife laughing at me through the kitchen window and I grin back, feeling like a boy again. I shove some old baseballs into the head of the snowman for eyes and then pound a little flowerpot into his face for a nose. While I pose beside the snowman, Sharon takes my picture. The dark spell of winter is broken. The rest of the week I am relaxed, chirpy, and I begin to sleep again.

"There is something about play that engages a different part of the mind," I say to Sharon. "It frees up energy that has been under tension, you know?"

She nods. "No wonder children have so much energy. Play is their work, their career."

I reflect on how I used to play more when I was younger. I used to play practical jokes on my fellow teachers. I used to go fishing almost every day. I used to play catch with the neighbors' children. And so I prayed:

Lord, teach me again to play so that I don't break during the storms of life. —DANIEL SCHANTZ

Digging Deeper: ZECHARIAH 8:5, MATTHEW 11:28

Thu 22

Look at the birds of the air; they do not sow or reap or store away in barns, and yet your heavenly Father feeds them....
—MATTHEW 6:26 (NIV)

I was planning a trip to Israel and was extremely worried about the two-hour drive from the airport to the Birdsong Bed-and-Breakfast in a tiny settlement near the Sea of Galilee. My anxiety about finding the place went through the roof as I read the innkeeper's directions: "There's no house number. Just look for the bird statues on the gate."

Then a tidbit of information about how the bed-and-breakfast got its name caught my eye. Apparently, Israel is at the crossroads of three continents and every year one billion birds from 540 species fly over in the spring and autumn!

Jesus told us that when we start to worry to "look at the birds of the air." I'd always pictured a few tiny sparrows. Now I understood that when Christ's listeners looked up into the sky over Galilee, they saw thousands and even millions of birds filling the sky. Only a god of vast and unimaginable resources could actually feed all of those birds winging their way across huge continents.

I closed my eyes, tucking away the image of a sky darkened with birds in flight over the Sea of Galilee. It would serve me well as a prayer for trust and peace, not only as I drove to the B and B, but also whenever worry started to stress me out.

Dear Jesus, I trust You to provide for me. Amen.
—KAREN BARBER

Digging Deeper: 1 KINGS 17:1–6

Fri 23   *Assuredly, at such a time the prudent man keeps silent....*
—AMOS 5:13 (JSP)

I can't catch my breath."

The moment I heard my husband, Keith, say that, I ran for the phone and dialed 911. Before he retired, Keith was a swimming pool technician, and we were paying the costs of his having spent forty-four years breathing in chlorine fumes. He had had a stroke in May, but it was minor and left no lasting effects. Now it was July, and suddenly his lungs weren't working.

The doctors hospitalized him, and for the second time in three months I had to go home without him. The first time had been terrifying; this was, I could tell, no better. Our home is *our* home—to me, it isn't a home unless we're there together.

I didn't realize how poorly I was coping with being in the house without him until I noticed that I'd been turning on the TV sets in every room and forgetting to turn them off when I left. I wasn't watching or listening; I just needed the sound so that I didn't feel alone.

Looking for something else to distract me, I pulled out the journal of my trip to Italy. I'd had to go without Keith, and the journal began in fear. But as it went on, I began to see more evidence of blessings, because the trip had been filled with wonders.

I finished the journal, got up, and turned off the televisions. Keith might not have been there, but I'd just been reminded that I wasn't really alone.

Please keep reminding me, Lord, that You're in the silences, waiting for me to notice. —Rhoda Blecker

Digging Deeper: 1 Kings 19:11–12, Zechariah 2:13

Sat 24

"Do you look at things according to the outward appearance?..."
—2 CORINTHIANS 10:7 (NKJV)

Because I work in retail, I try never to be annoyed when someone holds up a line that I'm waiting in as a customer. Yet the woman ahead of me in the supermarket had an overflowing cart and two fistfuls of coupons. Even her son was in on the act with a small handful. I was getting impatient when I saw how long it was taking the clerk to finish. I didn't shout, but I did roll my eyes and tap my fingers on my plastic basket. *I only need these two things. If I'd gotten here a minute sooner, she might have let me go ahead of her.*

Finally, the cashier was done matching the items to the coupons, the tower of selections was rung up, and the mother and son gathered up their purchases. "How about that?" the cashier said to me.

Assuming she was as irritated as I, I was about to blurt, "How annoying!" when she continued, "They do this at the end of every single month, just when food-bank supplies are getting low."

At that moment, the boy piped up, "Mama, can we go to the food bank now?"

The coupon lady's eyes met mine. "I'm trying to teach him a lesson about kindness," she said quietly.

He's not the only one who could use a lesson, I thought.

God, today, may I excuse rather than accuse the people around me when I don't know their motivations. Let me see everyone through Your kind eyes.
—LINDA NEUKRUG

Digging Deeper: PSALM 28:1, JOHN 9:11, ROMANS 13:10

Sun 25

"So stay awake and be prepared, for you do not know the date or moment of my return."
—MATTHEW 25:13 (TLB)

The phone rang. It was my Realtor. "Bill," she said, "we have buyers who want to see your house today."

"Today?" It came out as a croak. "What time?" We hadn't shown our house in months. Preparing it would be a huge effort.

"One thirty."

As a pastor preaching multiple services every weekend, I look forward to nothing more than my Sunday afternoon nap. I did a quick calculation: by the time church was over and we got home, that would leave all of thirty minutes to make the beds, do the dishes, and achieve the miraculous transformation. We negotiated a 3:30 PM showing.

The afternoon was a blur of straightening, cleaning, hiding, vacuuming, dusting, folding, and otherwise perfecting our house. As a final touch, my wife loaded our two kids and two dogs into the car and drove off, with ten minutes to spare.

During those ten minutes, I sat and prayed for a strong offer. I also reflected on how hard it was to get ready for a showing. At first it wasn't; we stayed in a state of readiness. But months had gone by, showings dwindled, and our home took on its comfy lived-in vibe.

How much easier to stay ready than to get ready from scratch . . . just like with Jesus, I thought. Was I staying ready for Him? How much scrambling would I have to do if Jesus knocked on my door today?

We didn't get an offer that day, but I got something better.

Thank You, Lord, for the reminder to stay ever ready for Your appearance. —BILL GIOVANNETTI

Digging Deeper: MARK 13:35–37

Mon 26

"From where, then, does wisdom come? And where is the place of understanding? . . . God understands the way to it, and he knows its place."
—JOB 28:20, 23 (ESV)

This winter, our nine-year-old, Stephen, decided that he wanted to learn the Greek alphabet.

He's been reading children's detective stories set in ancient Rome; one of the main characters is Greek, and a few Greek letters form a clue in one of the stories. So with a printout of the letters he found on the Internet, Stephen went to work. In a couple of weeks he was able to recite the Greek alphabet, if not always in the correct order.

I'd been taking him on weekly homeschool field trips, and it seemed like a good time to visit the Greco-Roman galleries at the Metropolitan Museum of Art. We had a great time. We looked at a whole range of objects, from archaic Greek weapons to a complete room from a Roman villa. But what really fascinated Stephen were the inscriptions. He couldn't group the letters into words, and after calling them out, he'd look up at me and I'd try to make some sense of them; suffice it to say that my brief foray into Greek was a *long* time ago. Trying my hardest, I'd be able to make out a word here or a name there, but the grammar, as always, defeated me. Then we'd make our way to the next.

Lately it's been hard for me to see what message God is writing in my life. There are bits here and there that I think I understand; I can make out the letters, but I stumble over the sentences. And when that happens, the best thing I can do is stop relying on my own resources, trust the Author, and keep moving on.

> *Lord, even when I can't understand them,*
> *I know Your words are living truth.*
> —ANDREW ATTAWAY

Digging Deeper: PROVERBS 3:5

Tue 27

"But if you forget about yourself and look to me, you'll find both yourself and me."
—MATTHEW 10:39 (MSG)

I gripped the steering wheel of my vehicle as I flew down the highway. Mile after mile of gray wooden fence posts supporting strands of barbed wire flashed past. The road wound through large ranches with cattle grazing in the grassy meadows. The scenery looked peaceful, but I wasn't. I churned like a volcano ready to erupt. I'd been involved in a situation where I'd been repeatedly wronged and was driving to calm down.

I shook my head and raised my voice. "But, God, I . . ." On and on I ranted about my upsetting situation and then I slapped the steering wheel and yelled, "I'm finished!"

Finally I grew quiet. Only the humming of the tires on the road broke the silence. *It's really not about what you want,* I heard. *It's about what I want to do through you. When you talk about I, I, I, each one of those I's is like those miles of fence posts. When you rant and rave, you're stringing barbed wire between us. You've been fencing Me out.*

Tears streamed down my face. "Oh, God, I'm so sorry. What do You want me to do?"

Stay and be a witness for Me.

So I stayed. My situation didn't change. But I took control of my thoughts; I refused to let them lead me down the dark road of rage. Trusting the Lord and obeying Him despite my own desires brought me more joy than I ever could have imagined.

Lord, nudge me when I start putting I's where there should be Yous. Amen. —REBECCA ONDOV

Digging Deeper: JAMES 1:5

Wed 28

These commandments that I give you today are to be on your hearts. Impress them on your children. Talk about them when you sit at home and when you walk along the road, when you lie down and when you get up.
—DEUTERONOMY 6:6–7 (NIV)

On the entry gate of the fence that surrounded my great-aunt's house was a small metal box with what looked like squiggles to my seven-year-old eyes. "*Mezuzah* on the post lets everyone know we are Jewish," Aunt Frieda explained. Laughing, she added, "Mezuzah also reminds us that we are Jewish."

Hebrew for "doorpost," mezuzah is a small container placed by the doors of Jewish homes. The word *Shaddai* ("Almighty") adorns the box's exterior in Hebrew lettering.

My grandfather and his family are Jewish, but I'm a Christian. Yet on my porch, no emblem professes my religion or love for God. My house looks like every other on the block. Inside are furnishings, photographs, and figurines, but nothing shows my faith. God may be first in my life, but where is He in my home?

Finally, evidence of my belief: I have several Bibles, biblical references, and Christian titles. In all, I have at least ninety books that could give the impression that I am a woman of God. Yet, would ninety books in a library of more than six hundred volumes be enough to convince someone of my faith?

I love the Lord with all my heart, but there is little evidence of Him where I live. Maybe I should redecorate with God in mind. Not only will all who pass by know I'm a Christian, but like Aunt Frieda, I, too, could use visual reminders of my faith.

Lord, help me to be mindful of what I believe and how I show it. —STEPHANIE THOMPSON

Digging Deeper: EXODUS 20:2-3, PROVERBS 16:3

Thu 29

All things belong to you, and you belong to Christ; and Christ belongs to God.
—1 CORINTHIANS 3:22–23 (NAS)

I'm soon trading my familiar, cozy front porch in central Minnesota for our new home in northern Idaho. Our present home on a small acreage is angled toward a cornfield. From my front porch I have followed the farmer's planting and harvesting and watched wild deer and turkeys roam the fields. One autumn morning I was startled by a half dozen geese materializing from the fog, flying low over our house with a quiet *whoosh* of their wings. At twilight I've watched critters creep around in the low darkness, hoping that they weren't skunks!

Saying good-bye to my front porch is bittersweet. It's been friend and shelter for fourteen years. But there's a new place, near my elderly, frail mother, waiting for us. Still, I'm a lingerer. Since childhood it's been hard for me to let go. I do want new adventures, but I cling to what's familiar too. Jesus said, "The foxes have holes and the birds of the air have nests, but the Son of Man has nowhere to lay His head" (Matthew 8:20, Luke 9:58).

My life is not tied to a front porch. Neither does it depend on the dwelling or town that I live in. My life belongs to Jesus, wherever He takes me.

*When I think of Your itinerant journeying, Jesus, the
lives You touched and transformed in each place,
it gives me courage to pick up and go!*
—CAROL KNAPP

Digging Deeper: LUKE 18:28–30

Fri 30   *But those who hope in the Lord will
renew their strength. They will soar
on wings like eagles; they will run and
not grow weary, they will walk and
not be faint.* —ISAIAH 40:31 (NIV)

Good night," I said to my colleague. It had been
a long day, my body was tired, and the thought
of having to walk to the subway felt like torture.

I plodded along as I thought about everything I
still had to do. It made me want to stop right there
and stretch out on a park bench. For weeks, my
days had played out exactly like this one: I'd rush
in the morning to get my sons ready for school,
negotiating what they'd eat, what they'd wear, who
would press the elevator button. I'd sometimes be
too busy to stop for lunch. Back home my sons
would run around like little tornadoes as I'd fix
dinner, do laundry, straighten up, wash dishes, and
get them ready for bed.

Is my life always going to be this hectic and exhausting? I wondered.

I slumped onto a bench to wait for my train. Suddenly, a gentleman began playing his accordion. The music took me back to when I lived in France years before. My body relaxed, and the heaviness lifted from my eyes, my shoulders, and my heart. I thought of Paris at night and all the wonderful people I'd met during my stay. There was such adventure, wonder, and discovery then.

The man played on, and I felt a sense of hope. My memories reminded me that life wasn't always a struggle and wouldn't always be.

Lord, thank You for hope of a new tomorrow.
—KAREN VALENTIN

Digging Deeper: PHILIPPIANS 1:6

Sat 31

You make known to me the path of life; in your presence there is fullness of joy; at your right hand are pleasures forevermore. —PSALM 16:11 (ESV)

The single moment in the thirty million moments I have been allowed to live on this bruised, blessed planet that filled me most with joy? The moment our first child was hauled, startled and displeased, from the salt sea of my lovely bride. Talk about your miracles. I wept helplessly. My lovely bride was groggy but beaming. Our new daughter glared at me, a laser blast I would see all too often in the years to come, and then she fell asleep. That was the happiest I ever was. Ever.

I have been crammed and thrilled and overwhelmed and doused with joy from the waters of the Lord more often than anyone, I sometimes think: My daughter's mother said *yup* when I proposed, and our sons slid out of that same wild sea in later years, and I have been handed joy by the barrel as a writer, in letters and notes from readers who were moved and elevated somehow by my sentences. And no man ever was granted cooler, more gracious, more generous parents and siblings than I, and my lovely bride said *yup* again, with amusement, when I asked her to marry me this morning at breakfast.

But for sheer joy—unadulterated unprecedented, permanent, untrammeled, inimitable, holy beyond words? The moment when our first child slid into the world with her huge dark eyes clapped on mine. Meeting our twin sons as they emerged like circus clowns three years later, that was sweet and wild and astonishing. But the first time I saw a miracle with my own naked eyeballs and gently said, "Hello, Lily"—that was the day I was most filled with joy. So far.

Dear Merciful One, thanks. You know and I know my lovely bride and I did not think we would ever be able to have children and then You gave us a daughter! And then sons! And even when they are surly and grumpy and testy and sneering, I remember the vastness of Your gift and have nothing in my mouth but thanks. —BRIAN DOYLE

Digging Deeper: PSALM 127:3–5

DAILY JOYS

1 _____

2 _____

3 _____

4 _____

5 _____

6 _____

7 _____

8 _____

9 _____

10 _____

11 _____

January

12 _____

13 _____

14 _____

15 _____

16 _____

17 _____

18 _____

19 _____

20 _____

21 _____

22 _____

23 _____

24 _____

25 _____

26 _____

27 _____

28 _____

29 _____

30 _____

31 _____

FEBRUARY

For the joy of the Lord is your strength.

—NEHEMIAH 8:10 (KJV)

Sun 1

When they landed, they saw a fire of burning coals there with fish on it, and some bread.
—JOHN 21:9 (NIV)

It was an ordinary morning. I had a to-do list, breakfast to eat, and the weather was somewhat gray. I reached into the carton for an orange and saw on the side of the box in big letters: Fresh from the Field. The oranges were grown in Israel. *Quite a long journey from the fields*, I thought with a touch of cynicism.

Then I saw a smaller line, almost illegible: "Galilee Export."

The oranges suddenly seemed to glow. It was possible that these very oranges had grown somewhere Jesus might have walked! *Maybe He ate an orange. Did they have oranges in those days?* We hear a lot about Jesus's humanity and how He was "made man," but the paintings of an ethereal figure in a white robe don't always feel very human.

"He left Judea and went back once more to Galilee" (John 4:3). For me one morning in gray New York City, my breakfast transformed Jesus from Son of God and Savior of the world to a man walking in an orchard eating a juicy orange.

Jesus, You were human as we are human.
While we pray and worship, help us not to forget.
—BRIGITTE WEEKS

Digging Deeper: 1 JOHN 2:5–6

GOD OF JOYFUL SURPRISES

Mon 2 *The time of the singing of birds is come....*
—SONG OF SOLOMON 2:12 (KJV)

BIRD-WATCHING

I used to think bird-watchers were pretty ridiculous, but now I am one of those obsessed bird stalkers. The change happened the day my husband brought home a black case and pulled out a pair of large binoculars. He suggested: "They'll bring things up close."

But I resisted: "By the time I get them focused, the dumb bird will have flown away."

Patiently, he showed me how to twist the wheels to adjust for each eye. "Now look at something out the window."

The trees jumped wildly as I learned to steady the glasses. I picked the clothesline to practice on. Finally, I got a small stretch centered in both lenses.

Nothing, as I expected, only a metallic bluish blur. I twisted the wheels again and found myself staring at a tiny iridescent-blue bird.

What were the chances that I should have picked that particular spot and that a breathtakingly beautiful bird should have chosen that instant to land there? It was an indigo bunting, we learned when we borrowed a book from a neighbor, a species he'd never seen in ten years of bird-watching. And I heard God say: *You've seen My mountains and My starlit skies. Now let Me show you My birds.*

God of joyful surprises, what wonders will
You show me this day? —ELIZABETH SHERRILL

Digging Deeper: PSALM 40:5

Tue 3 *Become as little children....*
—MATTHEW 18:3 (KJV)

I was at the end of my rope. Driving home from work, I divided my immediate projects into two categories: the ones I could handle with a few intense hours at the office and those that were beyond my control, like the plum account I had knocked myself out to get and was now being decided by others. It was that big account that was stressing me out.

Sitting with my family at our favorite pizza place, my wife, Corinne, told me about her day, and fifteen-month-old Mary Katherine lavished her attention on my thirteen-year-old son, Harrison.

Mary Katherine adores Harrison, calling "Da" at the sound of his voice and following every step he takes. He reciprocates her adoration, reading books to her and playing tea party with her, an amazing sacrifice for a seventh-grader.

Now, with her high chair next to Harrison, Mary Katherine laughed as the waitress handed her a bright pink balloon. All was right with her world until a little boy from a nearby table reached over and grabbed the string. Mary Katherine gripped it with both hands, giving it her all, but it was obvious who the winner was going to be.

"Da. Da." She set her eyes on Harrison. Within seconds, the scrimmage was over, the little boy was back at his own table, and Mary Katherine had her balloon.

All she did was let go and call out her brother's name. I thought back to that choice account at work and knew what it was time to do.

Father, I've worked hard and given
it my all. Now I let go and trust You.
—Brock Kidd

Digging Deeper: Psalm 50:15, Nahum 1:7,
Luke 11:11

Wed 4

Comfort, oh comfort my people, says your God. —ISAIAH 40:1 (JPS)

Our cat L.E. is a talker and has an extensive vocabulary. She does have a normal meow and a soft purr, but she also yowls and howls, barks, warbles, chirps, squeaks, and makes a variety of different sounds for which my husband and I make up words like *murfing*.

She is most definitely Keith's cat. When it's clear he's going to leave the house, she complains by "chittering." She stares at him until he looks her way, then she deliberately turns her back on him and goes on complaining, biting off her chitters with apparent annoyance that he would dare go off and leave her.

So when Keith was in the hospital, L.E. did not know how to behave. She was surprised when I came home without him again and again. She wandered from room to room, searching. Now and then she'd let out a sharp call, as if summoning him to her presence. When he didn't come, the call morphed into a piteous meow of loss.

I had to comfort L.E. "It'll be all right," I found myself telling her. "Keith is being taken care of. He'll be back home with us before you know it."

Soon it became evident to me that because I'd had to convince the cat that there would be a good outcome, I was convinced as well. It was as if L.E.

had decided that the only way I'd have faith in Keith's coming home was if she made me keep saying it over and over again.

Thank You, God, for giving me ways to grow my faith and trust in You. —RHODA BLECKER

Digging Deeper: PSALMS 94:18–19, 119:50

Thu 5

Not that I have already obtained it or have already become perfect, but I press on so that I may lay hold of that for which also I was laid hold of by Christ Jesus. —PHILIPPIANS 3:12 (NAS)

I was striding through the whirl of humanity at Grand Central Terminal one morning, brooding on a typo I had discovered in something I had recently published. The fact that I could fix it on the digital version was of no comfort. I hated making mistakes, especially ones that everyone could see.

I glanced up at the big departures board to check the train schedule and found my gaze wandering to the magnificent vaulted ceiling arching over the main concourse, a dazzling depiction of the zodiac...except that it's all wrong. The nineteenth-century artisans misread the blueprints and mistakenly inverted the constellations to create a mirror image of the heavens. The Vanderbilt family, builders of the great beaux arts structure, was mortified but quickly concocted a charming explanation: what was portrayed was actually God's view of the sky from above and beyond the cosmos.

If you look closely enough, there are a couple of dark, grimy panels left by the restorers who lovingly cleaned the ceiling over a decade ago to remind us of what time and neglect will do to beauty. That whole gorgeous canvas is a kind of accidental tribute to the inherent imperfection of human endeavor.

I thought again about my typo. My attack of perfectionism was really an attempt to steal from God an attribute possessed only by Him. I stood there for a moment amid the swarm of morning commuters and smiled. Maybe I wouldn't fix that typo in the digital version after all.

God, from Your heavenly view You forgive all my many imperfections. Don't let me forget I'm only human. —EDWARD GRINNAN

Digging Deeper: ECCLESIASTES 7:20, 1 CORINTHIANS 13:12

Fri 6

I will protect those who know my name. —PSALM 91:14 (NRSV)

It was a long hike for a five-year-old. The trails in this California state park were steep and overgrown. I was thrilled my daughter liked the outdoors as much as I do, but I wondered if I was being irresponsible.

"Daddy, can I play by the creek?" Frances asked.

"Yes, just don't go in the water. Wait till I'm with you to swim." There had been no ranger at the park entrance. It was early in the season, and state budget cuts had left parks understaffed. We were alone in the wilderness.

Suddenly, I felt overwhelmingly vulnerable. What on earth had I been thinking when I planned this trip? Frances and I had backpacked before but never this far. What if something happened to her? What if something happened to me? We'd talked about what to do in an emergency, but how much does a five-year-old remember?

"Frances?" I called. I strode toward the creek. "Frances!" No answer. "Frances!"

A blonde head poked out from some reeds. "Daddy, come see! There's a caterpillar." I ran to her, trying not to show my fear. She tugged me toward a leafy plant where a caterpillar inched along. "I love it here," she said. "Can we have hot chocolate now?"

"After dinner."

We explored the creek, ate dinner, drank hot chocolate, told stories, and fell asleep to a chorus of frogs. In the morning, we hiked back to the car. "That was the best," said Frances. "Can we do it again?"

Yes, I seemed to hear. *I'll keep you safe next time too.*

Help me to trust You always, Lord. —JIM HINCH

Digging Deeper: LUKE 10:21

Sat 7

Because of the Lord's great love we are not consumed, for his compassions never fail. They are new every morning; great is your faithfulness.
—LAMENTATIONS 3:22–23 (NIV)

Today when I flipped the calendar page I thought, *Let's see how my New Year's resolutions are going.* I was going to swim one mile every week; I've given up my pool membership. I was going to blog daily on my Web site; I post sporadically at best. My plans have definitely not gone the way I thought they would.

So I decided to flip them around. I don't swim anymore, but I've taken up walking. I push myself, so my pedometer reads ten thousand steps a day. I have trouble posting consistently on my Web site, but I set deadlines to keep me blogging twice a month.

I usually beat myself up for not following through with my grand plans. Instead, I will look at what I have accomplished and smile. My resolutions may become a habit, or I may fall short of my goals. Either way, I am a child of God, loved and cherished. And I get a fresh start every morning, even if it's not New Year's Day.

Dear Father God, I want to start fresh this morning. I'm going to hold Your hand, and we'll tackle my goals together. Amen. —LISA BOGART

Digging Deeper: PSALM 86:11, EPHESIANS 1:7–8

Sun 8

Nor should there be . . . foolish talk . . . but rather thanksgiving. —EPHESIANS 5:4 (NIV)

After having lunch with a new church member, my husband and I were in the kitchen, discussing our first impressions. "She seems really full of great ideas," I said.

"And she's so friendly and easy to talk to," Gordon added.

"On the other hand . . . ," I began, ready to say that she'd probably run into resistance with some of the powers that be who wouldn't be very open to new ideas if they weren't their own. Before I could get in my next word, the telephone rang. Gordon answered the phone and began talking to a contractor who was doing some work in our basement.

That interruption was enough for me to feel a twinge of guilt about the statement that had been ready to roll off of my tongue. I remembered a book called *Three Simple Rules* that our church had urged every member to read. It was based on John Wesley's admonition to "do no harm, do good, and love God." When I read it, I thought that the "do no harm" section was simplistic. But now I saw with clarity that it was easy to open my mouth and do plenty of harm. Judgmental comments. Negativity. Saying that things won't work out before they even get going.

When Gordon hung up the phone, I decided to do the simplest yet the hardest thing in the world. Instead of continuing the conversation, I asked Gordon about the basement project and thanked God for the interruption that had helped me curb my tongue.

Dear Father, help me "do no harm" when it comes to the things I say about others today. Amen.
—KAREN BARBER

Digging Deeper: 2 CORINTHIANS 13:11, JAMES 3:3–12

Mon 9

"Follow Me, and I will make you become fishers of men."
—MARK 1:17 (NAS)

Yesterday I was visiting my high school buddy at his office and said, "You know, John, you taught me something years ago that I use every day of my professional life."

He looked at me with an incredulous grin and said, "Well, what in the world was that?"

I asked John to remember a moment forty-five years before when he and I were in the cast of our high school's play *Barefoot in the Park*. We were in the final round of the state competition at the University of Georgia when I encountered an embarrassing predicament. I wore a sports coat and tie but didn't know how to fix my tie. My father died when I was young, and he had not been there to teach me to do simple male things like shave, select clothes, polish shoes, or tie a tie. So I screwed up my courage and said, "John, will you teach me how to tie my tie?" I still remember his words: "Sure, sport, I can do that in a skinny minute." And he did!

"I'll be doggone," John blurted. "I don't have the least memory of doing that."

"Well, you sure did, and I've quietly thanked you a thousand times over the years." Two old friends just sat for a few seconds, grinning at each other.

We are all teachers, Father. Today, show me the opportunity to be a teacher of good things.
—SCOTT WALKER

Digging Deeper: MATTHEW 13:52, EPHESIANS 2:10

Tue 10

We also glory in our sufferings, because we know that suffering produces perseverance; perseverance, character; and character, hope.
—ROMANS 5:3–4 (NIV)

John and I planned to go on a walking tour of historic Harlem today. My son was eager to go, yet when the time came to leave, he was sullen and difficult. It was major work to get him out of the house. One of our goals this year is to help John overcome his dislike of new places and things. He's a senior in high school and needs to expand his comfort zone.

Eventually, the two of us made our way to 135th Street and Lenox Avenue. Our first stop was an exhibit about East Africans who became generals and leaders in India. Then we went on the walking tour, which lasted two hours and ended up at the Apollo Theater. Afterward, we found a place to have something to eat and rest our weary legs.

My son smiled at me, and I smiled back. Conversation flowed easily. It was so good to see John happy and engaged. I knew, though, that as soon as we got home his preferences would revert to what's familiar, and that the next time I attempted to get him out and about, he'd balk again. But a mom's job is to think in terms of how to help her child grow instead of about how much work is involved.

As I thanked God for a good day, I remembered to thank Him for grace and perseverance too. We can only pass on what we already have.

Father, help me to step out of my comfort zone,
so I am able to grow and do the work
You've set aside for me to do.
—JULIA ATTAWAY

Digging Deeper: 2 THESSALONIANS 3:5,
HEBREWS 12:1

Wed 11

The king's heart is in the hand of the Lord, like the rivers of water; He turns it wherever He wishes.
—PROVERBS 21:1 (NKJV)

Presidents' Day is coming up in just five days. It's a special day. That morning I'll be sitting in my prayer chair, with the Bible in my lap and a steaming cup of coffee on the table. I'll tie a short piece of pink curly ribbon around the cup's handle so that all day, when I glance at it, I'll remember to pray for our president.

What a change from just a couple of years ago when I was fed up with politicians. Honestly, I wasn't interested in praying for them. Then one day while I was doing a Bible study, God revealed to me Proverbs 21:1. It zinged in my spirit. *Wow, if*

God holds the heart of a king in His hand, that means He holds the hearts of our president and politicians, directing them wherever He wishes. If I want to see changes, I need to invest time in prayer for them and watch God do the rest. That was the beginning of my renewed hope for this nation and my prayers for our leaders.

So join me on February 16. Tie a ribbon on your coffee cup (or teacup... or water bottle) and pray this prayer with me throughout the day—and perhaps every day—for our president:

Lord, direct our president's heart toward You. Give our president spiritual wisdom and understanding to lead this nation according to Your precepts and into all truth. May the president be filled to overflowing with Your depth of insight into all situations. Surround the president with godly advisers. Inscribe on their hearts the knowledge of Your will so that they may know You better. Thank You. Amen. —Rebecca Ondov

Digging Deeper: 1 Timothy 2:1–8

Thu 12   *"For man looks at the outward appearance, but the Lord looks at the heart."* —1 Samuel 16:7 (nkjv)

I'd been dreading Valentine's Day for weeks. On my way to work, I braced myself for the floral bouquets and candy that would surely be delivered to everyone but me.

"Help me to just get through this, Lord," I prayed on my drive to the Veterans Affairs Medical Center, where I'm a nurse. My ex-husband's new girlfriend worked at the hospital, and I got queasy at the thought of running into her. But God's answer was quick, unmistakable, and very personal: *If you'll just pay attention, Roberta, love will touch you in the most unlikely of places.*

So that's what I did as I made my rounds. On 4 South, I watched transfixed as an eighty-something wife of a veteran who had recently suffered a stroke zipped her beloved into his jacket. The two were headed home to begin their long journey of rehabilitation. It would be challenging but not impossible, for this team had weathered many storms in their sixty-four years of marriage.

In Primary Care, I took note of another veteran's wife who helped her husband complete a tedious form. The gentleman, who had served in Korea, had broken his arm and was having trouble writing.

Next, in Mental Health, the young boyfriend of a woman who had recently returned from Afghanistan offered comfort as she cried tears related to her head trauma.

Valentines, all—and not a single posy or chocolate in the bunch. Such is the nature of Valentine's Day in a place where US heroes are served.

Is there any more loving place than a VA hospital? I'm looking, Lord. —ROBERTA MESSNER

Digging Deeper: PSALM 63:3; 1 JOHN 3:1, 4:7

Fri 13

Let each one of you love his wife as himself. . . . —EPHESIANS 5:33 (ESV)

My thesis was due on February 13. Then, that night was one of the big senior parties as we celebrated completing our last major hurdle before graduation. I scrambled to get my paper finished, spending days cooped up in my room or the library, reviewing draft after draft.

Through all of this, my girlfriend was supportive. Emily helped with the things you sometimes forget to do when you're busy, like cook dinner, and accepted that I had less time for her than usual.

"What do you want to do for Valentine's Day?" she asked me.

"I don't know," I said. "I might want to rest that day. Maybe we could just hang out together."

She seemed okay with that. I thought of Valentine's Day as a holiday that existed to sell cards and had nothing in common with true holy days like Easter or Christmas.

I turned in my paper, and Emily and I had a great night with our friends. The next day I was feeling lazy and assumed she was too. We were walking through the student center as a classmate of ours opened her mailbox, found a candy cane with a heart-shaped note attached, and smiled. I noticed Emily frown. Valentine's Day *did* matter to her! I had been blind and selfish.

I found time to slip away and bought sunflowers, Emily's favorite. It was then that I understood that every day is a holy day, a chance to express love.

Thank You, Lord, for reminding me never to waste a chance to love. —SAM ADRIANCE

Digging Deeper: PSALM 18:24

Sat 14

Do not withhold good from those who deserve it when it's in your power to help them. —PROVERBS 3:27 (NLT)

My husband changes the kitty litter. He took on the chore twelve years ago when I was pregnant with Solomon and has been doing it ever since. With our three cats, it's an ongoing stinky job, but Tony does it every day without complaining.

And though it might sound weird, when I pass the clean kitty litter pans in our mudroom, I love my husband just a tiny bit more.

Not long ago I watched a TV show about relationships. The specialist said it's the everyday blessings that make a marriage and the everyday grievances that break one. The specialist looked at the husband on the panel and said, "When you take out the garbage or make the bed, it says, 'I love you.'"

Exactly! I thought of the many times I was ready to put away a load of clean dishes and opened the dishwasher to discover it already had been done, and it felt just like I'd found a love note.

Tony and I aren't big Valentine's Day people; sometimes we don't even exchange gifts. But we do things for each other every day. In the folded laundry, the mopped floor, the stack of paid bills, and every unromantic chore are caring whispers of affection.

Dear God, help me to joyfully approach
housework as an opportunity to show
my love to those I love most.
—SABRA CIANCANELLI

Digging Deeper: 1 CORINTHIANS 13:4–8,
PHILIPPIANS 2:4

MAKING MARRIAGE WORK

Sun 15   *"Keeping covenant and steadfast love—do not treat lightly all the hardship that has come upon us...."*
—NEHEMIAH 9:32 (NRSV)

A STAYCATION?

I can't do this," I said, looking up at my husband, Charlie, from the floor where I was zipping my suitcase closed.

We were due to head to the airport for our annual four-month winter sojourn in California from Connecticut. But I'd gotten sick, and now, despite my doctor's assurances that I could travel, I still felt lousy.

Charlie looked relieved but uncertain. "You sure?" he asked.

"Yes, I just can't. I'm sorry."

Charlie and I had started taking these trips eight years ago when he had partly retired, fearing he'd be lured back into the ninety-hour workweeks that had caused grief in our marriage. Surely we could find a way to stay home, still have some of the fun we'd found in California, and negotiate between my need for privacy and Charlie's social nature.

While unpacking, I felt panic rising. *Will this hurt our marriage?*

I went to find Charlie. He was on the couch, phone in hand. He looked up a little sheepishly. I sat down next to him, we clasped hands, and I prayed: "Lord, help us to use this time to grow closer to You and to each other. Bless and protect our marriage. Amen."

Charlie turned off the phone, and I looked at the silver river outside our window. A peace stole over me. God had brought us through so much together; I would trust Him now.

God of all circumstances, help us to know we are where You want us to be. —MARCI ALBORGHETTI

Digging Deeper: JOB 38:4

MAKING MARRIAGE WORK

Mon 16   *Surely I am too stupid to be human; I do not have human understanding. I have not learned wisdom....*
—PROVERBS 30:2–3 (NRSV)

LEAVING IT TO GOD

L et me get this straight," our pastor said, smiling. "You want to know how to live as if you're in sunny California, away from all of the demands on both of you, without leaving cold, bleak Connecticut where everyone knows where and how to reach you 24–7?"

He knew us well, having witnessed our years-long "tug-of-love" between my yearning for solitude and my husband's easygoing sociability and workaholism. Our pastor prayed with and for us, but as usual, I wasn't able to wait for God to show me the next step.

"We need to make a list," I told Charlie when we got home. We'd learned lists helped us compromise and gauged our progress.

"Ready!" Charlie said, fingers poised above the laptop keys.

I began reeling off all of the things that would make staying home work: movies, walks, books, do-it-yourself projects, "no electronics days" . . . the keys had stopped tapping. I looked at Charlie. "What?"

He looked uncomfortable. "Couldn't we just wait to see what happens?"

No, we can't! I wanted to shout because waiting to see what happens usually meant nothing happened, and I was sick and tired of leaving everything to chance, and . . . and . . .

The silence shimmered. *Little one, don't you understand?* I heard God saying. *You're not leaving it all to chance; you're leaving it all to Me.*

"Let's try," I said to Charlie, knowing this time we really would.

Father, remind me to wait—quietly and calmly—upon Your will. —Marci Alborghetti

Digging Deeper: Psalm 7:1

MAKING MARRIAGE WORK

Tue 17 *She is clothed with strength and dignity; she can laugh at the days to come.* —Proverbs 31:25 (NIV)

SILVER LININGS

To shake ourselves out of our winter slump, my husband and I decided to combine work with pleasure by going to see the film *Silver Linings Playbook.* Pleasure, because it was a movie night out; work, because some of our friends live with mental illness and the film revolved around this issue.

No surprise that Hollywood made things a little simpler than they were in real life. Discussing the movie's title afterward over coffee, I said, "We're always complaining about what we've lost in not going to California. What about if we thank God for our silver linings in staying in Connecticut this winter?"

Charlie looked dubious. "Okay," he said, "you start."

I closed my eyes, thought for a minute, and started to laugh. "Dear Lord, thank You for keeping me home so that when I woke up with a full-body rash, I wasn't 2,500 miles away from my doctors."

Charlie opened one eye to check my sanity. Then he got into the spirit. "Father, thank You for making sure I was home during that second blizzard so that when the snow turned to rain and came blowing through the windows, I could spend the day keeping the wood floors dry."

My turn. "Lord, thank You for keeping us up all night with that last nor'easter so that when the heat went off in our building, we could call the management company before every pipe froze."

By now we were both laughing about our lopsided silver linings.

> *Lord, let me laugh at life's absurdities, secure in the knowledge of Your loving care.*
> —MARCI ALBORGHETTI

Digging Deeper: ZEPHANIAH 3:15

MAKING MARRIAGE WORK

Wed 18   *Therefore my heart is glad and my tongue rejoices; my body also will rest secure.* —PSALM 16:9 (NIV)

LEARNING TO SEE

As part of our plan to find the silver linings in our situation, my husband, Charlie, and I decided to attend opening night of New London, Connecticut's premier winter event, a film festival at the historic Garde Arts Center. But the mild December weather had morphed into the worst winter in recent history. Forecasters were predicting a foot of snow. "I can't believe it," I groaned to Sharon on the phone. "I'm not going out in that."

Sharon is one of those blunt, faithful friends whom everyone needs but who sometimes seems a bit unsympathetic. "You're just not used to the winter weather," she said. "Once you get there, you'll have fun."

"I'm not going," I said mulishly. "I'll stay home and work."

"Right, work on your book about living one's faith. We're lucky the disciples didn't stay home and write about their experiences with Jesus."

Charlie and I had a great time. It seemed the whole city had come out despite the snow. When the theater owner took the stage and called New London "the greatest city in the universe," the collective shout could have been heard on the moon.

Afterward, as we rushed to our car, Charlie leaned in and shouted over the gale, "Do you wish we were in California?"

"Sometimes," I said, taking his arm. But at that moment, I didn't want to be anywhere else.

Lord of joy, thank You for opening my eyes to Your many opportunities for rejoicing in my world.
—MARCI ALBORGHETTI

Digging Deeper: PROVERBS 13:20

MAKING MARRIAGE WORK

Thu 19

"And if you greet only your brothers and sisters, what more are you doing than others?..."
—MATTHEW 5:47 (NRSV)

WHAT WOULD JESUS DO?

Let's have a Super Bowl party!" Charlie declared. I stared at my husband. Never mind the short notice, our apartment's minuscule size, or even the fact that we didn't have a television. Neither of us watched football... ever!

"Do you even know who's playing?" I asked.

"Uh..."

"Hon, I don't want a bunch of people here on such short notice and..."

Charlie stopped me. "I don't mean a party-party," he explained. "I mean just us, down in the theater room with takeout."

I narrowed my eyes. "So this hasn't got anything to do with the fact that tomorrow is a 'no-electronics day' and you don't know what else to do with yourself?"

He gave me that *Who, me?* look.

On game day, we settled downstairs in front of the big screen. Shortly, another resident opened the door. "Oh," he said, "I was hoping to watch *Downton Abbey*. My TV's not working."

He did look tired and disappointed, and "What would Jesus do?" kept circling in the back of my mind.

There was a smaller TV in the exercise room, so we moved there. It was a good game, a great "party," and what Jesus would have done.

Compassionate God, show us the many
small ways to do good and feel good.
—MARCI ALBORGHETTI

Digging Deeper: JOHN 2:2

MAKING MARRIAGE WORK

Fri 20   *But grow in the grace and knowledge*
of our Lord and Savior Jesus
Christ.... —2 PETER 3:18 (NIV)

LEARNING TO STRETCH

One of the best things about our winter in Connecticut has been time with our pastor, Michel, before his sabbatical. Also, this would be our first Lent and Easter at Saint James in many years, a real treat.

During Evening Prayer, we were comforted with ancient prayers of praise and thanksgiving that focused us in today's loud and often thankless world. We listened to Lenten music and heard a choir that had prepared for months to bring us closer to God.

We walked the Stations of the Cross around a cold church made warm by the companionship of the handful of us who shared prayer books and huddled together contemplating Jesus's extreme sacrifice for us.

We participated in healing services and closed our eyes when Michel made the sign of the cross on our foreheads on Ash Wednesday. We shared the holy Eucharist on Sunday evening and spent time in church afterward with Michel and our small group, discussing his upcoming sabbatical.

I was surprised to learn that our pastor was planning to walk the five-hundred-mile-long Camino de Santiago in France and Spain.

"I can't picture you roughing it," I teased Michel.

Aware of our challenges these past weeks and months, he replied, "Sometimes you have to stretch yourself a little."

And sometimes God uses others to help us stretch.

God of all provision, thank You for providing
us with people who strengthen our faith
in You and each other.
—MARCI ALBORGHETTI

Digging Deeper: JOHN 2:9

MAKING MARRIAGE WORK

Sat 21 *The Lord looks down from heaven on*
humankind to see if there are any who
are wise, who seek after God.
—PSALM 14:2 (NRSV)

FINDING OUR BALANCE

Where should we go next winter?" Charlie asked one evening after we'd changed the clocks and the daylight was lasting longer.

The fact that my husband could ask it at all was a good sign. We already knew that we wanted to start spending winters away again. But God had led us through this and, for the first time, our plans for next year didn't seem as pressing or as cut in stone.

"Don't you want to go back to California?" I asked. Three months ago we'd considered our time there integral to finding balance in our marriage.

"That would be okay," Charlie mused, "but it doesn't have to be California. Should we try a new place?"

I smiled. We talked about various possibilities, and I got excited at the thought of a new adventure. "Or we could just stay here," I joked.

Charlie looked at me. "Are you serious?"

"I'd like to go away," I answered slowly, "but it's kind of a relief to know that we can stay here and be okay."

God had brought us through a long and sometimes difficult winter. How many times had we said, "We have God and each other. The rest will sort itself out"? And it had.

God of wisdom, we bless and praise You for all You give us. Continue to show us how to maintain the necessary balance in our marriage.
—MARCI ALBORGHETTI

Digging Deeper: 1 CHRONICLES 29:11

Sun 22   *Weeping may linger for the night, but joy comes with the morning.*
—PSALM 30:5 (NRSV)

Today, I sat by my six-year-old granddaughter Mia and my son Christopher in church. When the music began, Mia quickly reached up for her daddy to hold her when he stood up. With a big smile on her face, she bounced in his arms to each song.

I stood up next to them, though I had none of Mia's enthusiasm. It had been a difficult year. My husband had passed away one year ago, my heart was still heavy with sadness, and I was sure I'd never feel happy again.

Before the start of the next song, the song leader prayed, "Lord, let this music open our hearts so that we can worship You in all of Your goodness and glory. Amen."

Another song began, and Mia just couldn't contain her exuberance. She threw both of her arms into the air, smiling and singing as loudly as she could.

As I watched her, a feeling of joy rushed through me. It coursed through my veins, catching me completely off guard. "Thank You, Lord," I prayed. "Thank You!" I was so relieved to know that I could actually feel happiness again. I reached over and gave Mia a big hug. I knew there'd be difficult days ahead, but I also knew, thanks to Mia, that there would be good days ahead too.

Thank You, Lord, for this moment of joy
that is surely a promise of more.
—MELODY BONNETTE SWANG

Digging Deeper: NEHEMIAH 8:10, JOB 8:21,
PSALM 30:11

Mon 23

As cold water to a weary soul, so is
good news from a far country.
—PROVERBS 25:25 (NKJV)

We may be getting old, but my wife and I still have races. Sharon works in her sewing room at the north end of the house. She is the first to hear the low rumble of the mailman's truck. My study is at the south end of the house, so I am the last to hear the truck, but when I do, the race is on! Two old turtles run down the lane to the mailbox, a race that ends in joy.

"You bum. You beat me again."

"Ha ha ha ha!"

My younger friends scoff at snail mail, but I prefer to call it paper mail and I love it. Every envelope is a treasure chest to me. Every day I am sure that this will be the day when I get good news from some publisher with a check for one million dollars or a job opportunity that will take me to exotic places. Sharon is more realistic. She is just happy for what's not in the mail, like a tax audit or stratospheric credit card bill. A letter from her friend Carolyn is icing on the cake.

The mail gives us something to look forward to, and that's important, I think. I heard about a centenarian who revealed the secret of his longevity: "Every evening I make a list of things I want to do the next day. As long as I have my list, I have a reason to wake up."

So every evening I jot down some things I will enjoy doing on the morrow, like my quiet time with God, or setting out those tomato plants, and, of course, getting the mail. I sleep better just knowing there are some happy things on tomorrow's docket.

Thank You, Lord, for a reason to wake up each new day. —DANIEL SCHANTZ

Digging Deeper: JOSHUA 3:5, MICAH 7:7, ROMANS 8:25

Tue 24   *For the Lord is our judge, the Lord is our lawgiver, the Lord is our king....* —ISAIAH 33:22 (NIV)

When Jack and I got married in 2012, I was sixty-six years old and he was seventy-five. I didn't change my name, and we decided to keep both of our condos, which are just fifty-seven steps from each other. *What will my family and friends think of our living arrangement?* I worried.

We sleep and eat breakfast at Jack's condo but almost always have dinner at mine (I like my kitchen stuff better than his). I work in my office in my condo while he works on volunteer projects in his. We put our guests in the bedroom in my place. After dinner, Jack sometimes watches sports on TV at his condo while I watch something else in mine. We're back and forth every day, all day.

While browsing through the New Testament, I began to wonder how Jesus felt walking the land, gathering hundreds of people at a time, trying to talk them into living their lives in a completely different way...His way. Jesus was a renegade marching to the sound of a different philosophy.

Thinking of how Jesus lived His life gave me courage to live my life in a different way from that of my neighbors, friends, and family. I needn't have worried. Now that Jack and I have been living in both condos for a few years, many of our married friends wish they had two places to live in too!

Father, thank You for the courage to live my life the way it works best for me and for the blessing of having two homes and one loving husband.
—Patricia Lorenz

Digging Deeper: 1 Corinthians 7:32–40, Titus 1:8

Wed 25

And they mourned over him, saying, "Alas, my brother!"
—1 KINGS 13:30 (ESV)

Another thing about joy is that you never stop being surprised by the deeper levels of joy and how joy is like an elevator that keeps going down another floor farther than you knew there were floors and how what you thought were the pinnacles of joy were only mountains beyond which there are many more mountains, some of them shrouded in darkness.

For example, this odd, painful, strange, subtle, awful, sweet joy last year: my oldest brother was dying of cancer. He had cancer everywhere. He lost a hundred pounds. He lost his hair. He lost his balance. But he never lost his sidelong grin—never. Right near the end he and I went driving through his favorite forest, and even though he could hardly speak and his death was sitting companionably in the backseat, we were both filled with joy. We were brothers for fifty-five years, and about ten years before he died we got to be the same age finally, as sometimes happens with brothers if they are lucky, and we were happy together watching birds and playing chess and trading silly postcards.

He died on the first day of summer. There is a hole in the world the size of the man he used to be before cancer ate him. There will always be that big grinning hole in me and in his family and in his thousand friends. But here is a joy persistent and insistent, a joy that death cannot steal: I was graced to be that man's brother, and he loved me and I loved him. What used to be his body is now ash in the dense soil of Illinois. But who he is, who he always is, is in me and those he loved, and every time I think of this lovely terrible truth, I grin . . . as he would, sidelongingly.

Dear Profligate Deliverer of Brothers, well, You were especially generous to me, insofar as I was given six of them. But You have seen fit to retrieve four over the years, which was hard for me to endure, but I am pretty sure it is You whispering in my ear that I will see them again in the fullness of time and that will be a day of unimaginable joy. —BRIAN DOYLE

Digging Deeper: PSALM 133:1

Thu 26

A gentle answer turns away wrath, but a harsh word stirs up anger.
—PROVERBS 15:1 (NIV)

My husband woke up grumpy this morning, which made me grumpy. Lynn came into the kitchen way earlier than usual, which interrupted

my sacred time of solitude at the counter, surrounded by my Bible, journal, devotional book,
special pens—all my stuff.

"What are you doing up so early?" I asked.

"I don't feel well."

"You don't ever feel well when you first wake up,"
I reminded him.

"And I don't like these jeans. They don't fit right,"
he said.

"We spent a whole afternoon at the store, trying
on jeans and getting just the right ones. That's how
they're supposed to fit."

"Well, they don't fit. You might like them, but I
don't."

I knew my patience was waning, so I gathered my
stuff and stomped off to a place where I could be
alone and get holy.

I could still hear Lynn in the kitchen, so I talked to
God. *You can change the tone of this day,* I imagined
God saying to me. "But it's not my fault. Why
should I apologize for Lynn's grumpiness?" There
was silence. Nothing in me wanted to be the one to
take the first step.

I went back in the kitchen to refill my coffee cup.
Lynn looked at me with a sort of question mark on
his face, which made me laugh. "I'm sorry you don't
feel well," I said.

"Thanks for understanding," he replied. And the
day got better from there.

Lord, thank You for helping us change
the tone of the day to one of joy.
—CAROL KUYKENDALL

Digging Deeper: COLOSSIANS 3:12–14

Fri 27

"Let not your hearts be troubled;
believe in God, believe also in me.
In my Father's house are many rooms;
if it were not so, would I have told you
that I go to prepare a place for you?"
—JOHN 14:1–2 (RSV)

We stood at the cemetery by my father's open grave. The day before, we'd had the memorial service at church with hymns and eulogies and hundreds of people bidding Dad a fond farewell. Now it was just family and that aching sense of loss.

Our friend Rick Thyne led the graveside service. "At church when I was a kid," he began, "we had a balcony that wrapped around the sanctuary. If I had to lead a prayer or read a psalm, I could look up and see the people who cared about me. They were my encouragers, urging me on. They believed in me and looked out for me. I thought of them as my balcony people."

I thought of Dad, asking me about my job or school or the kids and then hanging up the phone with his standard line, "Love ya."

"Your dad is not here," Rick went on, "but he can become one of your balcony people. He's there watching it all, taking it in." I could see Dad's smile, hear his laugh, remember his kiss on my forehead when he'd put me to bed. "You can let go of him in life as you hold on to all the good things he wished for you and made happen when he was here."

The front row of my balcony. Still there. Love ya.

Thank You, Lord, for all the people who formed me.
May I honor in life all they gave me.
—RICK HAMLIN

Digging Deeper: 1 CORINTHIANS 15:54–57

Sat 28

As a father has compassion on his children, so the Lord has compassion on those who fear him; for he knows how we are formed, he remembers that we are dust.
—PSALM 103:13–14 (NIV)

The kitchen table looked like a laboratory. My son, age ten, and I shared a mission: save one hundred dollars by repairing his gaming system ourselves. The Internet video made it look easy, and we were handy and brave, so why not?

We cracked open the case and followed the directions step by step. Small paper plates held tiny screws. We laid out parts in the order removed. My son did all the steps he could. Then I took over. He kept track of parts and was my chief adviser.

At the most delicate stage, we replaced the laser—the walnut-size, ten-dollar heart of the machine. Laser installed, we began reassembly. With the cover snapped into place, my son looked at me with glowing eyes. I stood a little taller. We set it up. I held my breath. My son's hands quivered as he inserted a disk. Success! All was well with our world . . . for two whole hours. That's when my tearful son informed me that the same problem had recurred: his machine wouldn't read disks.

Fast-forward to a conversation with a repair technician: "Your machine is fried. We can't fix it. Did somebody replace the laser?"

"Yeah, that was me," I answered.

"When we do that we use a sterile environment and all kinds of antistatic technology. It only takes a little spark to fry the motherboard, and that's what happened. Sorry."

I felt deflated and broke the news to my son. He touched my arm. "Well, at least we tried."

Sweet kid. Reminds me of my Father in heaven.

Father, I take comfort in Your—and my son's—tender heart. —BILL GIOVANNETTI

Digging Deeper: PSALM 145:9, MARK 5:19

DAILY JOYS

1 _____

2 _____

3 _____

4 _____

5 _____

6 _____

7 _____

8 _____

9 _____

10 _____

11 _____

12 _____

February

13 _____

14 _____

15 _____

16 _____

17 _____

18 _____

19 _____

20 _____

21 _____

22 _____

23 _____

24 _____

25 _____

26 _____

27 _____

28 _____

March

"These things I have spoken to you,
that my joy may be in you,
and that your joy may be full."

—John 15:11 (ESV)

GOD OF JOYFUL SURPRISES

Sun 1

"There is more happiness in giving than in receiving." —ACTS 20:35 (GNT)

LIFTING THE BLUES

Recently retired and feeling low, a *Daily Guideposts* reader wrote to tell me she'd prayed: "Show me three people today, God, who need my caring." Kay couldn't believe how fast opportunities came! Within a day, a neighbor had disclosed that she had cancer and asked for prayer; she'd spent time with a recent widow; and she'd looked after the children of a friend delayed at work.

On a blue day of my own, I tried Kay's prayer. Three needs showed up almost immediately. An elderly man struggling with the heavy outer door of our building had dropped his grocery sack. It was quick work to collect the rolling cans from the sidewalk.

I was barely back in our own apartment when a neighbor called to say her car battery was dead and did we have a jumper cable. We did, and soon her engine was rumbling reassuringly.

I went to the mailbox, sure I'd find a cry for help. It was a serious one: a friend from our former church asking prayers for her daughter's baby, born prematurely. I phoned two intercessor groups as I began my own prayers.

And my blue day? It vanished like a passing cloud as I focused outside myself. The joy of God, Kay's letter showed me, is as close as the next person who needs help.

God of joyful surprises, show me how to take my small part today in Your joyous, eternal self-giving. —ELIZABETH SHERRILL

Digging Deeper: JEREMIAH 15:16, ROMANS 14:17

Mon 2
"How can someone be born when they are old?".... —JOHN 3:4 (NIV)

At fifty-four, I'm among the oldest in my yoga class. I started between the end of my daughter Charlotte's spring semester and the beginning of her summer internship. She'd been doing yoga in Boston and didn't want to stop, so she'd found a class in the town where I teach.

"Come with me," she begged. "I've always wanted to try 'hot yoga,' but I don't know anybody there."

So, ever the compliant mother, I agreed. First, we bought mats: $21.69 plus tax, each. Then, after the first slippery night, another $29.45 each for rubberized mat liners.

When Charlotte left, she took her gear with her. Whenever I saw my mat and liner, furled together in my closet, I regretted the waste. Finally, I decided the only way to make good on the expense was to use them. So I returned to yoga class and haven't quit since.

Mostly, class consists of skinny college kids who grunt and giggle together for an hour every Monday night. Often, it takes everything in me to heave myself into the right pose. But I'm improving.

Because the local university is Christian, or perhaps because the teacher's pastor-husband joins in, we often discuss our progress in stretching and meditating in spiritual terms. Our forty-day restoration program coincided with Lent. Meditation was prayer.

The best part for me is that when I master some new skill—side-plank, crow-pose, wheel, whatever—everyone claps. For a moment, in my "old age," I am reborn.

Thanks, good Father, for our bodies.
And for the young who grow us. And for how,
in the end, everything is about You!
—PATTY KIRK

Digging Deeper: JOHN 3:1–21, 2 CORINTHIANS 5:17

Tue 3

Day and night they never stop saying: "Holy, holy, holy is the Lord God Almighty, who was, and is, and is to come." —REVELATION 4:8 (NIV)

Don't sing here, Daddy!" my kids would tell me when I was tempted to sing out loud on the streets or in the car or at the dinner table or in the subway. "Okay, okay," I'd say, but that's the irrepressible power of music.

The other morning I was on the subway heading to work, closing my eyes, meditating on a passage from the book of Psalms, when, above the rumble of the train, I heard a woman singing one of my favorite hymns: "Holy, holy, holy, merciful and mighty, all thy works shall praise thy name from earth and sky and sea...."

I opened my eyes to see a handsome West Indian woman in a black coat, singing as she was handing out tracts: "God in three persons, blessed Trinity."

"I love that hymn," I told her, "but that's not the tune I usually sing it to. Do you know this tune?" I sang it back to her. She hummed along with me. Then I sang along with her version, the two of us forming an impromptu choir. The train was coming to my station.

"Amen, brother," she said as the doors opened.

"Amen to you too, sister," I said, darting off.

When I got to the office I e-mailed my now-grown sons. "You can be glad you weren't with your old man when he burst into song on the subway today. Just to let you know, I wasn't alone. Sang 'Holy, Holy, Holy' with a woman on the train." I could picture them rolling their eyes, but just so they'd get the message I added: "Music is a great way to connect."

It is. With the best parts of yourself, with your neighbors, and with our Creator.

Thank You, Lord, for giving us music
to make our spirits sing.
—RICK HAMLIN

Digging Deeper: PSALM 104:33

Wed 4 "*Bless me, even me also, O my father!*"
—GENESIS 27:34 (NAS)

Last year, in the midst of blooming hibiscus, hanging ferns, and multiple forms of flowering plants, one ceramic pot remained fallow and empty. Borne by the wind, a tiny seed penetrated the soil and soon a tall, vigorous stalk was growing and vibrant green leaves sprouted. When a neighbor visited, I pointed to the nomadic plant and asked, "Do you know what this is?"

She smiled and said, "Yes, it's a weed! It will take over a garden in a minute. You need to get rid of it."

The next day I picked up the potted weed and headed to the garbage can. But as I did, I felt a pang of sadness. This plant was truly beautiful, and just because someone declared it "a weed," I was discarding it and ending its life. I returned the weed to the porch, watered it, and decided to name my plant Esau, who was supposed to inherit his father Isaac's blessing and heritage until, in a moment of classic deception, his younger twin brother, Jacob, tricked his father and stole Esau's blessing. As a result, Esau was spurned by his family, cast away, and rejected without inheritance from the garden of rich Jewish history.

Today, I keep Esau prominent in my front porch garden to remind me that in the kingdom of God, everyone receives a blessing, everyone has worth, and everyone can reflect the glory of God.

Father, help me not to reject "a weed" in whatever form it may take. Amen.
—Scott Walker

Digging Deeper: 2 Corinthians 5:17

Thu 5

*Then Peter came to Jesus and asked,
"Lord, how many times shall I forgive
my brother or sister who sins against
me? Up to seven times?" Jesus
answered, "I tell you, not seven times,
but seventy-seven times."*
—MATTHEW 18:21–22 (NIV)

I was at dinner with my friend Sarah when an older gentleman walked over to our table and said hello.

"Hi," Sarah said. "How are you? I hope things are going well."

"Yes, they are. And you?" he asked.

"Good," she replied. "Thanks for asking."

He paused for a moment and, with a slight nod of his head, went on his way.

I looked at her, puzzled by what I'd just seen. "Isn't that the guy you used to work with?" I asked.

"Yes, it is," she replied.

"I don't understand," I said, recalling that he'd made her life difficult at work. "You were so polite to him! Don't you remember how horribly he treated you?"

"No," she said, shaking her head, "I don't." She paused. "I distinctly remember forgetting that."

"What?" I asked, confused.

"Clara Barton, the nurse who founded the American Red Cross, made it a rule never to hold on to resentment," she explained. "When a friend reminded her of a cruel incident from years earlier, Barton seemed not to recall it. 'Don't you remember what was done to you?' the friend asked. 'No,' Barton replied, 'I distinctly remember forgetting that.'"

> *That's a tough task, Lord, but Your Word*
> *tells us that the choice to forgive can't*
> *happen just once but over and over.*
> —MELODY BONNETTE SWANG

Digging Deeper: HOSEA 14:4, HEBREWS 12:24

Fri 6

Share with the Lord's people who are in need. Practice hospitality.
—ROMANS 12:13 (NIV)

By New York City standards, my one-bedroom apartment is spacious enough for my boys and me, and this wonderful little home has the ability to open its arms far and wide.

I've always loved having guests; it must stem from my childhood. Growing up, we'd always be a host family with a sofa bed in the living room, mattresses on the floor, and sleeping bags in any space we could find. When I got my first apartment, I continued these cozy sleepovers, inviting friends from California to Europe. This stopped when I was married. The tension in our relationship made having guests over awkward; even visits from my parents became uncomfortable.

After the divorce I struggled with the word *family*. A family of three with no husband for me, no father for the boys, felt empty. But opening my home again became part of my healing. A young woman from my church who wasn't sure where to go between apartments became my roommate for a few months. A family member's in-laws needed a place to stay as they hunted for an apartment after their move from Vermont. Free temporary housing was a blessing for them, but their presence was a blessing for us.

I've since made my peace with being a family of three, but our open door continues to be our little ministry. Days ago, my cousin told me about a friend who would undergo surgery in New York City; they live in Connecticut. "His wife needs a place to stay while he recovers. Could she stay with you?"

"Of course," I said without hesitating. "That's what our home is for."

Lord, thank You for the opportunities of service You place in our hearts and for the blessings You pour out in our obedience. —KAREN VALENTIN

Digging Deeper: MATTHEW 10:40

Sat 7

It will burst into bloom; it will rejoice greatly and shout for joy. . . .
—ISAIAH 35:2 (NIV)

I do not have a green thumb and have managed to kill even the hardiest of herbs. So it should come as no surprise that my simple wish would be met with anxiety. "I want to plant tulips," I told my husband.

"Sounds like a plan," Brian said, looking doubtful, if supportive.

I picked out bulbs, then checked gardening blogs for step-by-step tips. I even filled my planters halfway with foam in order to make them lighter.

The first rain came, and I noticed the dirt rising in my planters. *That's interesting,* I thought. *The foam must be absorbing the water and swelling.* The next rain came and the dirt rose higher, leading Brian to realize that my step-by-step pointers had missed one: cut holes in the planter to allow rainwater out. He helped me load the bulbs, now strewn across our deck, back into the planters.

When Brian's dad came to visit and inquired about the planters, I told him we'd encountered some trouble. "Oh," he said, "did you plant the bulbs upside down?" My face fell; now I quite possibly had waterlogged buds growing down into our pots instead of up.

Spring came quickly and tips of green began to poke through the soil. A few weeks later, the planters overflowed with bright bursts of color. In spite of my gardening shortcomings, God made something beautiful. It's by His Spirit that my meager works come to bloom.

Lord, bless my handiwork this day and always. It is through You that bulbs turn to blooms and the earth is renewed. —ASHLEY KAPPEL

Digging Deeper: ZECHARIAH 4:5-7

Sun 8

As iron sharpens iron, so one person sharpens another.
—PROVERBS 27:17 (NIV)

The question I've heard the most in my work for the church is a simple one: How do you grow in your faith? It's an easy question but a difficult answer.

The latest response came from a stranger who was sitting next to me on a small jet as we waited for thunderstorms to clear the Asheville, North Carolina, airport. After we'd both finished the one newspaper we were sharing, he pulled out a Bible. I asked him, "How do you grow in your faith?"

Here's what he said: "I can't grow unless I'm willing to do something I haven't done before." For him that meant intentionally reading a challenging author and being alert to a new idea. Or joining a different ministry team at church, perhaps one he wasn't very good at; or making that phone call or visit he didn't want to make; or even talking about his faith with strangers on airplanes.

And that's how Max came to be my growing-deeper trainer this year, through his simple discipleship principle: do one new thing to challenge yourself.

What am I doing? I'm meeting regularly with two people of different faith backgrounds from mine, sharing stories and experiences and Scripture and practices. It's a way to go deeper into how God is working in this world.

> *Challenge me, God, to see how I might see*
> *You more clearly, love You more dearly, follow*
> *You more nearly, day by day.*
> —JEFF JAPINGA

Digging Deeper: ACTS 8:26–40, GALATIANS 6:6

Mon 9 "*Yet man is born to trouble, As the sparks fly upward.*" —JOB 5:7 (NKJV)

I work with a family on a remote cattle ranch in Oregon. We'd been hauling cow-calf pairs to our summer pasture when we drove onto the ranch for another load and found an unattended brush pile burning out of control.

Armed only with irrigating shovels, we dug frantically through the duff and sagebrush, trying to dig a bare ring of dirt around the perimeter to stop the spreading flames. The wind gusted relentlessly, causing the wildfire to jump our hurried fire lines repeatedly.

Heat blistered my face and hands. Smoke choked and blinded me. For four long hours we battled the blaze. Flames shot up juniper and pine trees like torches. Neighbors saw us and hurried over to help. At one point I collapsed to the ground, too tired to stand, and got up only when the fire burned against my boot. It took eight of us to get the fire under control.

But later at home, once the adrenaline ebbed, my back ached, a constant throbbing. I headed to bed, sure I was hurt. I just didn't know how badly.

The next morning it took forty-five minutes to get out of bed. I couldn't walk. I could barely crawl. *I'm in big trouble,* I thought.

"You've ruptured a disc spilling fluid into the nerves in your spine," the doctor said later that day. "You're going to need surgery to alleviate the pressure." He wasn't sure I'd ever fully recover. Oddly, the scalpel didn't scare me; it was the sudden shattering of my safe, familiar world.

Lord, please comfort me as I face the unknown.
These are the times that make it hard to remember
You are still here. But You are still here.
—ERIKA BENTSEN

Digging Deeper: ISAIAH 13:10, MARK 13:24,
LUKE 16:24

Tue 10

"Ask and it will be given to you...."
—LUKE 11:9 (NIV)

Several months before my husband's health crisis, I had agreed to teach a class in and about the synagogue, showing the high school students the ritual objects, explaining how we use them and what they mean, and answering their questions. The class coincided with the day after Keith went into the hospital. The rabbi offered to find someone else to take over, but I took a deep breath and said I'd do it. I'd promised, and a last-minute replacement would not be easy to locate.

I left the hospital right before the class was scheduled to start and entered the sanctuary just as the students were arriving. Many of them were looking around, wide-eyed. Some had been in a synagogue before, but most had not. I tried not to be distracted by worrying about Keith.

All of the students were seated, and I began explaining about the kippah I was wearing, the prayer shawls, the Eternal Light, the menorah, the Ark, the memorial boards. By the time their teacher and I unrolled the Torah, the students had fully captured my attention, and standing with the Torah always fills my consciousness. Not until the class was over, the ritual objects put away, the Torah locked safely in the Ark, and I was getting into my car to drive back to the hospital was I aware that for the first time since the paramedics had taken Keith, I had become calm. I might have been giving to others, but I was getting much more in return.

Thank You, Lord, that in giving to others I have received so much. —RHODA BLECKER

Digging Deeper: PSALM 119:97

Wed 11

The Lord thy God is with thee whithersoever thou goest.
—JOSHUA 1:9 (KJV)

I'll admit it: for years I've been a nervous driver. Bridges. Mountains. Wet roads. Parking garages. Narrow streets. Interstates. Rush-hour crush. Any number of scenarios makes me grit my teeth as I grip the wheel. My tension abates as I ease off the gas, coasting into my own street.

Home and safe, I thought, sighing, on a recent evening. Setting down my umbrella, I glanced at the ceramic plaque hung years ago right inside my front door: "Peace be with you." In my decorative scheme, its message was meant for visitors. But as I turned the lock and settled in for the night, I claimed the motto for myself, here in my home, within my sturdy brick walls.

Later in the week a young neighbor girl, who struggles to read and whose family speaks Spanish, stopped in after school as she does every day. "We can talk and play for half an hour," I explained, "but then I have to go out."

As I gathered up my purse and gloves, dreading my drive toward rush-hour dusk, she stood by the door and nodded toward the plaque. "What does it say?" she asked, as if seeing it for the first time.

Drawing close and pointing out each word, I read out loud the four one-syllable words. Then I heard a second question: "What does *peace* mean?"

"Well," I proposed, "peace is the opposite of fighting and peace is the opposite of being afraid." Before I could think of a third explanation, she interrupted. "It means God be with you."

Was it a statement or a question? I wasn't sure. But as I reached for the doorknob, I heartily said, "Yes!"

God be with me. As I leave my own home, as I drive into the night, as my heart opens to accept His peace.

*Lord, be with me today. Enfold me in
Your presence. Fill me with Your peace.*
—EVELYN BENCE

Digging Deeper: ISAIAH 26:3

Thu 12 *Love thy neighbor as thyself....*
—LEVITICUS 19:18 (KJV)

I'm always in a hurry for spring to arrive. The sky was solid gray and the limbs of the trees naked. I was bundled up, entering the grocery store. En route to the fruit section, I passed the florist. Flowering bulbs had arrived on this rainy afternoon. Daffodils, tulips, and hyacinths sat in neat rows along the shelves. The fragrances brought me back to my childhood.

We had lived next door to a widow who grew magnificent flowers. As a child, I got down on my hands and knees to smell the hyacinths. Many years later, standing in the grocery store, a silent voice seemed to urge, *You can have one!*

I placed the white hyacinths in my cart by my purse. When I checked out, the woman in line behind me offered, "Oh, who's the lucky person to receive those? How lovely!"

"It's for me." I responded. "From myself!" I hand-carried my sweet-smelling promise of spring to the car.

Father, sometimes I forget about loving myself.
Thank You for this tender reminder.
—MARION BOND WEST

Digging Deeper: EPHESIANS 5:2, 1 JOHN 4:7

Fri 13

I long to see you so that
I may impart to you some
spiritual gift to make you strong.
—ROMANS 1:11 (NIV)

When I received a letter from my dear friend Roberta, who lives hundreds of miles away in West Virginia, I noticed that she had written something in neat letters along the V-shaped seal on the back of the envelope. It was a quote from the author Phyllis Theroux: "To send a letter is a good way to go somewhere without moving anything but your heart."

Inside the letter, Roberta wrote, "I have a bad headache and can't sleep, but am thinking about you and your prayer ministry. Thank you so much for praying me through so many seasons of my life."

Have I really done that much for her? I wondered. *I rarely know what's going on in her day-to-day world, and we haven't seen each other in several years.* But we weren't so far out of touch after all. Every morning I was in contact with God about Roberta because I pray for her at the same spot near some rose bushes on my morning prayer walk. I took out my journal, inspired to change Theroux's quote ever so slightly: "To say a prayer for someone is a good way to be there for her without moving anything but your heart."

Dear Father, take my heart on a prayer journey
today to erase the distance between those
I love and me. Amen. —KAREN BARBER

Digging Deeper: ROMANS 15:30–33,
EPHESIANS 3:14–21

Sat 14

"You shall be near me, you and your children and your children's children...."
—GENESIS 45:10 (RSV)

I can't believe it's almost over," my son, Harrison, said. We were in Snowmass, Colorado, enjoying a father/son ski trip over spring break. Harrison is shuttling between two families. He has a stepmom and a stepdad and new siblings on both sides. I felt I needed to make every effort to stay close to my son.

"I know, buddy, time really does fly when you're having fun."

As we boarded the lift for one last run, we sat together quietly. I couldn't help but wonder what

Harrison was thinking. Tomorrow we were headed home to Nashville, Tennessee. A flood of worries came over me. Being thirteen is hard enough on its own. In addition to a tough schedule at school and legs and arms that seem to grow an inch a night, we were scheduled to see the orthodontist to get braces for Harrison. *God,* I prayed, *help me give my son the stable foundation he needs.*

"Holy cow, Dad!" Harrison yelled, pointing behind us. As the lift carried us toward the top of the mountain, the sun broke through the gray sky, illuminating a pristine snowcapped scene. Harrison put his arm on my shoulder. "Seeing that mountain lit up like that makes it hard to understand how a person might not believe in God," he said.

It seemed, too, like God was answering my urgent prayer with a gentle reminder: *Be still. Trust. Remember I am here.*

> *Father, I claim Your promises for my children.*
> *Please stay close and wrap them in Your love.*
> —BROCK KIDD

Digging Deeper: 2 CHRONICLES 16:9, 3 JOHN 1:4

Sun 15

"Look, the Lion of the tribe of Judah, the heir to David's throne, has won the victory...."
—REVELATION 5:5 (NLT)

I walked through the door of the sanctuary, glancing through the congregation. All were taking their seats before the music started. *Where should I sit today?* I enjoyed taking a different seat each week, so I could meet new people. There was one place I'd wanted to sit for a long time but hadn't. The first few rows on the right side always brimmed with Native Americans. I hadn't ever seen anyone else sit with them. *Why not today?*

Cradling my Bible, I walked up to Debbie. I knew that she was a tribal member of the Salish Kootenai and the notoriously fierce Blackfoot nations. "Do you mind if I sit next to you?" I asked.

"Please do," she said, looking pleasantly surprised.

As I settled in, I chuckled. "I figured that I could sit here because I'm from one of the fiercest tribes that the world has ever known." Debbie's brows furrowed. "I'm Norwegian. The Vikings were a warring tribe that terrorized the earth."

Debbie and I burst into laughter until tears formed in the corners of our eyes. Everyone around us turned to look at us. Then Debbie shared the miraculous words: "Rebecca, we're both part of the same tribe—the tribe of Judah."

Lord, thank You for binding us all together in Your family. Amen. —REBECCA ONDOV

Digging Deeper: EPHESIANS 2:19–22

Mon 16

Thus says the Lord: "Keep justice, and do righteousness...."
—ISAIAH 56:1 (ESV)

Maggie glared across the table at John. "You got the biggest portion. That's not fair!" My children have a problem with portions. When it comes to dessert, one of them always tries to get the biggest piece of cake, the most generous serving of ice cream. And another has a sharp eye out to make sure the portions are all equal, that everyone has what's due to him or her, no more and no less. And making sure that's so, in much more than desserts, is one of the challenges of being a parent.

"How come he gets more screen time than me?" "How come I got a time-out for that and she didn't?" "Why couldn't I go along on her special time with Dad?"

Yes, I've read plenty of parenting books, and I know that fairness and consistency are important in raising my children. But it doesn't always work out like that. If I'm irritable, or still annoyed from the last time one child transgressed, or charmed by a particularly fulsome apology or creative excuse, I'm inclined to bend the rules just a tad. And nobody is as quick to focus on a perceived injustice as a child.

I'm sorry to say that my justice problems aren't confined to parenting. Whether it's a question of spending my time at the computer and not sharing it with others, or taking that bit of extra money and spending it on myself, or, sad but true, eating an extra cookie or spoonful of ice cream, I'm too often giving myself more than my due and others less. Learning "to keep justice" can be a lifelong lesson.

Lord, I come before Your judgment seat.
Thank You that Your justice is tempered with mercy.
—ANDREW ATTAWAY

Digging Deeper: PSALM 50:5–7

Tue 17

"Do not be afraid or discouraged. For the Lord your God is with you wherever you go."
—JOSHUA 1:9 (NLT)

Saint Patrick's Day—what a cliché, what a marketing coup for the color green and all the tinny faux-Irish twaddle for sale, what an unfortunate prompt for off-key caterwaulings of "Danny Boy." But every year I take solace in the fact that at least it is a day for bending hearts and minds toward the brave wet green rock from which my forebears came. Attention and concentration is a form of prayer, yes?

I find myself, every year, praying quietly for poor Patricius, kidnapped at age sixteen from his Scottish village, thrown into a foul slave ship, and sold to a warlord in Ireland. A boy the age of my sons, sent by his master to watch sheep for six years on Sliabh Mis, the lonely mountain, with no companions but the birds of the air and the creatures of the crags. "Humbled every day by hunger and nakedness," he later wrote, "in snow, in icy coldness, in rain," offering hundreds of prayers day and night. There are many among us who would end up suicidal or homicidal after six years of solitary slavery. But there came unto him a vision, and he was filled with joy and followed instructions to leave Sliabh Mis and walk to the sea, where freedom awaited.

Here your usual dramatic story would end. But Patricius bravely, crazily returned twenty-five years later, baptizing thousands, seeding hundreds of churches, gently persuading the people of the land that love defeats violence, hope defeats despair, light defeats darkness. The joy that filled him on the lonely mountain never left him, and he changed the course of history without any weapon but his own wit and word. That is the man I celebrate today: joy-bringer, far-walker, mercy-messenger. *La fhéile Pádraig sona daoibh.* Happy Saint Patrick's Day to you and yours!

Dear Unimaginable Grace, how many times have You watched with pleasure as Your children endured and rose to their gifts, changed the world, shoved it an inch closer to Your light? And Patricius was a great one of these, was he not? —BRIAN DOYLE

Digging Deeper: JAMES 1:2–4

Wed 18

For now we see in a mirror, dimly, but then we will see face to face. Now I know only in part; then I will know fully, even as I have been fully known.
—1 CORINTHIANS 13:12 (NRSV)

Mom, I don't like the snow anymore," I overheard a tot say to his mother as they passed by me.

I'm right there with ya, kid, I thought as I bent my head down to protect my face from the blizzardlike snow flurries. Although the weather report had shown a late snowstorm in the forecast, I had dismissed it and forgotten to pack my umbrella. And as beautiful as the snow looked, I couldn't help but be annoyed. How could it be snowing when the spring equinox was exactly two days away? Even as March turned to April, I couldn't fathom the end of winter.

So, too, with my own personal winters: my sadness, my insecurities, my loneliness. Just as I could only see a few feet in front of me now, I can't always see to the endpoint of my trauma.

But as I experience the return of warm weather year after year, I know the end of the pain is coming. Even as I continue to cycle through the good and the bad, I have to trust and believe in the promises God has made. So I breathe, put one foot in front of the other, and try to stay focused on the One Who never changes.

God, give me the strength and courage to endure the winters of my life. —NATALIE PERKINS

Digging Deeper: ECCLESIASTES 3:1, 1 CORINTHIANS 13:9–10

Thu 19

Return to your rest, my soul, for the Lord has been good to you.
—PSALM 116:7 (NIV)

Electricity. It's all about electricity. That was my realization this morning when I came to work and found out my office had none. No lights. No phone. No computer. No way to charge my cell. This was a new office space, and our recent move had gone relatively smoothly... until now.

I'd been anxious to get to work early. I'd skipped the gym, barely eaten breakfast, and blown through my meditation time. These are the three things I do daily to keep myself connected physically and spiritually before I get distracted by the details of life. But I was in too much of a hurry. Too much to do. Not enough time.

And now, no electricity. Really? Today of all days? I drummed my fingers on my desk. What was I supposed to do? Sit here in the dark? A quiet inner voice seemed to answer: *Yes.*

That would be weird, wouldn't it? People would think I'd gone crazy. Didn't I need to take some sort of action? *Not at all,* said that inner voice. *Try it.*

I closed my door, then groped my way back to my chair in the pitch black. I sat down, tried to get comfortable, and wondered, *Why am I doing this?*

I waited. In the darkness my breathing slowed. My pulse decelerated. My irritation subsided. The anxiety that had been the driving force behind my morning receded. The world and its worries seemed far away, as if God had gently covered my eyes so I could see what was really important, what I'd failed to connect to—the true source of power.

I closed my eyes and said a prayer for serenity and for the strength I would need to face my day and a whisper of gratitude for the comfort of darkness.

Lord, it isn't really all about electricity. I know that.
Thanks for turning the lights back on.
—EDWARD GRINNAN

Digging Deeper: PSALM 119:105

Fri 20

As ye are partakers of the sufferings,
so shall ye be also of the consolation.
—2 CORINTHIANS 1:7 (KJV)

I was checking my e-mail when a new message popped up: "Emily passed away quietly at 5:50 this morning."

A few weeks earlier my husband, David, a former minister, had received a call from a friend asking him to visit Emily. She was dying, the friend said, and David might be of some help.

"Pam," David said after that first visit, "you've got to meet Emily! You have everything in common—optimism, community involvement, faith!"

I swallowed hard and shook my head, resolved to not get involved. "No, I've had enough death vigils. I can't do it anymore."

The next time David visited, he was adamant that I meet her.

"No," I insisted, and then for some reason I softened.

The moment our eyes met, Emily and I were friends. An honesty connected us that was completely natural. She wanted to hear about my study of angels, my belief in "the other side." She talked of death as a trip that led from here to that other place—a place she was eager to see. We laughed and forgot to feel sad.

The next week Emily came for dinner. I made our favorite comfort foods: lemon chicken, green beans, and chocolate pie. Then we stood out on the deck, imagining the Nashville skyline. "We should have known each other sooner," she said weakly. Now, she was gone.

I stood on the deck and looked up into the sky. I knew for sure Emily was out there. Our friendship hadn't ended. I would see her again. "And, yes, Emily, the view is glorious."

Father, I expected death. You showed me life. Thank You for allowing me a glimpse of glory through Emily's eyes. —PAM KIDD

Digging Deeper: LUKE 6:21, ROMANS 12:15, 1 PETER 4:13

Sat 21

He who finds a wife finds a good thing and obtains favor from the Lord. —PROVERBS 18:22 (ESV)

I felt married the moment Emily and I got engaged. There was no more decision to be made, no more soul-searching or foot-dragging. I had promised myself to Emily forever. So for a long time I thought our wedding would be just a nice celebration and a way to include our family and friends in our commitment to each other. I was so naïve.

Our wedding was on the grounds of a lovely restaurant in Austin, Texas, Emily's hometown. All of our family and friends were there, but once I saw Emily walk toward me in her white dress, as beautiful as I'd ever seen her, it was like we were the only two people there. I squeezed her hand, my heart pounding as we turned toward our minister. I knew Sarah's words were an authentic description of the love and commitment Emily and I had for each other, but only because I'd worked for so many weeks with Emily to have a ceremony that was right for us.

Then it was time to make our vows. We'd chosen traditional ones: "In the name of God, I, Sam, take you, Emily, to be my wife, to have and to hold from this day forward...."

I finally felt what was really happening. I was not making a promise to Emily alone or even to the guests. By speaking the same words so many of my ancestors had spoken in their moments of greatest reverence for each other and for God, the words had become hallowed. Before, I had promised myself to Emily. Now, I promised myself to God.

Thank You, Lord, for transforming my love into something heavenly. —SAM ADRIANCE

Digging Deeper: NUMBERS 30:2

Sun 22

> *I will speak of Your splendor and glorious majesty and Your wonderful works. They will proclaim the power of Your awe-inspiring acts, and I will declare Your greatness.*
> —PSALM 145:5–6 (HCS)

I was back at my alma mater, Princeton, for a conference. I arrived on campus a few minutes earlier than expected. So I did something I used to do as a student when I had time to kill: I went to the chapel to sit for a bit. Though built in the 1920s, the cathedral-like chapel has a soaring nave and flying buttresses that harken back to another era, not just in church architecture but also in its attitude toward God.

Back in the seventeenth and eighteenth centuries, when it was more customary to build those grand, Gothic houses of God, the building was intended to reflect divine majesty. Those spires pointing to the heavens, those windows telling stories of saints— they served at once to humble the worshipper and exalt the worshipped.

While the Bible tells us frequently that our God is gracious and good in an individual, deeply personal way, it also emphasizes that God is great beyond our comprehension. Just a few minutes on a hard wooden pew, seeing the morning light refracted through the resplendent stained glass, reminded me that part of God's divine mystery is how He can hold these qualities in perfect balance. There, sitting quietly, I returned to a place of wonder and awe, of true and utter worship.

God, You are majestic and great beyond human description. I praise You for Who You are.
—JEFF CHU

Digging Deeper: PSALMS 29, 93

Mon 23

But let all who take refuge in you be glad; let them ever sing for joy.... —PSALM 5:11 (NIV)

It was my mother-in-law on the phone. I had called her to plan my family's upcoming trip to her house in Minneapolis, where my husband grew up and where a big chunk of his heart still resides. Mom and I talked about plans for various meals, sleeping arrangements, daily comings and goings that might mesh with Prisca's nap schedule. Perry and I get to the Twin Cities only twice a year; each visit is priceless to us all.

Mom was eager for our arrival date to dawn, but quickly added, "Oh, but the time will fly once you're here and then you'll be gone again. How I hate to say those good-byes."

I was tempted to scold her but thought better of it. The truth is, I do the same thing. I did it just last night. I coveted the joy of hosting a dinner party and then unwittingly sabotaged it by being too busy to take in all the pleasure. I killed it before it even had been born. I'm constantly living this way, thinking more about my next to-do than about the delight that's right here at hand, racing from fretfulness to fretfulness rather than resting with one sweet moment.

I don't want to live like that anymore. I want my life to be an inviting guest room, where joy can walk in and stay awhile. I want to treasure her visit each time she comes, without wasting a lick of energy on the inevitable good-bye.

> *Father, let my day today sing not for sorrow,*
> *but sing—and sing loudly!—for joy.*
> —ASHLEY WIERSMA

Digging Deeper: PSALM 98:4

Tue 24

"But seek first his kingdom and his righteousness, and all these things will be given to you as well."
—MATTHEW 6:33 (NIV)

Retinitis pigmentosa," the doctor said, and finally the dreaded day came. I awoke, held my hands in front of my face, and saw nothing. At thirty-one, I was facing the rest of my life as a blind person. It terrified me.

"I can't do this, God. I hate my life," I whispered. How could God let a young mother go blind? Why would He refuse to answer my prayers for sight? Family and friends tried to support me, but none could understand the depth of my pain.

Then a friend called. "Come to my church. You'll enjoy the service." A trace of hope flickered, and I went. The message of Matthew 6:33 shook me. God was asking me to seek Him first. Tears rolled down my cheeks. I soaked in God's Word. He promised to be a lamp to my feet and a light to my path. I believed it. I received it. And I applied it to my every moment as a wife and mom.

My life is peaceful now. Rest comes knowing God guides my footsteps, holds my future, and erases my fear.

Father, no matter how dark our world gets, Your light of victory still shines. —JANET PEREZ ECKLES

Digging Deeper: DEUTERONOMY 31:6

Wed 25   *Surely your goodness and love will follow me all the days of my life....* —PSALM 23:6 (NIV)

When daylight is a gray sliver pressing through the bedroom drapes, I wake to my picture wall. I found the frames on clearance. "Best deal ever," I'd said to my oldest son. We snagged them and he helped me find pictures and hang them. They are beautiful.

But when I woke the next day, I ached over the passage of time as I looked at the framed photos of my family. There's a close-up of my youngest clinging to the shoulder of my oldest. The baby's fingers are still plump, and his wrists hold a deep crease. There's one of Gabriel, now eight, when he was two. His swim trunks graze his ankles, and the sandcastle he's standing beside is taller than he is. There's one of my husband, Lonny, and me, arms looped around each other; the freshness of youth still shadows our smiles.

This morning, though, I had a different feeling. Those pictures capture moments and memories that were made along our way. The children have grown and changed. Lonny and I have changed too. But our story isn't finished.

When I'd gotten those frames, I thought I'd found the best deal ever. But filling frames with life to come? That's the best deal yet.

Thank You, God, for special moments, for the sweetness of days, and for the days that are still to come. Amen. —SHAWNELLE ELIASEN

Digging Deeper: EZEKIEL 34:26, MALACHI 3:10, LUKE 12:32

Thu 26

"Consider the lilies, how they grow: they neither toil nor spin; and yet I say to you, even Solomon in all his glory was not arrayed like one of these." —LUKE 12:27 (NKJV)

As I was exiting the elevator at the hospital where I work, a coworker entered. "Love your outfit, Roberta," she said. "Must be nice to have a fancy wardrobe like that."

I smiled. "GW again." GW is short for Goodwill, known as the original recycler. I was wearing a linen foil-embroidered jacket I'd found there for $1.50, a glitzy white tank top with gold beads I'd discovered for $1.38, and a pair of ankle pants I'd snagged for $1.25.

Goodwill was founded in 1902 by a Methodist minister who collected used household goods and clothing in the wealthier areas of Boston, then trained and hired the poor to repair and sell them. His vision has now expanded into a four-billion-dollar nonprofit organization that sells gently used goods and hires people of limited employability. "A hand up, not a handout" is Goodwill's philosophy.

This pioneering recycler is great for the environment and terrific on my pocketbook. It's one of the Lord's wonderful provisions.

Thank You, Lord, for teaching me the pleasures of recycling. —ROBERTA MESSNER

Digging Deeper: MATTHEW 6:26, HEBREWS 13:5

Fri 27

"This is the bread that comes down from heaven, so that one may eat of it and not die." —JOHN 6:50 (NRSV)

My sister Maria always made Easter bread. Her braided bread wreaths topped with pastel-colored eggs were a festive treat we enjoyed every spring. Yet somehow I'd completely forgotten them until this year.

I was thinning down my collection of recipe books and flipped through one I inherited from Maria. It's hard to believe it's been five years since she died. The book opened to a page stained with dribs and drabs, the recipe for Easter bread. Maria was the baker, the cook, the family hostess. Her house was always decorated for every holiday and filled with her delicious goodies. My baking was a joke next to hers, so I didn't even try.

I touched the well-used recipe and thought of all the time Maria and I spent together. Growing up, she had been a second mother to me, helping me fall asleep when I was nervous about school, and later working for days, baking and decorating my three-tiered wedding cake. Throughout my life, Maria was the voice of encouragement, lifting me up and cheering me on. After Solomon was born, she visited to lend a hand. She looked at me with such love in her eyes and said, "I'm so proud of you. I knew you'd be a good mom."

This year I'll make Easter bread for my family, I thought. I'll do my best and ask Maria for a little help. Re-creating one of her traditions, I'll honor her life and the glorious promise of Easter—that one day we'll have the infinite joy of being reunited.

Dear Lord, as the years pass, the weight of grief lifts and old joys resurface to remind me that love and life are everlasting. —SABRA CIANCANELLI

Digging Deeper: 2 SAMUEL 12:3, 1 THESSALONIANS 4:17

A TURKISH LENT

Sat 28   *Evening, and morning, and at noon, will I pray....* —PSALM 55:17 (KJV)

SATURDAY BEFORE PALM SUNDAY: SHARING FAITH

Morning in Istanbul had dawned flamingo pink and gold, so when the *muezzin* called the faithful to prayer, I felt inspired to use the reminder to pray as well. Sure, I still said my morning prayers and grace at meals, even alone during this retreat, but a few more prayers throughout the day seemed a worthy Lenten practice. Alas, my good intentions lasted only a few days before I lapsed into my irregular prayer rhythm.

Weeks later during a break, I craned over my balcony to glimpse the Sea of Marmara, barely visible as eastern blue haze. Below, an elderly gentleman wearing a woolen skullcap carried a blue plastic tarp and rake across the lush lawn. I surmised he was a gardener for the apartment complex, as primroses bloomed in profusion and tulips, a colorful symbol of Istanbul, poked a few inches through the warming earth.

While I was absorbed in this tranquil scene, the call to prayer rolled fuguelike from all the mosques in the city. The gardener began to pray right there on the lawn. He stood with his back toward me, facing east, palms outstretched. His blue tarp had become a prayer rug. He kneeled on it, prostrated himself, rose, and repeated the sequence several times.

The gardener literally dropped what he was doing to pray. His devotion humbled me.

Minutes later, he resumed his duties. I watched him rake under another bush, mound the debris onto his tarp, and disappear around the building.

Without a word, this stranger, who did not share my faith, forced me to rethink my own slipshod prayer practices and taught me profound truths about my own faith as well.

Lord of all, may I always learn from those who love You. —GAIL THORELL SCHILLING

Digging Deeper: PROVERBS 20:6–7

A TURKISH LENT

Sun 29   *For you know that when your faith is tested, your endurance has a chance to grow.* —JAMES 1:3 (NLT)

PALM SUNDAY: AMERICAN CATHEDRAL IN PARIS

Pink blossoms bob on branches framing the Eiffel Tower, and yellow tulips sway along the Champs du Mars under blue skies. These delightful distractions, plus construction barriers and a few wrong turns exiting the metro, have made me late for church. Never have I been so eager to attend a service.

I dash into the American Cathedral in Paris and slide into a pew just as the procession begins. "All glory, laud and honor" fills the sanctuary with familiar melody; clergy and readers in recognizable red and white vestments wave the palms. Even the US state flags suspended over the sanctuary make me feel at home. Suddenly, here in this church where I know no one, I experience reunion so powerful I am too overcome to sing.

Until today, I have spent all of Lent in Turkey without any Christian fellowship. God, in His infinite wisdom, had a lot to teach me in the land of my Christian ancestors, where few spoke my language and fewer still understood my faith practices. It was during my recent sojourn in ancient Cappadocia that one of my traveling companions suggested, "You have to leave your country to understand it." Perhaps this is true of accidental pilgrims like me who learn truths about their faith communities by living without them, at least for a while.

As this Holy Week begins, I ponder my recent time of testing. Now Jesus begins His. Thanks to my solitary Lent, I begin to understand the loneliness, the endurance, and the faith of His Passion.

Father of all, wherever I am, You are there.
I can endure. —GAIL THORELL SCHILLING

Digging Deeper: PSALM 37:18

A TURKISH LENT

Mon 30 *A man's heart plans his way,*
But the Lord directs his steps.
—PROVERBS 16:9 (NKJV)

MONDAY OF HOLY WEEK: A JOURNEY IN TRUST

Why don't you visit Cappadocia before you leave Turkey?" e-mails my son's fiancée, who has lent me her apartment in Istanbul.

Good idea, I think. After two months writing my memoir, I need a break and begin to research some options.

When Ercan, my host, hears my plan, he insists, "I have a very good travel agent. I will take care of it."

Indeed, the itinerary will take me to the historical and geological wonders of a land I know only from the Bible. In the early darkness, we drive to the Olympiad Stadium to find a single car idling. My host speaks to the driver, then to me. "This is your ride to the airport. You're with a small tour group. No bus."

I trust my host, who has taken such good care of me, and climb into the sedan. The driver nods and merges into traffic while the friendly interpreter explains, "We drive one hour to the airport on the Asian side of Istanbul. I help you find your flight. Once you arrive in Kayseri, you will meet your guide and group. Easy!"

Predawn Istanbul glitters with a million lights and silhouettes of mosques as we streak across the bridge spanning the Bosporus. Low and exotic music drifts from the radio. With no itinerary in hand, a tiny

Turkish dictionary in my purse, and utter faith in my host, his travel agency, and God, I begin my Lenten pilgrimage, a solitary journey in trust.

> *Lord, I am so alone. Be with me.*
> —GAIL THORELL SCHILLING

Digging Deeper: EXODUS 2:22, PSALM 146:9, 1 PETER 1:1–2

A TURKISH LENT

Tue 31

> *For we are strangers before thee, and sojourners, as were all our fathers....*
> —1 CHRONICLES 29:15 (KJV)

TUESDAY OF HOLY WEEK: ON TO CAPPADOCIA

By the time I arrive at the Kayseri airport in Turkey and find the tour company's gleaming minivan and easygoing guide, I have already met my fellow travelers. Two sat next to me on the plane. All four travelers and guide are young professionals about my children's ages, and four of the five speak English. Serpil, a clothing designer, quickly draws each person into the conversation, shares apricots, laughs a lot, and even leads singing.

March

Our driver cruises through endless high desert a lot like Wyoming while Mehmet explains the topography. Though primroses bloom in Istanbul, here more than three thousand feet above sea level, snow banks the sides of the deserted roads and covers the rough plains that stretch to the mountains.

The first stop overlooks Pigeon Valley, a ravine edged by hundreds of eroded pinnacles pocked with caves and dovecots, homes for ancient people and their pigeons. Silence envelops us like a silken shawl. Then, as if on cue, a rustle of wings swoops overhead. Pigeons race across the valley as they have for eons.

As we sip glasses of hot tea, our guide sketches a brief history of this region. Christians lived here for seven centuries. Mehmet speaks in Turkish to my companions, remembers me, slides into English, and then back to Turkish. Because I cannot understand his Turkish words, I am often alone with my thoughts. Strangely, I do not feel lonely. In this magical land of cave dwellings and bizarre stone pillars, I sense the spirit of my Christian ancestors. No, I am not alone.

Heavenly Father, I begin to comprehend: You are, indeed, everywhere. —GAIL THORELL SCHILLING

Digging Deeper: GENESIS 23:4, DEUTERONOMY 31:6

DAILY JOYS

1 _____

2 _____

3 _____

4 _____

5 _____

6 _____

7 _____

8 _____

9 _____

10 _____

11 _____

12 _____

13 _____

14 _____

15 _____

March

16 _____

17 _____

18 _____

19 _____

20 _____

21 _____

22 _____

23 _____

24 _____

25 _____

26 _____

27 _____

28 _____

29 _____

30 _____

31 _____

APRIL

*My heart and flesh sing for joy
to the living God.*

—PSALM 84:2 (ESV)

A TURKISH LENT

Wed 1 *Now therefore ye are no more strangers
and foreigners, but fellow-citizens
with the saints, and of the household of
God.* —EPHESIANS 2:19 (KJV)

WEDNESDAY OF HOLY WEEK: GÖREME

In Göreme, site of early Christian cave churches, we follow our guide up icy stone stairs toward a six-foot opening in the ocher cliff. About 1,200 years ago, people in this valley found naturally eroded caves and carved them deeper to create hiding places and sacred spaces. We enter the Chapel of Saint Basil, a dim, vaulted cavern the size of a garage.

Our guide points out the low wall in the nave, a burial place for early believers, and keyhole-shaped doorways under the arches. I discern faded paintings on the earthen walls: pale-red geometric designs and indistinct human images. As my eyes adjust to the dim light, I can just make out the faint likenesses of the Virgin Mary and Baby Jesus. Mehmet explains in English that the painting is one thousand years old. I am transfixed by this image. After five weeks of Lenten solitude in Turkey, I have found a palpable Christian connection. My reaction surprises me: I weep. Mehmet regards me quizzically. "This painting is very special to me," I explain.

The next day as we travel to Avanos to watch potters at work, Mehmet says, "There are hundreds of Christian churches in Cappadocia. We accept this..." The conversation veers into Turkish.

He and my group are Muslim, yet they accept me as readily as the Christian artifacts abounding in their homeland. Within this ancient civilization of bizarre rock formations and an unfamiliar tongue, I feel increasingly secure in the roots of my heritage—and the kindness of strangers who are fast becoming friends.

Lord of all, ever strengthen my trust in the complexity of Your creation. —GAIL THORELL SCHILLING

Digging Deeper: MALACHI 2:10, MATTHEW 5:9

A TURKISH LENT

Thu 2

With stammering lips and another tongue will he speak to this people. —ISAIAH 28:11 (KJV)

MAUNDY THURSDAY: EXPLAINING EASTER

My companions and I savor a lavish Turkish breakfast at our hotel. Passover is in just two days. Over cheeses, tomatoes, olives, cucumbers, omelets, and breads washed down with glasses of hot tea, I casually remark that I will be home in time for Easter.

"What is Easter?" asks my companion, a microbiologist at a university in Istanbul.

"Is it eggs?" asks Serpil, the clothing designer. All eyes are on me now.

These women are curious to learn. I have taught Sunday school for years but never to scholars with PhDs. No matter, the truth is the same.

"Well, Easter is our most joyful celebration. Christians believe that on that day, Jesus rose from the dead after being crucified. So we, too, will rise from the dead. The Easter egg is a symbol of new life."

"Jesus died . . . and came back to life?" My new friend makes sure she has understood. I imagine how extraordinary this must sound.

"Yes. We call it the Resurrection." They nod, acknowledging they have heard me. After a few quiet moments, conversation turns to other things.

Later that day, we tour the five-story-tall stone cones into which the early Christians carved chambers to create a monastery. Somehow, the faith arrived here from the Holy Land. Somehow, it continued to be handed down for centuries. Somehow, the faith still endures. I do not aspire to proselytize, evangelize, or preach. Yet today I simply answered a question and, in a tiny way, added to the legacy of my faith.

> *Holy Father, I never quite know how You will use me. May I always be ready.*
> —GAIL THORELL SCHILLING

> *Digging Deeper:* MATTHEW 28:19, JOHN 11:25, 2 TIMOTHY 2:2

A TURKISH LENT

Fri 3
    They wandered in deserts, and in mountains, and in dens and caves of the earth. —HEBREWS 11:38 (KJV)

GOOD FRIDAY: GIVING COMFORT

By day three, our little group has spent hours together riding in the van, sharing meals, and chatting over tea. We now know a bit about one another's families, careers, and faith practices. We have grown close. In fact, we feel comfortable enough to admit to some anxiety about the next stop, the underground city of Derinkuyu, eight stories deep. Serpil discloses that she is claustrophobic. I'm anxious too.

Interior light dims as we follow Mehmet. Down we go over hand-hewn rock stairs, zigzagging along narrow corridors and into cramped chambers that graze the tops of our heads. Some tunnels are so small, we must stoop and waddle through them. Mercifully, gratings between floors and a central shaft provide plenty of air. Our guide points out carved tethers for animals, stones for kitchen use, a chapel. I try to imagine rolling that great wheel of stone to block the door against invaders. It looks like the one that blocked Jesus's tomb. We marvel at the stone's size and photograph each other next to it.

Soon I notice Serpil has stopped talking. "Are you okay?" She doesn't answer. I meet her boyfriend's glance. He takes one of her hands; I take the other. Together, we lead her through the cramped tunnels, toward light and space. We never let go until we emerge and Serpil breathes deeply again.

Many times now, I've relived this Derinkuyu experience, which has become for me a profound metaphor of familial love: We of different faiths—holding hands in dark, scary places—comforting each other.

Father of all, help us to find
You in each person we meet.
—GAIL THORELL SCHILLING

Digging Deeper: PSALM 133:1–3, 1 PETER 2:17

A TURKISH LENT

Sat 4

> *In thee, O Lord, do I put my trust; let me never be put to confusion.*
> —Psalm 71:1 (KJV)

HOLY SATURDAY: IN GOD'S HANDS

The evening of our last day, my companions and I wedge ourselves into the van now stuffed with souvenirs and reflect dreamily on mystical Cappadocia. At the Kayseri airport, however, afterglow gives way to practicalities. We find our departure information and enjoy one last Turkish coffee. Mehmet asks if I have transport back in Istanbul. I push down a prickle of panic. "I thought that was included in the tour package!"

"Ah." He frowns. "I will take care of it." He makes a quick phone call and smiles. "You will be met." Even once I'm picked up at the airport, I need to reach my hosts at the original drop-off point.

Stop worrying! I chide myself. *Keep trusting. You are in God's hands.*

My driver appears as promised. He speaks no English. Serpil makes sure he understands where I need to go before she leaves me.

I am the only passenger for the hour-long ride. Eventually, I recognize Istanbul landmarks. When we reach the roundabout near the drop-off point, my driver loops past my exit. I gasp. "*Bu.* This." He glances anxiously over his shoulder at me—and circles the rotary again. "*Bu!* This!" I plead. After a couple of loops, he understands my feeble Turkish and exits toward the Olympic stadium. I spot my host Ercan's vehicle.

"*Dür!* Stop!" He stops. "*Çok güzel!*" I assure him. "Very good!" I don't know who sighs with greater relief.

"You have had a pleasant journey, yes?" asks Ercan as he lifts my bag. "You see, you can trust my good travel agent."

"Yes." I smile. *And my faithful God.*

Dear Lord, thank You for this Lenten lesson in trust.
—GAIL THORELL SCHILLING

Digging Deeper: PSALM 78:53; ISAIAH 12:2, 58:11

A TURKISH LENT

Sun 5 *But they did not believe the women, because their words seemed to them like nonsense.* —LUKE 24:11 (NIV)

EASTER: HALLELUJAH!

When I was twelve, Uncle Bub tried to convince the Sunday school class that once we were older, we'd love Easter more than Christmas. Though we didn't dare roll our eyes, none of us believed him. Surely, he was teasing us as he did so often.

Yet to me, the intervening years have proved him right. Uncle Bub knew that Easter grants spiritual gifts we gradually grow into, so unlike toys we quickly outgrow. Now, decades later, I find that my recent travels have blessed me with yet more appreciation of this glorious day.

This Easter morning, I am home. I sit in "my" pew, seventh back on the right, snuggled between my daughters. They are flanked by my granddaughter and son-in-law; my nuclear family fills the row. My parish family celebrates a rousing liturgy: organ, trumpet, chamber orchestra, and choir thunder "Hallelujahs" that nearly rattle the windows.

I last heard "Hallelujah" the Sunday before Lent at Saint Anthony of Padua in Istanbul, where the service was sung in Italian. Since then I have celebrated the Christian message in several countries and find that I need not speak the local language to understand it. Even in desolate regions of Turkey where the early Christians hid in caves, I have discovered a spiritual connection with my ancestors in faith.

Today we celebrate Jesus's triumph over death. I rejoice with my family and my parish community. And now I understand, as Uncle Bub hoped I would, that I am also part of a worldwide family of believers who glory in the astonishing Easter promise.

Giver of Life, hallelujah! Hallelujah!
—GAIL THORELL SCHILLING

Digging Deeper: MATTHEW 28:5–6; MARK 16:2, 4

GOD OF JOYFUL SURPRISES

Mon 6 *A friend loves at all times....*
—PROVERBS 17:17 (RSV)

FRIENDSHIP

It still hangs in my closet: a shapeless pink housecoat.

I'd flown from New York City to Covington, Georgia, to teach a one-day seminar. I knew Colleen, the organizer, only through e-mail, but in the motel room she'd thoughtfully laid out snack food and an electric pad for my troublesome back.

At the close of the seminar, I boarded the airport van for the hour-long drive to Atlanta. I checked my suitcase at the curb, inched through the endless security line, collected pocketbook and shoes on the other side, and dashed to the departure gate. Delayed One Hour read the monitor. The hour turned into two, three, and, finally, Canceled. Every flight to the Northeast had been delayed by a storm until the following morning, so I joined thousands lined up at airline counters to rebook. When I reached the desk at last, I found one of the few remaining hotel rooms nearby.

It was 11:00 PM when I picked up my room key. I was famished (the hotel restaurant closed at 9:00 PM) and my back hurt so bad I knew I wouldn't sleep. I had no bathroom bag, no night clothes, not even a toothbrush. I was debating whether to wear my clothes to bed when there was a knock at the door. I opened it to see Colleen holding a sack of sandwiches and hot tea; another with aspirin, toothbrush, and toothpaste; a packet of cotton underpants; and a pink housecoat. She'd heard the weather report and called the airport.

"They didn't have pajamas in the all-night pharmacy," she apologized.

I was crying, of course, for the joy of friendship. The housecoat made a perfect nightgown.

God of joyful surprises, teach me to be a friend.
—ELIZABETH SHERRILL

Digging Deeper: PROVERBS 18:24, JOHN 15:14

Tue 7

Above all, clothe yourselves with love.... —COLOSSIANS 3:14 (NRSV)

April

Laundry, laundry, a sea of laundry—it never ended.

Kate and I tried our best to run an egalitarian house. We split chores, child care, and cooking. For years I'd swept and cleaned bathrooms while Kate did laundry. I came to dread sweeping day and always envied what seemed like the meditative rhythm of folding clean clothes. *Much better than scrubbing toilets,* I thought. So after some prodding, we agreed to trade.

Boy, did I regret it! Sweeping and bathrooms could be done in a day; laundry was eternal.

I picked up Frances's shirt with the logo of her gym. How she loved gymnastics! And how I loved watching her tumble and cartwheel. I tossed the shirt in the washing machine. Next came Benjamin's orange shirt with a brown truck on it. It was his second favorite after his guitar shirt. I smiled, remembering driving him to preschool that day. "Daddy, let's look for garbage trucks!" he exclaimed. He was obsessed with wheeled vehicles.

I gazed at the laundry basket. It was a basket of memories too. Everything in it was imprinted with the kids' activities, and one day they'd do their own laundry and I'd be one step more removed from their lives. I turned the dial on the washing machine, musing that there is life and love in all things, even laundry.

All work is holy, Lord. Teach me to see that.
—JIM HINCH

Digging Deeper: PROVERBS 12:14,
EPHESIANS 2:10

Wed 8

In the morning, while it was still very dark, he got up and went out to a deserted place, and there he prayed.
—MARK 1:35 (NRSV)

This Lent, I joined my yoga class in a forty-day commitment to healthy eating, daily exercises, and meditation every morning and evening.

I was against the meditation part, at first. Strangely put off by—afraid of, even—the idea of not thinking, not doing something, for five whole minutes. When I admitted this fear, my teacher said, "It's no different from praying. Just commit five minutes to being alone with God. Present. Available."

Not much happened during my meditation attempts. No revelations or visions. Still, this new way of praying was curiously satisfying. I set the oven timer for five minutes, settled myself cross-legged on the living room floor, and sucked in air loudly through my nose, as I'd been taught, then shot it back out through my mouth.

"I'm here," I breathed. In. Out. Soon, I was no longer seeing breaths or saying mind-words but just being. Here. In. God's. Presence.

Immediately, it seemed, the timer shrilled.

That's, I learned, what prayer is. Or can be. Not a duty. Not achieving some holy purpose. Just being present, by myself, with God.

Father, I'm here.
—PATTY KIRK

Digging Deeper: PSALM 100

Thu 9

"Unless you change and become like little children, you will never enter the kingdom of heaven."
—MATTHEW 18:3 (NIV)

It was bedtime for Prisca, which is my favorite time of day. For my husband and me, her bedtime is the grand exhale, the long-awaited moment of peace and quiet, the fulfilling, albeit fleeting, opportunity for adult dialogue. For Prisca, not so much. Mention bedtime and what follows is a litany of "I'm-not-tired-I-don't-want-to-go-to-bed-I-want-to-stay-up-with-you-*foreeeeeever*."

So instead of mentioning bedtime, I simply dropped to all fours and said, "I'm a bear and I'm going to roar all the way to Prisca's room!"

Perry immediately followed suit, squatted, and said, "Well, I'm a frog, and I'm going to leap all the way to Prisca's room!"

He and I had barely gotten down the hall when Prisca said, "I'm a bunny, Mommy and Daddy, and I'm going to hop all the way to Prisca's room!"

And so we went, roaring, leaping, hopping all the way to her room. By the time we made it, we were a mishmash of animal sounds and giggles, overjoyed from play. Prisca climbed into bed, all sunshine and smiles, and laid her head on her pillow to rest. Same task tended to but with a playfulness that filled the soul. More of life should be so sweet.

Father, You Who thought to include rainbows and waving willows and duckbilled platypuses in Your grand plan, please remind me that efficiency and expediency aren't the only measures of a productive day. —ASHLEY WIERSMA

Digging Deeper: JOHN 10:10

Fri 10 "*That which is altogether just shalt thou follow....*"
—DEUTERONOMY 16:20 (KJV)

If I mention my home, Nashville, Tennessee, chances are you'll think of music. But in the annals of history, my city is known for something greater: the civil rights sit-ins of 1960.

Back then, if you were a person of color, you were welcome to spend your money in the white man's store. But when lunchtime rolled around, if you entered a restaurant, your next step just might be jail. However, a fair number of locals took the words of Jesus seriously and became advocates for equality through nonviolent protest.

Recently, I found myself sitting by one of the heroes of that era. He had been a student at a local university and was part of this move toward justice for all. He told me how he joined other black students to sit peacefully at a downtown lunch counter. Refused service, they sat for hours, returning the next day and the next. Angry mobs gathered. The students sat quietly, ignoring taunts, water poured on their heads, and cigarettes snuffed out on their skin. The police lined up the students and arrested them. Other protesters waited to take their place.

"How bad did it get for you?" I asked.

The man's smile surprised me. "One day, leaving the restaurant, a gang of thugs chased me into an alley. When a big car pulled up and blocked my path, I thought I was dead. Then the car door flew open and a white lady shouted, 'Get in!' and sped me off to safety."

I picture him there, a hero of one of history's most important nonviolent movements. And then I consider the woman in the car. We can't all be heroes, but we can be like her. When we encounter evil, we can move, speak, stand, drive to make it right.

Father, I hear Your call for justice. Show me how to be a part of Your movement. —PAM KIDD

Digging Deeper: LEVITICUS 19:18, GALATIANS 3:28

Sat 11

I will ordain My blessing for you....
—LEVITICUS 25:21 (JPS)

Since the time we brought Anjin, our greyhound, home from the rescue organization, she had never been crated for longer than three hours because Keith and I were rarely gone at the same time. But when Keith was hospitalized, I feared it meant Anjin would need to be crated for many hours. She doesn't like the crate; she starts panting and tries to run in the other direction when she suspects she's about to be locked in. I worried about that as I prepared to leave for the hospital, but then my friend Joan called to ask, "Do you need anything?"

I've always hesitated to ask people to put themselves out for me, but the timing seemed providential. "Have you got any time to sit with Anjin while I go to the hospital?"

"I can be there in a few minutes," she said.

Over the next few days, Joan sat with Anjin twice and word got around. Our neighbor Lu came up and spent four hours one day; our tai chi friend Dawn came and brought her hound, Nigel, to visit; the nuns sent one of their oblates to be with Anjin when our friends weren't free.

I was able to devote my full attention to Keith and his doctors without watching the time, now that I no longer had to rush home to let Anjin out of the crate. It was exactly the help we needed.

The blessings You give us come in unusual forms sometimes, Lord. Thank You for helping me to recognize them.—RHODA BLECKER

Digging Deeper: NUMBERS 6:24–26

Sun 12

He was delivered over to death for our sins and was raised to life for our justification. —ROMANS 4:25 (NIV)

I sat in church on Easter, observing people greeting one another, the beauty of the lilies, and the sound of the trumpets beginning the first hymn. But something was holding me back from totally entering into joy. I knew the reason: I didn't do Lent very well.

This year, I wanted to be more in-the-moment responsive to Jesus and obedient to His nudges to do or not do at least one different thing every day. Like not voicing that negative thought. Or giving more grace to that annoying person. Or reading instead of watching that mind-numbing TV program. But some days I made that negative comment anyway, or lacked the grace I meant to extend, or just plain forgot about Lent. So I entered church on Easter, feeling guilty about my inconsistent responses.

As the service progressed—through the words of the songs, confessions, prayers, and sermon—I began to experience a humbling awareness that I'd come to Easter exactly the way I should come, with a fresh understanding of how I so easily mess up. And I was freshly thankful that the truth of the Easter message is not about anything I do or earn, but about the powerful promise of forgiveness and hope and eternal life.

Lord, on this side of Easter, help me hold on to an awareness of Your message about the meaning of Jesus's Resurrection. —CAROL KUYKENDALL

Digging Deeper: ROMANS 8:11, COLOSSIANS 2:6–7

Mon 13

Do not think of yourself more highly than you ought, but rather think of yourself with sober judgment....
—ROMANS 12:3 (NIV)

The rap on my window almost made me spill my drink. I hadn't seen him coming. My hand shot out for the key, and I reflexively started the car.

Growing up in Chicago had given me certain street smarts. It also had made me jittery about being approached by strangers. So after visiting a local drive-through for lunch, I made a careful inspection of my surroundings before parking under a tree.

I had not been careful enough. A man motioned to me to roll down the window. I gave him a quick once-over. He looked harmless enough. I cracked the window an inch.

"Hey, man, can you spare some food?"

"No," I said and drove off.

By the time I was halfway back to work, I felt like such a heel that I turned around. I cruised the neighborhood, praying for direction, and found him.

I rolled down my window, called him over, and handed him a paper bag with my lunch. He thanked me. I felt proud and self-congratulatory at what an "extra-mile Christian" I was, practically ready for canonization. I couldn't wait to share my noble deed.

Then, I noticed the wrapped-up Polish sausage, which I'd thought was still in the bag. All I gave away that day were chips and a napkin.

I shake my head in embarrassment, Lord. The excellence is not in me; it's in You. Thank You for loving me anyway. —BILL GIOVANNETTI

Digging Deeper: PROVERBS 26:12, MATTHEW 18:4

Tue 14

"They will take up a lament concerning you...."
—EZEKIEL 27:32 (NIV)

That morning on my daily prayer walk, I eagerly approached the neighboring subdivision lane, thinking, *Bradford pear trees might be blooming by now.* I'd been waiting all year to again see the twenty trees that lined the neighboring road in full bloom, forming a heavenly tunnel of white blossoms. These magnificent trees were the reason I'd set aside this part of my walk to meditate daily on God's majesty and glory.

As I rounded the corner, my mouth fell open in shock. A landscaper had cut off every single branch, leaving only a few knots of main branches on bare, ugly trunks! I felt repulsed, saddened, robbed. *Lord, I know that Bradford pears tend to split in half when their branches get too heavy. I understand that the radical tree surgery is good for them in the long run. But why did we have to lose these beautiful trees? I hate walking here.* But I couldn't help wondering if it was okay to complain on a prayer walk.

I remembered a conversation I'd had with my friend Debra, who was in theology school. She told me that lamenting is a biblical prayer form. There were psalms of lament expressing sorrow, loss, injustice, grief, tragedy, or a deep concern about the state of society or the environment. Jesus Himself offered a dirge over the lost people of Jerusalem.

As I continued to walk, I prayed my lament and was comforted that this, too, was prayer.

Dear Father, I've been afraid to express my
unhappiness and sorrow. I now offer them to You,
knowing that You are the One Who weeps
with me and hears me. Amen.
—Karen Barber

Digging Deeper: Psalm 13:1–6

Wed 15

Never be lacking in zeal, but keep your spiritual fervor, serving the Lord. Be joyful in hope, patient in affliction, faithful in prayer. Share with the Lord's people who are in need....
—Romans 12:11–13 (NIV)

Our church likes to take care of its parishioners when they are suffering. However, one patient I visit doesn't seem all that thrilled to see me.

Annie has lots of needs and wishes, including wanting food that is clearly bad for her condition. Ethical dilemma: *She is sick and unhappy. Should she have the cookies and potato chips contraindicated by her illness?* I stew about that one and often end up buying the cookies. My logic involves thinking of myself confined to a nursing home with few outside contacts and even less hope of leaving.

Saint Paul tells us these things are sent to test us, and he's right. It is facing less than ideal situations and soldiering on that brings unexpected rewards. "I did it," you say to yourself. "I hung on." Giving yourself credit is very hard, but I give thanks for Annie, grumbles and all. She lets me give myself credit.

> *Sometimes, Lord, figuring out what the right thing to do is a challenge. Thank You for helping us do our best.*
> —BRIGITTE WEEKS

Digging Deeper: 2 CORINTHIANS 5:9

Thu 16

God is faithful, who has called you into fellowship with his Son, Jesus Christ our Lord.
—1 CORINTHIANS 1:9 (NIV)

Being pregnant has been difficult. Many of my friends already have children, and those who don't aren't the least bit interested. I try my best to keep pregnancy talk to a minimum.

So walking into a prenatal water aerobics class, I was surprised to see that everyone looked like me! The first class went quickly; we talked baby names, due dates, and sore backs while we kicked and stretched our way through the workout. When I left, I felt blissfully worn-out and at peace. I was hooked.

The Bible tells us how important fellowship is to our spiritual health. What I didn't realize is that I could bring the spirit of fellowship to other areas of my life, including my personal relationships and even my physical well-being.

The women in my class aren't the ones I talk to about problems at work or struggles in faith, but they are the ones I reach out to when I need support in making decisions about the sweet little girl growing inside me. What's more, I've been able to return the favor, showing God's love four days a week in a three-foot-deep pool.

Lord, bless You for giving us the gift of friendship.
How much sweeter life is when shared
with those in fellowship with You.
—ASHLEY KAPPEL

Digging Deeper: PROVERBS 18:24,
1 JOHN 1:6–7

Fri 17

"Then your light shall break forth like the morning, Your healing shall spring forth speedily...."
—Isaiah 58:8 (NKJV)

After rupturing a disc in my back while fighting a wildfire on the ranch where I work, my sciatic nerve was constricted, rendering my left leg useless. Sitting was impossible. Walking was excruciating. Even lifting my arm would make me nearly pass out. I couldn't prepare a meal or light my woodstove. I couldn't read, watch TV, or concentrate.

Constant, overwhelming pain became a way of life. Prayers were reduced to "Please, God." My tough, cowgirl independence was gone. Mom came to take care of me until I could have surgery.

I woke from anesthesia afterward to discover the searing pain was gone. When the nurse told me it was okay to get up, I tentatively lowered my trembling legs over the side of the bed. I was weak, but it didn't hurt. I wanted to cry with happiness. I could walk!

The nurse said walking was good for me, so I toured the hospital wing five times that night. I didn't sleep a wink because I wanted to savor the feeling of being pain-free after a long month of physical torment.

The surgeon was cautiously optimistic. "Go home and stay put. No bending, twisting, lifting. No stairs. Don't sit for more than twenty minutes. I'll see you in two weeks."

You answered the prayers I couldn't even speak, Lord. You eased my pain. Thank You for being there, even when I ached more than I could feel Your presence. —ERIKA BENTSEN

Digging Deeper: PSALMS 26:7, 105:2, 126:2, 136, 145:5; ACTS 13:52

Sat 18

Therefore, as God's chosen people, holy and dearly loved, clothe yourselves with compassion, kindness, humility, gentleness and patience.
—COLOSSIANS 3:12 (NIV)

I'm a Chicago Cubs fan, so it probably would have surprised you to hear me let out a boisterous cheer the night Cincinnati Reds player Todd Frazier hit the game-winning home run in a 1–0 win over the Cubs. But I did, and here's why.

In a game just days before, Frazier had also hit a home run, which became an instant sensation. That particular day, the Reds batboy, a thirty-year-old with Down syndrome named Teddy Kremer, let it be known that he was rooting for three things: the Reds to score eleven runs; to record eleven strike-outs (that meant free pizza at a local pizzeria); and for Frazier to hit a home run. Frazier did, a monster shot to center field that scored the tenth and eleventh runs. Then he gave Teddy a bear hug in the dugout and, in a postgame interview, looked at him and said, "This is one of my best buds right here."

I can't do what Frazier does on a baseball diamond, except for one thing: I can look for ways to live fully and love extravagantly, and bring something positive to the lives of others.

God, baseball players call it "leaving everything on the field." Help me to do that every single day.
—JEFF JAPINGA

Digging Deeper: PHILIPPIANS 4:4, JAMES 1:2–4

Sun 19

I can do all things through Christ who strengthens me.
—PHILIPPIANS 4:13 (NKJV)

I stood there trembling, breathing deeply, hoping to get control of my emotions, but to no avail. I was giving my first Easter sermon at my church's early morning service. I was retelling the story of Jesus's trial, His agony, His death, and His Resurrection. I was speaking through the eyes of those who loved Jesus—His friends, His family, and the apostles.

I got to the words *and when He died* and found myself unable to say more. I took a deep breath as the words on the page began to blur. I started again. "And when He died . . ." Again I couldn't continue. I looked up at the ceiling and concentrated on breathing. The death of Jesus had so moved me that I was stuck in the Crucifixion.

Suddenly I heard a voice in the congregation say, "It's all right," and it was. Jesus had allowed Himself this excruciating experience for my freedom. In His time of weakness, I found strength. And it's all right because on the other side is the Resurrection, our redemption, our salvation.

And so with tears streaming down my face and my voice cracking, I finished the sentence: "And when He died there was nothing else left to do but bury a friend."

Lord Jesus, please guide me as I follow Your example and bring Your Word to my world, however imperfectly. —NATALIE PERKINS

Digging Deeper: DEUTERONOMY 32:4, PSALM 18:30

Mon 20   *When I tried to understand all this, it troubled me deeply.*
—PSALM 73:16 (NIV)

Every Monday is movie night at our place. My sons and I open up the sofa in front of the

TV, snuggle under blankets in our pajamas, and eat popcorn. One evening, instead of our usual cartoon, I decided to show the boys a DVD of all my old home movies. The boys, I thought, would get a kick out of it.

"Look, guys," I said pointing to me as a little girl, "there I am when I was Tyler's age!" Three-year-old Tyler giggled under the covers. A different clip came up of my mother cradling a very upset baby. "That's me," I said with a laugh.

Brandon, however, wasn't as entertained. "Who was taking care of us when you were a baby?" he demanded to know.

"Oh," I said, "you weren't here yet." He looked confused. "You're only four years old," I tried again. "You weren't alive yet when Mami was a baby. I had to grow up before you could be born."

Brandon's big brown eyes welled up with tears. "This is scary!" he cried.

I never thought my old movies would be frightening, but the more I thought about it, the more it made sense. Brandon couldn't grasp the concept of having no mortal existence, just as we can't completely grasp the idea of our existence after life. It's a heavy subject, even for an introspective four-year-old.

I snuggled Brandon and put on a regular movie instead.

Help me have faith, Lord, when I don't have all the answers. And thank You for revealing them to me when I can better understand. —KAREN VALENTIN

Digging Deeper: PHILIPPIANS 3:21

Tue 21

The memory of the righteous is blessed.... —PROVERBS 10:7 (NAS)

Often a song will remind me of my mother, who died in 2001 at ninety-two. When I was growing up in the 1940s, she had several 78 rpm records that she played for me: "Sentimental Journey," "Go Tell It on the Mountain," and "Alexander's Rag Time Band," to name a few. When "Alexander's Rag Time Band" played, she'd often step into the living room from the kitchen and dance the Charleston. One of my fondest memories of her, at nearly ninety, is doing the Charleston at a wedding reception. Today I can tune the radio to a nostalgic station and hear her favorite songs.

Sometimes, though, I long for Mama to bend down and give me a hug. For the most part, I gave away everything of hers except for a couple boxes of her belongings. One rainy day, I really missed her and started digging around in her old clothes packed away in the back of the closet. I brought out her plum-colored chenille bathrobe, the one in which I used to watch her do the Charleston!

Almost ceremoniously, I slipped into it and tied the long, skinny sash. The robe came almost to the floor. I stood before the mirror—a perfect fit!

I hugged myself tightly and, amazingly, it felt as though Mama had reached down from heaven and embraced me. I could almost hear her happy voice saying, "I love you!"

Oh, Father, for sweet memories that never die, I praise You. —Marion Bond West

Digging Deeper: Philippians 1:3

Wed 22

"Ask the plants of the earth, and they will teach you . . . ."
—Job 12:8 (nrsv)

Deep enough?" a little girl asks. I nod. Carefully, she pushes cucumber seeds into the tiny hill of dirt we molded together and pats them down.

I volunteer weekly at the elementary school's garden project, a program where teachers bring their classes outside to learn about gardening and the earth. This group of kids is an inclusion class, which means that some of them have challenges. One boy beside me, with brown eyes and dark curly hair, doesn't seem to talk or make eye contact. He holds on tightly to his seeds and keeps his focus on the dirt.

"Here, I'll show you," I say, crouching beside him and planting one. Slowly, carefully, he positions his five seeds into the soil. Less than an hour ago I was stressed about a deadline, but squatting in the dirt with all of these helping hands, my anxiety has vanished, replaced by the sun and the children's excitement.

When it's almost time for the group to leave, we sit in a circle on the green grass. The teacher thanks everyone for helping and says, "Friends, let's have a gratitude share. If anything happened out here today that made you feel happy, you can share it with the group."

One girl raises her hand. "I'm happy for the garden because when I come here it's fun and I feel good. Oh, and I like to hear the birds sing." Another child shares, "I'm grateful that we get to play in the dirt and see worms and bugs." And then the boy who hadn't talked and was hesitant to plant his seeds raises his hand and in a loud, confident voice says, "I'm happy to grow stuff. I always wanted to grow something."

Dear Lord, thank You for today, for easing my anxieties and sowing seeds of Your glory that will take root and flourish in a child's heart.
—SABRA CIANCANELLI

Digging Deeper: MATTHEW 5:4, 16

Thu 23   *May your unfailing love be my comfort....* —PSALM 119:76 (NIV)

Finally, after mounds of paperwork, months of prayer, and hours of travel, my husband, Anthony, and I were in Russia to meet our son, Christian.

We entered the ancient, musty orphanage, and a worker led us up a cracked concrete staircase to a playroom. A few minutes later, a stout woman brought Christian to us. He was no longer a chubby-cheeked boy in a picture; he was a flesh-and-blood child. I fought back tears as I said hello.

Christian maintained a safe distance from us gawking strangers, but I broke the ice eventually by playing "roll the ball." A few minutes later, I scooted closer to Christian. I reached out and touched him tentatively, worried he might recoil; he didn't. I moved a little closer; he didn't move. I spread my arms wide; after a few moments of uncertainty, he moved toward me, allowing me to place him in my lap. I smiled wide at my husband; I had just met my son.

The door creaked open to reveal a short, stately man—the visiting physician. Christian let out a scream. Mortified, I looked at him, then back at the doctor. The doctor picked up Christian and placed him gently on a table. Christian's eyes searched the room until they landed on me... and then my son reached for me. The doctor smiled. "Wow, look at that! He's already looking to you for comfort."

As I think back on that remarkable day, I revel in the fact that I, too, have a parent I can reach out to for protection and safety. God loves me more than I can imagine and stands forever ready to comfort me and keep me, especially during the most frightening times.

Father, help me to look to You for comfort when life is scary, even for a big girl like me.
—CARLA HENDRICKS

Digging Deeper: PSALM 23, 2 CORINTHIANS 1:3–4

Fri 24

The Lord is my light and my salvation—whom shall I fear? The Lord is the stronghold of my life— of whom shall I be afraid?
—PSALM 27:1 (NIV)

I keep a Louisville Slugger baseball bat in my office, usually in close reach. It's not for personal protection or to enforce editorial deadlines. But, of course, there is a story behind it.

A few years ago the Peale Center, dedicated to the lives of Guideposts cofounders Ruth Stafford and Norman Vincent Peale, consolidated its collection of memorabilia. They held a charity auction, and the one thing that caught my eye was the bat, presented to Dr. Peale by the city of Louisville, Kentucky, on behalf of the Jefferson County public schools for all he'd done to instill positive thinking and self-esteem in young students.

What I loved most about the bat was where it read, "Personal Model, Norman Vincent Peale." Usually there is a star baseball player's name in that spot. I'd made no secret of my admiration for the item, but Guideposts employees had been asked not to bid.

I didn't stay to the end of the auction to see who got the bat, but my friend, retired chief of army chaplains General G. T. Gunhus, had bid on the bat and sent it over to me with a note: "Think positive. Swing for the fences!"

That bat's more than just a conversation piece. The greatest hitters the game has ever known barely succeeded one out of three times at the plate. That's a failure rate of nearly two-thirds. That's why I keep the bat close: to remind me that failure is part of success, often a necessary prelude to it. It is the message of positive thinking, based on a relationship with a loving God—the message Dr. Peale preached around the world. That despite our setbacks, reward awaits us as long as we keep trying and believing.

> *Lord, I must always trust that You will see me*
> *through my setbacks and my successes.*
> *Today, let me swing for the fences no*
> *matter what the outcome.*
> —EDWARD GRINNAN

Digging Deeper: 2 CORINTHIANS 13:11,
1 TIMOTHY 4:9–11

Sat 25

The plans of the diligent lead to profit
as surely as haste leads to poverty.
—PROVERBS 21:5 (NIV)

A light breeze brushed past my cheek. I sat on the only spot of the mountaintop that wasn't buried under a foot of snow. Unzipping my day-pack, I pulled out a granola bar and took a bite. A few crumbs fell. I lay on my side in the warm sun and sighed. It had been a tough week. Once again, I hadn't reached my goals; I felt discouraged.

Suddenly, a whole army of ants marched out of their tiny hole next to my face and swarmed the crumbs. I chuckled. Obviously, it'd been a long winter and they were thrilled with a new food source. They raced up and down their hole, each carrying a minicrumb—except for Muscles.

Muscles had spied the crumb of a lifetime. I watched it circle the crumb, which stood three times as tall as the buff ant. Muscles stepped behind it, and rearing up on its hind legs, it leaned its weight into the jumbo crumb and heaved. Nothing. Then it turned around and stood on its hands as it put its feet against the crumb and pushed. It barely budged. Meanwhile, all of its buddies ran up and down the hole, packing away treats.

Finally, Muscles shoved the crumb and it settled over the hole, sealing it shut. I laughed. "You bit off more than you could chew!" And then I heard, *Just like you.*

I inhaled. I'd been like Muscles, choosing gargantuan goals. That afternoon, I set bite-size ones.

Lord, help me to focus on achieving big goals
by setting small ones. Amen.
—REBECCA ONDOV

Digging Deeper: PROVERBS 15:22

Sun 26

We ought always to thank God for you . . . because your faith is growing more and more, and the love all of you have for one another is increasing.
—2 THESSALONIANS 1:3 (NIV)

There is a proverb that says, "As iron sharpens iron, so one person sharpens another" (Proverbs 27:17). Doc, the bass player in the worship band at church, sharpens my faith through his questions, reflections, and personal spiritual quest. It never fails after the Sunday service. Doc says something positive about my sermon: "You hit the ball out of the park!" or "Just what I needed to hear today." Recently he shared, "Pastor, every time I want to get closer to the Lord and grow in my faith, I pull away." It wasn't the first time I'd heard him confess this struggle.

"Doc, why do think this happens to you?" I asked.

"I'm afraid that God will ask me for something I cannot do," he replied. "I don't always feel confident about myself."

The more he talked, the more I tuned into my own fear. I finally said to him, "Sometimes I am afraid of being called by God. Who isn't afraid to do something beyond his or her skills, knowledge, or faith?"

Doc became at ease with the fact that he wasn't alone on this issue.

"Thanks," he said to me. "This helps me better understand my faith journey."

"Thank you," I replied. "You help me, too, to learn and grow in my faith."

Lord, thank You for surrounding me with friends who increase my faith and love for You.
—PABLO DIAZ

Digging Deeper: ECCLESIASTES 4:10, 2 PETER 3:18

Mon 27

My times are in thy hand....
—PSALM 31:15 (KJV)

As a child, I dreamed of becoming a nurse. In 1974, when I passed my RN boards, I saw my hands as an extension of God's, caring for those who were hurting.

For many years, I worked as a hands-on nurse in medical wards, intensive care, hospice care as a patient educator. But this morning, now as an infection preventionist, where my job is to coordinate activities in my Veterans Affairs Medical Center, it felt like the RN after my name no longer stood for "real" nurse, as we like to call ourselves.

Then Shawn dropped by my office to ask me a question. He also was doing a more administrative form of nursing but was transitioning better than I was. "How do you do it?" I asked.

"Well, it took me a while to realize," he said, "but one day I was praying, and the Lord impressed upon me that I take care of patients on a different level now."

I took a moment and surveyed my morning's activities. I'd reviewed the case of a patient who had developed a bloodstream infection, and followed up with his caregivers to make recommendations so that it wouldn't happen again. I'd written a patient education brochure on how to keep from passing the pernicious germ *Clostridium difficile* to others. And I'd drafted a memorandum on influenza, so patients would receive more timely treatment. Nursing care, all, but just of another type.

I said a prayer of thanks to God, Who sent me Shawn today. I have a renewed Monday-through-Friday purpose and now know for certain that I have never stopped being a real nurse.

Thank You, God, that there is a high calling in any line of work. —ROBERTA MESSNER

Digging Deeper: JEREMIAH 29:11, ROMANS 5:8, 1 PETER 5:7

Tue 28   *Rejoice in the wife of your youth.... Be captivated by her....* —PROVERBS 5:18–19 (NLT)

Filled with joy... oh dear, it would take me a lifetime to just report the highlights, the all-star moments, without even getting into the steady quiet joys like peanut butter and dogs and wood-hawks flying sideways through copses of trees.

But let us name a few superstar joys. Kisses from a lover who means it. Children learning to read suddenly, in a moment, and the way their faces light with amazement and pride—a look I saw on my daughter's face at age four, and I'll never forget it. My mother's hand on my face not only when I was a sobbing boy but also a sobbing man, a hand as tender and sturdy and fragile as any there ever was in this world. Watching each of my kids on playing fields and sport courts, their sweet wild physical grace and shy feats and patent joy in being a glorious mammal in the blessing of this holy air.

Hauling in that holy air again in a brilliant white hospital room filled with nurses and nuns in white after not being able to breathe in the dark at home and being rushed to the hospital where I woke up not dead.

Being on my knees on a hill by the sea and watching a woman's face as she smiled and said *yup*. The joy I felt this morning when I woke up and there she was in the bed, still, again, miraculously, unbelievably, smiling sleepily, murmuring *you* make the coffee and get the paper today, *I* am taking the first shower, for once, and we'll wake the kids together, that might work . . .

Dear Love Incarnate, I have spent thirty years trying to corral and shepherd words into the right order to sing Your creation, but even after all that practice I do not have words for how grateful I am for the small, vivacious, tart-tongued, amazing, confusing woman who still says yup every morning. Thanks.
I owe You big there. —BRIAN DOYLE

Digging Deeper: 1 CORINTHIANS 1:5–6

Wed 29

Moses answered the people, "Do not be afraid. Stand firm and you will see the deliverance the Lord will bring you today...."
—EXODUS 14:13 (NIV)

I'm miscarrying."

Those two words, texted to me from one of my best friends, stole all of the breath right out of my lungs. This was her second miscarriage in a matter of months.

Later, at the doctor, she discovered she hadn't miscarried but still might. All she could do was wait and see.

During that wait, my friend told me about a verse in Exodus she had underlined in her Bible, months before, about God's deliverance. It felt like a promise. Together, she and I prayed that God would deliver her baby, that He would spare that baby, that He would save that baby. A couple of weeks later, she miscarried.

"The thing is, Katie," my friend said to me afterward, "those words I read are no less true on this side of my miscarriage than they were on the other."

At the time, I'd been going through some trials in my own life: infertility and an unpredictable, emotionally exhausting adoption, just to name a couple. How often had I looked for God's deliverance in a specific outcome? How often had things not turned out as I'd hoped?

God continues to teach me that deliverance doesn't always look the way I think it should or want it to look. When Jesus died that violent, humiliating death on the Cross, His disciples and family didn't see that as deliverance either. I have to imagine they were confused and grieving and maybe even angry. Until three days later...

Lord God, help me to trust in You, even when I'm hurting and Your ways don't seem to make sense.
—KATIE GANSHERT

Digging Deeper: PSALM 91:2, ROMANS 11:33–36

Thu 30

Commit your way to the Lord; trust in him, and he will act.
—PSALM 37:5 (NRSV)

Thirty years ago, on April 30, Carol and I were wed. Every wedding requires a million decisions, and when you make them, they might seem mundane. But when I look back, I see a young couple determining just what they hoped their life together would be.

We chose to marry in our scrappy Manhattan church where the neighborhood was dicey and the stained-glass windows desperately needed cleaning. But here were our friends and here was our choir. This was our spiritual home.

"Let's process to a hymn," Carol said—not the usual Mendelssohn tune. We chose "The Church's One Foundation"; the message was for the people who were witnesses to this event, our firm foundation.

We invited the minister from my childhood church in California to give a homily, and we had the rector of our New York parish marry us and then the assistant agreed to join him.

We asked friends to sing, had a friend do the flowers, and insisted on having Communion at the service. It made for some awkwardness: the church was Episcopal; my family was Presbyterian; our friends came from a broad spectrum of beliefs and traditions. Never mind. Jesus would be at the center of the ceremony.

Some decisions were intuitive; some we stumbled upon; some involved long discussions. We made a few decisions and stuck by them, and God has stuck by us.

I commit my way to You, oh, Lord, and
accept all the good that follows.
—RICK HAMLIN

Digging Deeper: PHILIPPIANS 2:2

DAILY JOYS

1 _____

2 _____

3 _____

4 _____

5 _____

6 _____

7 _____

8 _____

9 _____

10 _____

11 _____

12 _____

13 _____

14 _____

15 _____

April

16 _____

17 _____

18 _____

19 _____

20 _____

21 _____

22 _____

23 _____

24 _____

25 _____

26 _____

27 _____

28 _____

29 _____

30 _____

MAY

Be full of joy in times of prosperity;
in bad times consider this:
one is the work of God; the other is too—
and because of this, no one can discover the future.

—ECCLESIASTES 7:14 (TIB)

GOD OF JOYFUL SURPRISES

Fri 1

We sailed slowly for a number of days. . . . —ACTS 27:7 (RSV)

JOY IN THE GOING

It was to have been a week's trip to Europe to celebrate the sale of our house. Then a routine doctor's visit turned up a recurrence of a heart problem. "Sure," my doctor said, "go celebrate. Just do it nearby."

My husband, John, looked for the positives. "We'll make it like our canal trip!"

The words brought a rush of memories. While living in England years ago, we'd rented a narrow boat, one of the long barges built in the nineteenth century to carry coal along the canals that crisscrossed the country. It was an adventure from beginning to end: learning to navigate through the locks; sitting on the boat's flat roof as church steeples, farmhouses, and grazing cows glided by; tying up at night along the banks.

A few months later, John and I decided to repeat the delightful trip by car. We drove to where we'd rented the boat and set out toward the town where seven days' traveling had brought us. We were there in half an hour. We'd sped past the flowering fields, the trees, the little hamlets we'd enjoyed so much. What at fifty miles per hour was an ordinary stretch of highway had been, at another pace, an unforgettable journey.

So that's how we took our celebration trip, a leisurely weeklong drive within a fifty-mile radius of Boston on the smallest roads we could find. We stopped when something caught our eye; we turned into inviting vistas, explored, and made discoveries. We learned that a journey isn't how far you go but the joy you take in the going.

> *God of joyful surprises, help me go observantly,*
> *joyfully through this day.*
> —ELIZABETH SHERRILL

Digging Deeper: PSALMS 16:11, 17:5

Sat 2   *Therefore confess your sins to each other and pray for each other so that you may be healed....* —JAMES 5:16 (NIV)

Driving to my exercise class early yesterday morning, my thoughts kept circling around a problem my husband was facing in his retirement, so it felt like my problem too. As I walked through the parking lot toward the gym, I ran into a friend I hadn't seen in weeks.

"What's going on in your life?" she asked. That's all it took to open the floodgates and let my problem flow out. It was so much more than she asked for, so much more than I needed to say.

By the time I got into class and started stretching, I began a whole new conversation in my head. *Why did I say all that? So unnecessary. So overly vulnerable.* My self-talk continued for most of the class.

When I got home, I called my friend. "I walked away from our conversation feeling bad that I dumped so much on you. I should have said less. I'm sorry."

"I was going to call you," she said. "I walked away from our conversation wishing I had said more. Trusting me with your honesty made me wish *I'd* been more honest and asked you to pray for my husband, who is facing a problem in his job."

She went on to tell me her story, and I felt grateful that she trusted me with her concerns.

Lord, thank You for the privilege of listening to my friend and for the gift of her loving heart. Bless us as we pray for each other's husband.
—CAROL KUYKENDALL

Digging Deeper: LUKE 18:1–8, PHILIPPIANS 4:19

Sun 3   *Whatever things are lovely... meditate on these things.*
—Philippians 4:8 (nkjv)

I have a profound need for beauty, but I don't live in the garden spot of the world. Nevertheless, I decided to try the Apostle Paul's advice for a day and meditate on what was lovely around me.

A big truck was backing up in our lane to deliver a load of gravel. Steve, our friend, guided his fifty-thousand-pound truck deftly to its target, tilted up the bed, and then pulled slowly forward, laying down a seamless river of white gravel. When he got out to take my money, I couldn't help noticing how handsome he was.

"Steve, you are a regular da Vinci with that truck!"
He laughed. "I've had a lot of practice, Dan."

Then I was off to get a haircut. My barber, Kelly, a smart brunette, was struggling with a boy who didn't want his hair trimmed. He screamed, twisted like a snake, and made threats, but Kelly's gentle voice charmed the little serpent and turned him into a beautiful little man. "Kelly," I said, "when it comes to children, you are a virtuoso."

She blushed. "It's just part of the job. I'm used to it."

In the evening, I stood in the doorway of my wife's sewing room, where she was working on a quilt. Hundreds of quilt pieces were stacked in small piles, awaiting her assembly into yet another beautiful tapestry like the ones that grace our walls and cover our beds. Sharon is an artist in thread.

At the end of the day, I had to admit that there was a lot of beauty around when I looked for it. I need to make every day a tour through the gallery of life, looking for the elegance that gilds the world around me.

> *Lord, I see Your beauty in everything and I love You for it.* —DANIEL SCHANTZ

Digging Deeper: PSALM 90:17, ECCLESIASTES 3:11, 1 PETER 3:3–4

Mon 4   *My soul waiteth for the Lord more than they that watch for the morning....* —PSALM 130:6 (KJV)

Weakness followed the surgery to repair a disc in my back that ruptured while I was fighting a wildfire on the ranch. The day after my follow-up appointment, with the surgeon's approval, Mom drove me to where I had grown up, 250 miles from the ranch. She and Dad took care of me for the next month.

I walked every day, making laps around the house and barn. Five laps equaled a mile. With stubborn will and determination, I built myself back up to walking six miles a day.

When I returned for the next doctor's appointment, he couldn't believe how far I'd come. *I'm going to be okay,* I thought.

But within one week I couldn't walk. I was bounced around the medical community, each doctor offering a different diagnosis. Finally, some answers: My disc had reruptured; my vertebrae were collapsing; disc fragments were floating around my spine; I had infected abscesses; I needed more surgery, injections, meds. I had inflammation; I didn't have inflammation. Use heat only; use ice only. Move; don't move. Listen to your body and stop when it hurts; power through the pain. Never bend or twist; you must bend and twist! On and on.

Would I ever get my life back? Would I ever feel good again? "Keep trusting, Erika," Mom would say. "Keep trusting."

I don't understand Your methods, Lord, but I still trust You. Please keep me strong through this trial.
—ERIKA BENTSEN

Digging Deeper: PSALMS 33:20, 119:147; ISAIAH 61:3

Tue 5   *But those who won't care for their relatives, especially those in their own household, have denied the true faith....* —I TIMOTHY 5:8 (NLT)

I was nervous when I met Emily's parents for the first time. Her dad, Mark, had a bit of a gruff demeanor and didn't say much, and though her mom, Nancy, was eager to make me feel comfortable, I was too focused on trying to impress them to feel anything but anxiety.

Over the years, Mark took me to University of Texas baseball games, and Nancy showed me some of the best Mexican restaurants that Austin had to offer. I still couldn't get over my anxiety; I just wanted them to like me.

During our wedding week, however, my feelings started to change. Mark was quick to offer any help he could provide, and Nancy was putting together welcome baskets with Texas-themed gifts for my family, practically doing the flower arrangements on her own, and attending to Emily's every need before the big day. Their helpfulness reminded me of what really mattered: not whether others like us, but how helpful we can be to others.

Finally, I was not anxious but grateful. I wrote them heartfelt notes, thanking them for their help and warm welcome. It was the most honest I had ever been with them.

After the wedding, Mark gave me a rare smile and said, "Welcome to the family." Now that I'd stopped holding back my gratitude and worrying about what he thought of me, I felt I belonged.

Thank You, Lord, for the gift of gratitude, which opens up the way to love. —SAM ADRIANCE

Digging Deeper: 1 THESSALONIANS 5:18

Wed 6

"Here are my mother and my brothers. For whoever does the will of my Father in heaven is my brother and sister and mother."
—MATTHEW 12:49–50 (NIV)

I celebrated Mother's Day in the most unlikely of places—my ex-mother-in-law's home. "Your relationship with my son has nothing to do with ours," Eleanor said when he and I separated. I wanted to believe that, and on one incredible evening she proved it to me.

I'd stopped by to drop off the boys at her home. Gary was there but never came out of the other room. Eleanor asked me to stay since she was having an evening of prayer and food with family and friends. It was my first time around his family after our separation. I felt funny but agreed to stay.

After many prayers, Eleanor spoke in front of her sisters and brothers, nieces and nephews, cousins and friends. "I'm just a little emotional right now," she said, "because my daughter-in-law is here. Karen, I want you to know that my son married a treasure of a wife. He may not be able to see it, but I do." Both of us had tears in our eyes, and I knew she really loved me and was dedicated to keeping me as one of her own.

As I celebrate this Mother's Day, I honor the woman who wasn't afraid to honor me so long ago.

Father, thank You for family that's bonded by blood and by love. —KAREN VALENTIN

Digging Deeper: JOHN 19:26–27

Thu 7

"When I shut up the heavens so that there is no rain . . . if my people . . . will humble themselves and pray . . . then I will hear from heaven . . . and will heal their land."
—2 CHRONICLES 7:13–14 (NIV)

The Scripture above was printed in the bulletin at the National Day of Prayer service I attended. *This is such a powerful promise,* I thought. *But sometimes when I'm praying, I'm not sure anything is really improving.*

The next morning when I ventured out on my prayer walk, it was misting ever so slightly, so I took an umbrella just in case. We were in the middle of a severe drought, and the grass was brown and burned up in the highway medians. Things had been dry for so long that I didn't want to get my hopes up. *Just like I feel when I'm praying,* I thought wearily.

An hour later as I neared home, I was surprised when big raindrops began to hit my face. I quickly opened the umbrella. Suddenly, I was walking through a downpour. I stopped and watched a fast-moving stream of rainwater cascading down the curb to the bottom of the hill, carrying with it dust, pollen, and dead leaves. I took a deep breath, drinking in the beautiful smell of the newly cleansed earth. As my feet made a satisfying splash along the sidewalk in rhythm with the rain beating against my umbrella, I remembered the promise from 2 Chronicles: *If my people... will humble themselves and pray... then I ... will heal their land.*

I smiled. God hears. God is always answering. So don't ever forget your umbrella when you pray for an outpouring.

*Dear Father, thank You for reassuring us that when
we offer our prayers as a country
You hear and answer. Amen.*
—KAREN BARBER

Digging Deeper: 2 CHRONICLES 6:26–27,
MALACHI 3:10–12

Fri 8   *He leadeth me beside the still waters.
He restoreth my soul....*
—PSALM 23:2–3 (KJV)

May

It is long past midnight, and tomorrow I am going to regret staying up so late. But I love these quiet hours when the house is still, my heart is calm, my thoughts are deepening, and I am alone with God.

I will let our three golden retrievers in through the back door, refresh their water bowl, and bed them down for the night. I also will not be able to resist plopping down in my lazy chair and reading a short chapter of a biography that fascinates me. And when I finally reach up and click off the lamp to head to bed and am embraced by darkness, for a moment I will feel the presence of God close by, lulling me into sleep and rest.

The psalmist writes, "Be still, and know that I am God" (Psalm 46:10, KJV). Sometimes we best commune with God by being quiet, by drifting off into slumber, by leaning back and abiding in God's presence. The Good Shepherd gives His sheep permission to rest, to be content, to be lazy, and to do nothing but enjoy the goodness of God.

Lord, in the midst of my chronically busy world,
may I learn to rest in Thee. Amen.
—SCOTT WALKER

Digging Deeper: JOHN 15:4–5

Sat 9 ...*A time to dance.*
—ECCLESIASTES 3:4 (NAS)

I don't like some of the music we exercise to at the YMCA. The songs are unfamiliar and don't have my kind of rhythm. One day we had a substitute teacher. She announced, "I've brought some new music. Hope y'all like it!"

I probably won't, I thought.

Suddenly, Julie Andrews's voice filled the room. "I could have spread my wings and done a thousand things I've never done before.... I could've danced all night...." I could've too! My soul and energy soared as I marched in place.

During a break, the man standing by me headed to the water fountain. Even though he moves rapidly, he has some trouble walking. All of us in the seniors class have something amiss with our bodies. He smiled to himself as though remembering and, with swooping perfect steps, waltzed over to the fountain.

For one crazy moment, I thought I was going to rush out onto the floor and shout, "Dance with me!" After moving like Fred Astaire, he floated back to his spot beside me. I smiled at him and did a quick thumbs-up. He smiled back. The man's joy reminded me of David dancing before the Lord.

Father, I can imagine You on Your throne and a host of us dancing before You with all our hearts and souls.
—MARION BOND WEST

Digging Deeper: 2 SAMUEL 6:14

Sun 10

*Be devoted to one another
in love....*
—ROMANS 12:10 (NIV)

I don't like to use the word *hate*. But I hate Alzheimer's. I saw my maternal grandfather die of it, though I was too young to understand why he never knew my name. I watched both my mother's older sisters die of it and one of her brothers. I lived through my mother dying of it. Now a couple of my older cousins on that side of the family—I'm the youngest in my generation—are starting to show symptoms.

I lingered over some photos of my mom taken a year or so before her death. We'd been at a summer cookout at my brother's house. Even in those frozen moments in time you can tell something's not right because she looks more than just old. Maybe it's the way her head is inclined or that certain limpness in her stance, as if there is physical confusion as well as mental. Yet there is one thing: her smile.

Research has shown that two completely different parts of our brain control smiling. There is the "smile for the camera" neurofunctionality, which is essentially artificial and social. But the smiles we can't suppress—the ones that burst forth when we are happy or in love or when we're infants— are connected deep within the so-called primitive brain.

That's how my mom was smiling. She didn't really know where she was or why she was there, but she knew she was with family, with people who loved her, people whom she had loved fiercely her whole life. Maybe that's the one thing Alzheimer's can never kill: love. Maybe nothing can ever kill love; there is a kind of immortality at its essence. Certainly my mother's love outlived her. I felt it more than ever looking at those pictures.

Jesus, You commanded us to love above all else for love is the greatest gift of God. Let Your love guide me through all things, from sorrow to joy, from life to death and beyond. —EDWARD GRINNAN

Digging Deeper: 1 JOHN 4:18

Mon 11

There is a time for everything, and a season for every activity under the heavens.
—ECCLESIASTES 3:1 (NIV)

With a little one on the way, a full-time job, and various volunteer engagements, I've been focusing my devotion on the act and choice of being busy. When I think of *busy,* I think of fluttering hummingbirds, buzzing bees, and Wile E. Coyote plotting to nab the Road Runner. But what does busy really mean?

I stumbled upon a breakdown of the Chinese character for *busy*, which is made by combining the characters for *heart* and *kill*. What an eye-opener! This definition painted the picture of a dying heart. No wonder my heart and soul always felt deflated when I returned home from four errands after work just in time to start dinner.

While I can't change that I am busy, I can change my perspective. My life is full. My schedule is wonderfully packed. My errands overflow. It's an excellent reminder to seize each moment with joy.

Lord, help me to use my time wisely today so that I can avoid the dreaded "b" word. —ASHLEY KAPPEL

Digging Deeper: PROVERBS 23:4, LUKE 10:38–42

Tue 12

I strain to reach the end of the race and receive the prize for which God is calling us up to heaven because of what Christ Jesus did for us.
—PHILIPPIANS 3:14 (TLB)

Raising four children, mostly as a single woman, meant I had to spread myself pretty thin. I'm sure at some point my children felt I didn't spend enough time, energy, or money on them. It bothered me for years. Then something amazing happened.

A huge carton arrived in the mail. Inside the triple layer of bubble wrap was a big black box with decorative bungee cords around each end. When I pulled off the cords and lifted the lid, there, nestled in black silk-covered foam, was a golden statue of a woman with wings, holding up a replica of Earth. It was an Emmy, from the National Academy of Television Arts and Sciences. The inscription said that my son Andrew had won it for his work on Major League Baseball on TV. "Andrew," I screamed into the phone, "you won an Emmy! But why did you have it sent to *me*?"

"We earned it together, Mom. Remember all those checks you mailed me in college, so I could fly to cities all over the country to work baseball or football games for different networks? That was the best education I could have had. I want you to have the Emmy."

And it is the first thing you see when you walk into my home. Every day it reminds me to keep plugging along and do the best job I can with the resources I have—and to be as generous as I'm able.

Father, when I think I'm not doing
enough for the people I love, keep me on track
doing what I can, believing in their potential.
—PATRICIA LORENZ

Digging Deeper: 1 CORINTHIANS 9:24–27,
TITUS 3:14

Wed 13

"Whenever the rainbow appears in the clouds, I will see it and remember the everlasting covenant between God and all living creatures of every kind on the earth." —GENESIS 9:16 (NIV)

Rainbows or sunshine?" Henry asks. My son is seven, and his latest habit is to hammer me with either/or questions about what I like better: reading or watching TV, going to the movies or being at the ocean, swimming or sleigh riding.

Most of the time I answer quickly, sometimes without even looking up from the vegetable I'm chopping or the clothes I'm folding. And just when I think Henry's not paying attention, he'll say something to prove me wrong. Like when I answered, "Being at the ocean," he said, "That's what Dad said too." Or when I told him I like dirt better than grass, he just laughed and laughed like it was the punch line of a joke.

Usually my answers are immediate, but "rainbows or sunshine" stumped me. "That's a hard one, Hen," I said. I love the feeling of sunshine, the way the warmth seems to come from inside me and meet the rays. But then rainbows—rainbows are the end of a storm. Brilliant colors appear like a miracle across the sky, a finish line of the struggle, a ribbon of hope.

"Rainbows. Yes, rainbows," I answer.

"Me too!" Henry shouts, jumping up and down. "I love all the colors. The colors of life are in rainbows."

The colors of life. I have to remember that for the next time the dishwasher breaks when I'm hosting a huge family party, for the next bout of stomach flu that strikes our entire household, or for the times when life seems gray. The brilliant colors of life, joy, and hope are just below the surface. I only need faith to weather the storm.

Dear God, thank You for the joy of a little boy's curiosity that gives me pause to reflect on Your covenant of hope.
—SABRA CIANCANELLI

Digging Deeper: GENESIS 8:1, EZEKIEL 1:28

Thu 14   *Each of you should use whatever gift you have received to serve others, as faithful stewards of God's grace in its various forms.*
—1 PETER 4:10 (NIV)

I hadn't heard from my dear friends John and Tib Sherrill for a while. They'd moved to a retirement community in Massachusetts, too far from New York City to visit regularly. Soon they would be celebrating sixty-five years of marriage. I gave them a call.

Tib answered on the first ring. She sounded weak. "What's wrong?" I asked.

"It seems that I have pneumonia. I've been taking medication, but I can't sleep at all. I'm waiting to be taken over to the nursing wing."

"Where's John?" I asked.

"You must pray for him," she said. "He's got a terrible case of diverticulitis and has been in the hospital for a couple of days. I can't even visit him in the state I'm in. Please pray that he won't have to have surgery."

I got John on the phone; he sounded subdued. He'd been on an IV drip and was up walking around. "Is there anything I can do?" I asked.

"Rick," he said, "Tib hasn't been able to eat very well and needs to get her strength up. Would you pray for her, that she can eat without getting nauseated?"

Neither John nor Tib asked me to pray for themselves. Instead, they each thought first of the other. Marriage flourishes on selflessness. So does the spiritual life.

Who can I pray for today, Lord?
—RICK HAMLIN

Digging Deeper: JOHN 15:17

Fri 15

But perfect love drives out fear....
—1 JOHN 4:18 (NIV)

"We'll pay for your travel expenses and meet you at the airport," the meeting planner wrote in her e-mail to me.

I'd been invited to be the keynote speaker at a church in Virginia, to share my story of triumph over blindness, something I'd done many times. But since losing my eyesight, I'd never traveled alone from my home in Florida. This time I had to and I was terrified. *What if I end up in the wrong place? What if I miss my connection? What if I don't connect with the person scheduled to pick me up?*

Then slowly, out of my dark thoughts, I heard *Trust Me.*

"If traveling is what God has in His plans for me," I said out loud, "I need to change my what-ifs." So I began: *What if God removes all the obstacles? What if He knows the people who will help me? What if I can share the Gospel with anyone who asks about my blindness?*

My panic eased. My heart slowed. I smiled with expectation. A renewed passion for adventure fluttered in, and soon I was holding onto God with one hand and gripping my white cane with the other as I kissed my husband good-bye and walked into the airport alone.

Thank You, Lord, for being my divine guide. Your promises take me to destinations that delight my soul.
—JANET PEREZ ECKLES

Digging Deeper: PSALM 27:1–3

Sat 16

Though he may stumble, he will not fall, for the Lord upholds him with his hand. —PSALM 37:24 (NIV)

In the midst of planning our daughter's wedding, I butted heads with her wedding consultant. I was upset by her less than cordial attitude toward my attempted contributions to planning. Then I got a call from my daughter telling me her consultant had reserved a limousine I thought would be too small.

"Who does she think she is?" I muttered and hung up the phone.

Still fuming, I sat at my computer, checking e-mail, when a video caught my eye. I clicked Play. It showed a soldier returning home from deployment to his wife and kids. His six-year-old son had cerebral palsy and had never walked. The wife had an amazing surprise for her husband. As the soldier knelt down with arms outstretched, their son slowly, haltingly, walked toward his father. Finally, the boy reached him and the father picked him up and hugged him tight. I cried.

And here I am fretting over a limousine! I thought. We were blessed by a joyful daughter who was marrying the man of her dreams. It didn't matter how they got to the wedding. I forwarded the video to the wedding consultant with an apology. To my surprise, she responded in kind.

Thank You, Father, for lovingly and gently getting me back on track when I slip. —KIM HENRY

Digging Deeper: PSALM 119:34–37, PROVERBS 14:10

Sun 17

For surely I know the plans I have for you, says the Lord . . . to give you a future with hope.
—JEREMIAH 29:11 (NRSV)

In North America, the majority of churches don't have as many members as they did ten, twenty, or fifty years ago. Some experts say there's no hope for the church.

My friend Bill is not one of them. Pastor of one of those small-and-getting-smaller churches in the Midwest, he never seems discouraged about that reality. So one day I asked him, "How do you stay so positive when your membership keeps shrinking? Aren't you afraid you'll close?"

Bill smiled. "I don't know what you're talking about. We're not shrinking. We're growing—up ten percent from last year."

"Can't be," I said. "I've seen your membership numbers. Down every year for the last ten."

"You count members," Bill said, "but we count *touches*. Anytime anyone in our church does something for someone else in the name of Jesus, that's a touch: a card sent, a phone call made, a meal delivered, a donation to the food pantry. And our goal is to increase touches. In the five years that we've counted this way, we've grown every year."

Bill's wisdom has changed the way I live my life. My initial goal was one touch per day; too small. Now it's five. And here's what I've discovered: when my touches grow in number, I grow in faith.

Show me, God, where I can bring Your hope and love to someone else today. —JEFF JAPINGA

Digging Deeper: LUKE 12:22–32, ACTS 9:31

I SURRENDER ALL

Mon 18

Those who know your name trust in you, for you, Lord, have never forsaken those who seek you.
—PSALM 9:10 (NIV)

OPENING UP

I immediately spotted my cousin Laura—long blonde hair and a smile a mile wide. "It's great to see you! We should've done this a long time ago."

We settled into a booth and could hardly eat for talking. We caught up on our children's lives and then our conversation focused on God. Turns out, Laura's a managing nurse at a pregnancy resource center. She helps mamas-to-be by administering pregnancy tests, counseling, teaching parenting classes, and even leading Bible studies. "We're always looking for volunteers."

Holy goose bumps covered me. My mentor, DiAnn, had suggested I get out more, but should I take time away from work to volunteer? "What am I qualified to do?"

"What sorts of ministry do you enjoy?" Laura asked.

"I like listening. And I taught Sunday school for almost twenty years."

"Wonderful! We need teachers, counselors, people to organize our baby boutique, knitters . . ."

"Can I pray about it?" I said tentatively.

"Wouldn't want it any other way."

Before we left, I shared my one-word theme for the year: surrender. "I thought I surrendered everything to God years ago," I told Laura.

"We never stop surrendering, do we?" she said. "Guess what God's been teaching me lately?"

*Lord, thank You for teaching me to surrender
the use of my time to the path You have for me.
It's a far better path.* —JULIE GARMON

Tue 19

"You shall walk in all the way that the Lord your God has commanded you, that you may live...."
—DEUTERONOMY 5:33 (ESV)

It hit me: next year my oldest, Elizabeth, will graduate from college.

I knew this before, of course. I knew it but hadn't grasped the reality. My mind zeroed in on peripheral issues like the budget we'd need for a trip to Boston for the whole family, a new dress for Elizabeth, dinner out. Then I contemplated the bigger things like having my daughter living on her own somewhere. I tried to imagine Elizabeth with a full-time job, completely independent of me. My brain hurt, not to mention my heart.

I've always known my kids would grow up, yet it comes as a surprise that they have. I suppose this myopia is a mercy. If God had showed me everything that parenting involved in advance, I'd most assuredly have said no. I'd have protested, "I can't *do* that!" I'd have been certain about my inability to persevere. I'd have given up before God could help me grow up myself.

One day, a year from now, Elizabeth will walk across a platform in cap and gown and walk off to a new stage in her life. I'll walk on, with an aching heart, to a new stage in mine. Not because I chose this transition but because God has other things in store for both my daughter and me.

Father, walk with me in the places I don't
want to have to go but must.
—JULIA ATTAWAY

Digging Deeper: PSALM 23

Wed 20   *"Indeed, the very hairs of your head*
are all numbered...."
—LUKE 12:7 (NIV)

"Normally when someone dies, his or her influence is over," a speaker at a conference said. "Not so with Jesus. His life didn't end on the Cross. And now His influence is stronger than ever after two thousand years."

The comment started me thinking. I'd lost my husband recently. He'd spent two years in Africa, educating young people. *Is there something I could do to carry on John's positive impact in the world?* I wondered.

During the break, my friend Anne and I walked over to a table representing an organization that offers sponsorships for children in developing countries. I turned to Anne. "I'm going to sponsor a child. What a great way to continue the work John began."

During the lunch break, I pulled out my laptop and logged on to their Web site. Up popped hundreds of pictures of children. I scanned them quickly until my eyes settled on one boy. *I'm not sure why, but I know he's the one.* I signed up to be his sponsor.

Before the conference ended that day, I logged back on to the Web site to learn more about my new friend. Anne walked up to me. "I loved the session about asking God into the details of our lives, but do you think God really has time for that?" she asked.

"I think so," I replied.

"How do you know?" she asked.

"I prayed about finding just the right child to sponsor and guess what?"

"What?" she asked.

I smiled. "I just found out his name is John."

Thank You, Lord, that in spite of Your enormity,
You find the time to take care of even the
tiniest details of my life.
—MELODY BONNETTE SWANG

Digging Deeper: MATTHEW 6:25–26

Thu 21

Thanks be to God, who ... through us spreads in every place the fragrance that comes from knowing him. For we are the aroma of Christ to God....
—2 CORINTHIANS 2:14-15 (NRSV)

A former neighbor stopped by. Briefly back in town from her overseas posting, Angela smiled big and handed me a gift bag. "Open it!" A little white box contained a pink vial of exquisite French perfume—sweet, robust, maybe a hint of cherry.

Angela and I caught up. She'd acclimated to a new job and recovered from a car wreck. I listened. Like an older sister, I encouraged her and then she me. We laughed and eventually said good night. *God be with you till we meet again.* As a reminder to pray for Angela, every morning I place the tiniest dab of the perfume on the back of my neck; the rich fragrance lingers for hours.

Today it awakened a pleasant memory. Lifting the stopper transported me back to my first Sunday school classroom. What was in the wooden box set in the center of a circle of preschoolers? As Mrs. Nightengale told the Bible story—a woman washed Jesus's feet with perfume—she opened the box, revealing a small bottle of cologne. The dank smell of the church basement disappeared, over-whelmed by one scented drop on each ankle that we thrust toward our teacher, as if she were the center of a circle of grace.

Saint Paul says that through us God can and does spread the aroma of Christ. I know He used Angela's personal warmth and fragrant gift, which draws my heart to prayer—even wafting back around, prompting petitions for her well-being half a world away.

God, give me the privilege of being the aroma of Christ. —EVELYN BENCE

Digging Deeper: 2 CORINTHIANS 3:2–6

Fri 22

Carry each other's burdens, and in this way you will fulfill the law of Christ. —GALATIANS 6:2 (NIV)

Finally. It's Friday. Knit Circle Day! I get to head out to my favorite coffee shop and settle in for an afternoon of fiber fun and giggles. My knitting group makes me smile in a way no other can. These are women I might not have met without knitting. In our group we have a casting agent, a software engineer, an accountant, a new grandma, an author, a collection of nurses, and several teachers. We also have an explorer, a photographer, an animator, and a life coach. Knitting brings us all together.

Yes, we *ooh* and *aah* over each other's projects, but this group has been together long enough to go a little deeper. We share life. We worried with Ruth as she prepared to put her house on the market. We encouraged Annie as she searched for a new job. We cried with Mary when she brought hospice in for her mom. We rejoiced with Marti when her son got into college. We celebrated with Maureen when her new grandson arrived. All of these events were richer for having been shared.

Not everyone in our circle is comfortable with prayer. I am. Our little group knows that. I often will tell someone I am praying for a situation that's been shared. And every now and then someone will ask me to pray about something too tender to share out loud. It is an honor to pray for my knitting friends.

Dear Father God, shouldering the burden of another sometimes requires a physical effort and sometimes carrying the burden means quiet prayer. Let me see how I can carry the concern of someone else today. Amen. —LISA BOGART

Digging Deeper: LUKE 10:33–34, ACTS 20:35, COLOSSIANS 1:9

Sat 23   *Remember how fleeting is my life....* —PSALM 89:47 (NIV)

O kay, fine, I'll take him for a walk."
We were in Ashland, Oregon, and lucked into a free outdoor Shakespeare performance by a drama troupe from Iraq. I was fascinated. Benjamin, two, was not.

Sometimes I get tired of shepherding small children. Frances, five, was old enough to enjoy the performance. She and Kate sat on the grass, laughing and applauding. I followed Benjamin toward some stairs. As I often do, I fell to calculating how much longer he'd be a toddler. *Hurry up and grow,* I wanted to urge him.

Benjamin was in no rush. He stopped to swing on a railing. He bent to inspect a bug. Painstakingly, we descended step by step. Finally, we reached the last stair. Before us spread a magnificent view: pine-clad mountains soared behind the town; a rocky creek dashed and swerved beneath a footbridge; a public garden burst with flowers.

Suddenly, I remembered something a relative had told Kate and me. "The one thing I most regret saying to my kids was hurry up. They grow so fast. You have to savor each moment."

"Daddy, a street sweeper!" I crouched and put my arms around Benjamin. Together, we watched the sweeper hiss past. We waited until it disappeared. Then, step by step, we climbed back toward Kate and Frances. We didn't hurry.

Today I will savor the life You give, Lord.
—JIM HINCH

Digging Deeper: HABAKKUK 2:3

Sun 24

In the days of His flesh, He offered up both prayers and supplications with loud crying and tears....
—HEBREWS 5:7 (NAS)

When she was three years old, my granddaughter Grace astounded me with an unusual comment. She took two marbles, one clear and one blue, from a game I'd brought on my visit. Holding one beneath each eye, she said, "Look at my tears."

Gazing into her bright blue eyes, I responded, "I didn't know eyes could cry blue tears."

Colored tears are something I'd never thought of apart from Grace's creative interpretation. I once had blue tears cried for me: my mother's. She suffered with me through a "hurting season," as I called it. Not one to cry easily, she told me much later, "There was a time I cried just for you."

All of this made me think of Jesus. The Bible speaks of Him, in His earthly years, offering deeply felt tearful prayers to His Father. At the tomb of His friend Lazarus, "Jesus wept" (John 11:35). The prophet Isaiah writes that Jesus came as "a man of sorrows and acquainted with grief" (Isaiah 53:3, NAS).

But these were beautiful tears, just like Grace's. Jesus loved all people and anguished over broken lives, over "hurting seasons." He suffered as Savior on behalf of all people, for the forgiveness of sins and the promise of resurrected life. If tears come in colors, like blue, I believe the tears of Jesus are every color of the rainbow.

Lord, in Your bottle are my tears (Psalm 56:8). One day You will pour them out ... and crying shall be no more (Revelation 21:4). —CAROL KNAPP

Digging Deeper: HEBREWS 2:17–18

Mon 25

You keep him in perfect peace whose mind is stayed on you, because he trusts in you.
—ISAIAH 26:3 (ESV)

I'm currently in the throes of a waiting season, and it's not fun.

My husband and I are adopting a little girl from the Congo. I've met our little girl. I've held her. I've fallen in love. But she's there and we're here, and we have no idea when that will change. Finally, I reached a snapping point.

Thankfully, God puts people in our lives who can help us through our meltdowns.

"I can't do this anymore," I said. I was sitting on my friend's couch in her basement while our two boys played. "I honestly feel like I'm going insane."

She listened, as good friends do. Then she reminded me of one of my favorite names of God: El Roi, the God Who sees. She reminded me of a comforting truth—He sees my past and my present and my future, even when I can't. He sees my daughter's too.

I don't know what is on the other side of this waiting season, but God Who is faithful and good does. I'm finding peace in that.

Jesus, thank You for knowing. Let that be enough for me. —KATIE GANSHERT

Digging Deeper: PSALM 121:3, 5–8; JOHN 14:27

Tue 26

Shout for joy to the Lord, all the earth. Worship the Lord with gladness; come before him with joyful songs. Know that the Lord is God. It is he who made us, and we are his; we are his people, the sheep of his pasture. —PSALM 100:1–3 (NIV)

I had the great privilege of welcoming my new niece, Alma, into the world yesterday. She came fast (in a flurry of nurses and doctors running and my sister's screams) and strong (surrounded by tears of joy and laughter, a crowd of loving voices cheering as she let out a scream of her own that let us all know she had arrived).

I will treasure those moments always—moments so powerful, so extraordinary, and so beautiful that I can only turn to God in praise. And this morning, as I contemplate the miracle that is Alma, I'm praying that I never allow the miraculous in my life to turn into the ordinary.

I have three miracles of my own: precious babies whom God knit together in my womb—one by one—with unique personalities, precious spirits, priceless souls. Yet how often do I look at them and see runny noses? Toys all over the floor? Piles of dishes in the sink? Interruptions to my day? Too often.

But not today, because today I'm begging God to remind me that each word, each cry, each hug is a glimpse into the miracle that He performed for me, a glimpse into His heart. Today, my heart is filled with joyful gratitude for the incredible treasures that He gives in the things that sometimes seem all too ordinary.

Lord, thank You for each child whom You have blessed me with. Fill me with a desire to cherish them. Amen.
—ERIN MACPHERSON

Digging Deeper: PSALM 118:24, PROVERBS 17:22

Wed 27

"How can a mortal be just before God?"
—Job 9:2 (NRSV)

Brian's death took me by surprise and broke my heart. He'd died alone, in another state, at age twenty-eight.

Brian had been in and out of our church's homeless shelter for years. He was tall, thin, charming, courteous, and clever, probably to a fault. He was a Christian and knew his Bible better than any book. He liked happy endings.

He'd had few in his life. In fact, several months before he left, he'd been banned from the shelter. I'd arranged to have him allowed in for the book club, but I had to meet him on the street and escort him. He'd been sleeping in a large box in the rainy weather before getting a bunk at a temporary shelter. Winter was coming, and he was anxious to have a plan.

One evening he greeted me with a bear hug, declaring, "Say good-bye because I'm leaving tomorrow. I'm starting a new life!" He was moving to Virginia to live with his dad; even better, he had a job waiting for him. He told me that the staff members who'd banned him had greeted him enthusiastically. "Now that they know I'm leaving, they love me." But his quick smile was an instant too late to hide the pain in his eyes.

May

When news of his death moved through the community, I wondered how those staff members felt. Then I caught myself. How many times had I felt relieved to be free of a troubled person? How many times had I been of service only halfway? How many times had my actions caused another person pain?

I prayed for Brian—and for me to be a better servant of God.

Lord, help me to be selfless when I feel most selfish.
—MARCI ALBORGHETTI

Digging Deeper: PSALM 22:7, ISAIAH 9:1

Thu 28

Inscribe them on the doorposts of your house.
—DEUTERONOMY 6:9 (JPS)

The last thing we did after moving into our house was to fasten mezuzahs on the jambs of every exterior door. Some people think that mezuzahs are there to protect the house, but I think that they remind us to say a prayer every time we leave home. Touching the mezuzahs and kissing my fingertips as I go into the garage, lingering to say a prayer of thanks, sometimes to add whimsically, "And how are You today, God?" has become a ritual for me.

While my husband was in the hospital, though, I crazily rushed around. I couldn't spend time pausing at the mezuzah, and when there were errands to run, I felt even more pressure to move quickly.

I wanted to find something that wouldn't demand any lingering but would nevertheless convey to God that I remembered Him and needed His attention and help, even if I didn't have the luxury of unhurried prayer. One day, I started reciting the twenty-third Psalm, and when I got to "Thy rod and thy staff, they comfort me," it gave me an idea.

Every time I had to leave the house, I touched the mezuzah quickly, put my fingertips to my lips without slowing down, and said, "Rod and staff, Lord, rod and staff!" That seemed to say all I needed to.

I'm thinking that You understand the condensed version of a prayer as well as the unabridged version, God. In fact, I'm counting on it! —RHODA BLECKER

Digging Deeper: PSALMS 4:1, 17:6, 23:4

Fri 29   *You shall eat the fruit of the labor of your hands; you shall be blessed, and it shall be well with you.*
—PSALM 128:2 (ESV)

And the carpentered hewn planed polished workmanlike joy of making a thing well, with attention and craft and patience, and then when you are finished there it *is,* finished and inarguable, a new thing in the world that was never before in that form, be it a chest of drawers or a sculpture or a garden or an essay. There's a great, deep, quiet, proud pleasure and thrill and satisfaction in making, creating, tinkering, laboring. We do not salute and celebrate this joy enough, I think.

We are so good at adulating the finished thing, but not so good at singing the greater feat: the careful meticulous *making* of it, be it a child or a church or a country. It's the process that is the pleasure, not so much the product, the verb and not the noun. For we are always in the process of making and being made, and the greatest joy is the slow simmering one, not the sudden epiphany, yes?

The happiest I have ever been in life were the three moments that my children emerged, dewy and moist and astounding, from the middle of their mother. But the long joy of their growing up is even better than the wild startle of their arrival. I love them for who they are when I am not barking at them. But I love them more for *how* they are who they are and how they will be better at being themselves, I hope, day by day, year by year. In the same way that my greatest ambition as a male being is to be half the man my dad is, I hope to be twice as proud of the men and woman my children may become by the grace and gift of the mercy.

Dear Unimaginable Imagination, for many years I thought I was thankful enough that You made me. Then I was a hundred times more grateful when You gave me my lovely bride. But then a thousand and a thousand thousand times again filled with thanks that You sent us our children. Keep them in Your mercy, give them good work, give them joy and peace. Please?
—BRIAN DOYLE

Digging Deeper: PSALM 139:13–16

Sat 30

And he said unto them, Go ye into all the world, and preach the gospel to every creature. —MARK 16:15 (KJV)

This year, when my brother Robert and his wife, Ellen, were planning a mission trip to Poland, I asked how I might help. "These people will have memories of Auschwitz, so trust will be an issue. Our focus will likely be on building relationships rather than outright evangelism," Robert said. "We just need you to pray."

"But praying doesn't feel like I'm *doing* anything," I countered.

"Sometimes prayer is the real work," he answered.

When the group returned from Poland, I visited Robert and Ellen's church to hear them recount their experiences. "At first, they didn't even smile," Ellen said. The people of Poland had been hesitant to hear the Gospel and more receptive to simple friendship.

I couldn't help but reflect on my personal attempts at evangelism here at home. Aren't people more open to hearing about Jesus when they know me as a real person, when they've seen evidence of Him in my life? And isn't prayer the real work here too?

Help me to remember, in sharing the good news, God, that it's prayer and people first, and presentation second. —ROBERTA MESSNER

Digging Deeper: PSALMS 86:6, 141:2; PHILIPPIANS 4:6

Sun 31

Open thou mine eyes, that I may behold wondrous things....
—PSALM 119:18 (KJV)

As I walk along a country road, thoughts of my mother fill my head. A recent surgery has slowed her down; still, she never complains.

Ahead is a field of perfectly white cotton. Seeing it makes me sad. Mother told me about how she was made to pick cotton as a child. On impulse I break off a fluffy flower of cotton that has burst forth from the boll and carry it home.

Later, I head over to Mother's house to check in on her and her husband. I hand her the cotton.

"Have you ever told Herb about your cotton pickin' days?" I ask.

"You have no idea how prickly it is," she says. "By the end of the day, my hands would be red and swollen."

"So, Herb," I ask, "did you pick cotton too?"

"Sure did, in Spruce Pine, Alabama, right alongside my sisters, my mother, and my daddy. We picked row to row until we were weary. Then my daddy would shout, 'Why, look at that! A watermelon vine right in the middle of our cotton patch!'

"Sitting in the shade, relishing slices of juicy melon, it never occurred to me that this was Daddy's plan. Along with the cottonseed, he had planted watermelons where he knew we would need them most."

My mother and Herb were laughing, rehashing precious memories. And just like that my sadness was gone, replaced by something too marvelous to understand. God had planted His own surprises in between the cotton rows of my mother's difficult childhood, things that I will never know, things that helped my mother become the wonderful person she is today.

Father, even in hard times, You spread Your wonder and plant Your seeds. Open my eyes; help me see. —PAM KIDD

Digging Deeper: DANIEL 4:3, 2 CORINTHIANS 9:6

DAILY JOYS

1 _____

2 _____

3 _____

4 _____

5 _____

6 _____

7 _____

8 _____

9 _____

10 _____

11 _____

12 _____

13 _____

14 _____

15 _____

16 _____

17 _____

18 _____

19 _____

20 _____

21 _____

22 _____

23 _____

24 _____

25 _____

26 _____

27 _____

28 _____

29 _____

30 _____

31 _____

JUNE

Let us make a joyful noise
to the rock of our salvation!

—PSALM 95:1 (ESV)

Mon 1

"Where two or three gather in my name, there am I with them."
—MATTHEW 18:20 (NIV)

Several years ago, our son Kirk, a US Air Force officer, was deploying to Afghanistan. Months of uncertainty stretched before us. It was so far away, so fraught with danger. He couldn't guarantee when we would hear from him or how often, but he had an idea.

"While I'm gone, let's start with Psalm 1 and all read a psalm a day and pray together," he suggested. Nine of us agreed to do it: my sister, my mother, and my niece in New Jersey; Kirk's fiancée in Georgia; her mother in Tennessee; Kirk's sister in Ohio; my husband and me in Colorado; and Kirk, continents away in Afghanistan. We coordinated time zones. To the greatest extent possible, we would read a psalm and pray at the same time every day.

Marking the days with the Psalms became a lifeline for me while Kirk was deployed. Across the miles we were all joined in spirit with God and His Word.

On day 126 of Kirk's deployment I read Psalm 126:1–3 (AMP): "When the Lord brought back the captives...we were like those who dream.... Our mouths filled with laughter, and our tongues with singing.... The Lord has done great things for us! We are glad!"

That same day my phone rang. It was Kirk, calling to tell me that he and his team had arrived home safely.

You, Lord, have shown us the power of hearts united in prayer. I am filled with joy.
—KIM HENRY

Digging Deeper: PSALM 119:89–98, 105; HEBREWS 4:12–13

Tue 2   *And the leaves of the tree are for the healing of the nations.*
—REVELATION 22:2 (NRSV)

I'm one of those people who can get really discouraged when I can't see how the things I do are making a difference. But there's an antidote to my occasional descent into self-pity. His name is Nelson Henderson.

A friend lent me his dog-eared, slim volume of Henderson's *Under Whose Shade: A Story of a Pioneer in the Swan River Valley of Manitoba.* "It might help," was all he said, something I was seriously doubting halfway through the simple story. Until I hit the punch line of the book: "The true meaning of life is to plant trees under whose shade you do not expect to sit."

Henderson's medicine is simple. On those days when I know I'm especially susceptible to discouragement, I'll take a fifteen-minute break in the shade of a beautiful, nearly hundred-year-old maple tree just outside my home, where I can pray and be reminded: God will indeed use what I do in His name...in His own time...the right time. I let the majesty of the tree remind me of the majesty of God.

God, help me to see my work not only for its immediate outcomes but for its impact generations from now, when someone else will enjoy its shade.
—JEFF JAPINGA

Digging Deeper: PROVERBS 3:5,
1 CORINTHIANS 15:58

Wed 3

What do people get for all the toil and anxious striving with which they labor under the sun?
—ECCLESIASTES 2:22 (NIV)

The noisy clatter of the keyboard filled the room as I typed, trying to catch up. My workload soared off the charts. Last week I'd tuned up my schedule and gained several hours by consolidating errands. At the end of each week, I accounted for every minute. I was wound up like a clock.

I sensed Sunrise, my golden retriever, walk behind my chair. I ignored her. I was dog-sitting a friend's golden retriever, Shanny, so that I could work and Sunrise would have Shanny to play with.

A long, exasperated whine issued from Shanny. I twirled around, looked, then laughed. Sunrise had formed a body block between Shanny and me; she didn't want the other dog to get any of my attention. Both dogs stared at me with their big, sad brown eyes. My heart ached. I'd hurt the dogs' feelings, and last week I'd snapped at a friend. I'd been letting work consume my life and snuff out friends, fun, and even the dogs.

I stood up and scooted Sunrise to the side. Shanny barged in alongside me, and I scratched both dogs' ears. I had some rearranging and apologizing to do, but first I put a big X on the calendar for the next couple of hours. I needed to refuel, so I wasn't wound so tight.

> *Lord, when I get totally zoned out on work,*
> *remind me to use the body-blocking*
> *technique to guard relationships that*
> *are precious to me. Amen.*
> —REBECCA ONDOV

Digging Deeper: PROVERBS 18:24

Thu 4

"Choose for yourselves this day whom you will serve, whether the gods your ancestors served beyond the Euphrates, or the gods of the Amorites, in whose land you are living. But as for me and my household, we will serve the Lord."
—JOSHUA 24:15 (NIV)

My seven-year-old son is into choose-your-own-adventure books. Joey will sit for hours, reading through one storyline, and then go back to the beginning and choose another path for a completely different outcome. He loves seeing how one choice will lead his character to greatness (fifth-grade president, anyone?) and the other will lead to utter failure (or at least a week of detention). If Joey makes the wrong decision, he can just go back to the place in the book where it was made and make a better choice.

Oh, how I wish life were like that! If only I could erase those hurtful words that slipped out in a moment of impatience, or helped when I opted to stand back, or chosen joy instead of anger.

Of course, there are no redos, but we are living in a choose-your-own-adventure-story world. We have free will to choose our own path, whether it leads down the road to joy or destruction.

I wonder how differently I would choose today if I spent a few minutes before making each choice to consider the outcomes. Will I choose patience instead of grumpiness? Will I choose hope instead of desperation? Will I choose love instead of anger?

It's up to me what I choose and up to God how He moves with my choice.

Lord, help me to consider the path I'm heading down with each decision I make today and to choose what You want instead of choosing what's easy for me. Amen. —ERIN MACPHERSON

Digging Deeper: PROVERBS 6:6–8, ISAIAH 64:8

Fri 5 *The sea is his, for he made it....* —PSALM 95:5 (NRSV)

Daddy, get out of the water! Get out!" Benjamin's voice whipped away in the wind. We were on the beach in Monterey, California, and Kate, Frances, and I stood in the shallows, letting waves wash over our feet.

Reluctantly, I returned to my three-year-old. "It's okay, Benji," I said, picking him up. "Come with me. I'll show you."

"No!" he screamed as I stepped toward the waves. I stopped and stood, undecided. At last I put him down. "Let's pretend we're tractors," he said, vrooming his hand through the sand.

I gazed at the water. A huge breaker fell on itself with a boom. Something in the sound cast my memory back long ago. I remembered panic gripping my body when my mom, over my protests, carried me out into deeper water. She'd done it to accustom me to waves. All I remembered was a scary sense of the sea rising to snatch me away.

I looked at Benjamin. He saw the world like that too—a looming place full of incomprehensible powers. I still saw the world like that sometimes. Maybe that's one reason I prayed, one reason I leaned so hard on God.

"Okay, tractors," I said to my son. "We'll stay right here and play tractors."

> *When I'm anxious I lean on You, Lord. You are always faithful. —*JIM HINCH

Digging Deeper: PSALM 139:23, PHILIPPIANS 4:6

Sat 6

You are to rejoice before the Lord your God in everything you put your hand to.
—DEUTERONOMY 12:18 (NIV)

Today was finally the day; it was time for my baby shower. My sister had flown in. My mother and mother-in-law drove for hours to attend. My friends had gathered to celebrate the coming birth of Brian's and my baby girl.

I remember sitting in the same seat four years earlier as I anticipated my wedding day. Overwhelmed with the feeling of being loved by so many, I'd blushed as I opened presents meant to help set up my new home with my husband-to-be.

Now, I sat in the same place, surrounded by the same family and friends. Again, I was humbled. Who was I to receive such a blessing? What had I done to deserve such a perfect partner in life? How could I ever have been good enough to earn the right to parent a pint-size child? How could I have earned such a celebration from beloved friends?

The answer was simple: I had done nothing and could do nothing to be worthy of these precious gifts. God's love is great, vast, and endless, and He wants my joy to be as well.

Lord, help me to remember all that You have given me and all that I have to be thankful for.
—ASHLEY KAPPEL

Digging Deeper: 1 SAMUEL 2:1–3,
PHILIPPIANS 4:4–9

Sun 7   *Now you are the body of Christ, and each one of you is a part of it.*
—1 CORINTHIANS 12:27 (NIV)

One of the recent trends in the food world is what's called nose-to-tail eating—creating dishes from *all* parts of an animal. Hence the rise of foodie-favorite dishes like crispy pig's ear, spicy beef-tendon chips, and "buffalo-style" pigs' tails.

As I revisited some of my favorite meals of years past, it occurred to me that such cooking is redemptive. Chefs take cuts that might otherwise have been neglected and wasted. They find the good in them. And they transform them into culinary pearls. Might there also be a lesson here for the church?

In the church, we often fail to honor all parts of the diverse body of Christ. We engage in an ecclesiastical version of what, in the kitchen, would simply be called waste.

Of course, it takes effort to cook nose-to-tail, and it likewise takes effort to build a church where the individual gifts and skills of its members are not just honored but also well utilized. It's not easy, but it certainly is right. As believers invited to sit at the Lord's banquet table, we're asked to share His bounty with the world. If we don't use all the resources we have, how much harder might it be for others to taste and see that the Lord is indeed so very good?

Dear God, help us recognize the good in one another and the gifts with which You have equipped each of us.
—JEFF CHU

Digging Deeper: 1 CORINTHIANS 12:4–31, REVELATION 7:9–10

Mon 8

"Then Jesus placed his hands over the man's eyes again ... and he saw everything clearly...."
—MARK 8:25 (TLB)

My husband, Don, painted the basement a dingy tan. The color irritated me every time I went downstairs, and I let him know it at least once a week. Then one night I was driving home from my granddaughter's volleyball game and noticed that the headlights of oncoming cars wore halos. To make matters worse I missed my turn because the intersection faded into the surrounding countryside.

An eye exam revealed cataracts that needed to be removed. The surgery went well, and when I could see clearly again, headlights lost their halos, intersections reappeared, and the basement walls were a rich, lovely cream color.

I thought I had been seeing clearly. Clearly, I was wrong. I began to wonder, *Does my spiritual vision need correcting too?* I was ready to write off a friend who didn't acknowledge the gift I'd sent, only to get the package back marked "Insufficient Postage." And what about the time my feelings were hurt when one of my sons didn't reply to my text request for information? I later learned his phone had crashed.

A line from a song played in my mind: "Open the eyes of my heart, Lord. I want to see You." I closed my eyes and prayed the words over and over. Then I made a most sincere apology to Don.

Lord Jesus, thank You for restoring my physical eyesight and opening my spiritual eyes as well.
—PENNEY SCHWAB

Digging Deeper: PSALM 119:18, MARK 8:22–25, LUKE 6:41–42

GOD OF JOYFUL SURPRISES

Tue 9

"The word is near you, in your mouth and in your heart" (that is, the word of faith that we proclaim).
—ROMANS 10:8 (ESV)

RHEMA

Such a dismal day for our son's wedding! Not actually raining, but soggy, damp, and gray. We had planned an outdoor reception; tables and chairs were already set up in our yard. Since the bride's family came from Scotland, that was the theme for the day, complete with bagpiper. Would he even play in such conditions?

The service ended, and people filed from the church into a near-drizzle. My mood was as bleak as the skies, when my friend Marilee caught up with me. "What a perfect day!" she exclaimed. "Even the weather is Scottish."

And with those words, my outlook changed from distress to joy. The reception, in fact, went beautifully. The piper played—bagpipes, it seemed, were designed for just such weather—and the drifting mist cast a romantic haze over the scene.

Bible scholars have a name for the phenomenon of utterances like Marilee's: *rhema* or God's Word. Not *logos,* God's Word spoken eternally to all, but His intimate, personal Word spoken to a specific situation.

I suspect Marilee didn't even know she was speaking rhema. No matter: the power is not in the speaker but in the One Who, through human words, speaks God's unquenchable joy into our need.

God of joyful surprises, help me listen for Your voice of joy in the multitude of words I'll hear today.
—ELIZABETH SHERRILL

Digging Deeper: MATTHEW 4:4, JOHN 14:26

Wed 10

Therefore we do not lose heart. Even though our outward man is perishing, yet the inward man is being renewed day by day.
—2 CORINTHIANS 4:16 (NKJV)

Ever since I was a child, raising cattle in the big country was all I wanted to do. After rupturing a disc in my back while trying to save the ranch's forest from a wildfire, depression engulfed me as I watched my dream life slipping away. I'd been to a litany of medical experts, but there was only one point they could agree on: "Give up ranching. Your back will never be the same again."

This was my whole life. I'd sacrificed everything for this. I didn't get married and start a family. I didn't take time off. I didn't go to town or hang out with friends. I put my whole heart, my whole being, into the ranch.

Now my life was measured by daily pain indexes and pills. I was put on a walker and couldn't leave my house. On good days I could use a cane or crutches and stand outside for a few minutes. In my eyes, my purpose, my value, my identity were all gone.

Faith is believing that God has a direction in mind for you when you can't see the future. I couldn't see it then. I didn't even want to see it, but I knew God was there in it.

God, You know how hard this is for me. Help me to let go of what I've lost and treasure what I am to gain. —ERIKA BENTSEN

Digging Deeper: PSALMS 56:3, 91:4, 115:9–11

Thu 11

Behold, how good and pleasant it is when brothers dwell in unity!
—PSALM 133:1 (ESV)

I had been a little worried when I chose my brother, Ned, as my best man. As I do, he has a tendency to put off important things until the last minute, and I wanted everything to run smoothly at the wedding. Also, Ned isn't religious like Emily and me, and I didn't want the spiritual aspect of our wedding to be diminished.

But he is my brother. Neither of us does a good job of expressing our love to each other, so when I asked him, the way he said "Of course I will" and hugged me was worth more than any of my concerns.

Still, I didn't know what to expect from his reception speech, and my anxiety increased when he said he was still working on it the morning of the wedding. But by the time we all sat down to our meal, just a few minutes after Emily and I said "I do," I was so happy and everything was so perfect that I knew I would love Ned's speech.

He started with my favorite writer, David Foster Wallace, and his idea that even though we may live in "dark times," the only noble response to that is to seek more truth, more love, and more spirituality. Ned called Emily and me "soldiers against the dark times."

Ned made the perfect speech. And in communicating his love for me so openly, he showed me that even those who don't use God's name can be soldiers in His army.

Thank You again, God, for Your servants, both knowing and unknowing. —SAM ADRIANCE

Digging Deeper: 2 TIMOTHY 4:7

Fri 12

Be kind and compassionate to one another....
—EPHESIANS 4:32 (NIV)

My daughter Lindsay is the mother of an eight-, five-, and three-year-old, with a carefully planned schedule of preschool and elementary school that gives structure to her days. She lives in our neighborhood, and I often see her when I'm out walking the dog.

She and the kids spilled out of her front door as I walked by at 9:00 AM on the first no-school day of summer. "I'm done with summer!" she announced. "I can't do this!"

I laughed and without any sympathy said, "Summer gives moms the opportunity to grow their perseverance."

My motherly wisdom was not what Lindsay needed just then. "You just don't remember what it's like, Mom," she shot back as she gathered the children into the house and closed the door.

My immediate reaction was defensive because these days I'm sensitive about being told I'm forgetful. But I had time to think about her comment while walking. Maybe the passing years have edited out some of my memories of feeling tired, frustrated, invisible, and insignificant. Maybe I have lost touch with some of those emotions. Maybe what I remember most is having to get a grip and get through the chaos, so I expect my daughter to do the same. Maybe I want to fix Lindsay instead of listen to her feelings. I want to rush her back into "happy," so I don't have to experience her unhappiness.

Just maybe, summer is the time when this mom can grow the kind of empathy and compassion her daughter most needs and wants.

God, help me remember to listen without lecturing or fixing, so I can be more the kind of person You want me to be. —CAROL KUYKENDALL

Digging Deeper: ISAIAH 49:13

Sat 13

The righteous gives and does not hold back. —PROVERBS 21:26 (ESV)

I have a surprise," my son Samuel said.

"What's that?" I asked. His hand came forward, and his fingers uncurled. In his palm lay a few wadded, crumpled dollar bills and an assortment of change. "Wow!" I said. "What are you going to do with it?"

"What I'd like to do is take you for a ride on *that.*" A street fair had come to our small town, and Samuel turned toward the Ferris wheel curving just over the trees in our front yard.

"But that's your Tooth Fairy and birthday money, Samuel. Are you sure you want to spend it like that?"

"I'm sure," he said, but as we waited in line, I began to feel guilty. Maybe I should have offered to pay.

"C'mon up!" the man on the platform called. We headed straight for the sky. Around and around we went, in and out of the blue. We held our breath on the way up and giggled like mad on the way down.

"Are you having fun, Mom?" Samuel asked the final time we went around.

"I am," I said. "Thank you for the gift."

Samuel nodded. His hand wrapped around mine. His smile came straight from his heart. I didn't need to feel guilty. My little boy was learning to give.

Lord, help me learn to accept the kind gifts of others. Amen. —SHAWNELLE ELIASEN

Digging Deeper: 2 CORINTHIANS 9:6–7, PHILIPPIANS 2:3

Sun 14

For I am the Lord your God who takes hold of your right hand and says to you, Do not fear; I will help you. —ISAIAH 41:13 (NIV)

My friend Linda needed to talk, so we walked over to the park and sat down on a bench. "Business is slow, and I'm considering returning to school to finish my degree," she confided. "I'm full of fear about it though. I really think it's God's plan for me, but I can't seem to move forward on it. I don't know why. God has always been there for me. Yet..." Her voice trailed off.

"Let's pray about it, okay?" I offered.

We sat in silence for a moment and then both looked over in the direction of the playground. A father was coaxing his little girl down the slide— she at the top, clutching tightly to the rail, and he at the bottom, his arms outstretched to catch her.

"Honey," he said, "I'm right here."

"I'm scared," she replied.

"But, honey," he said gently, "have I ever let you fall?"

She shook her head.

"Then give it a try, okay?" he asked.

"Okay," she said reluctantly. With that, she let go and slid right into his arms.

"Daddy, that was fun!" she exclaimed. "Let's do it again!"

Linda looked over at me with a big smile. "Looks like I just got a perfect lesson in faith," she said, laughing. "Okay, Lord, here I come! Just make sure You catch me, okay?"

Father, help me to let go of the fear in my life that stops me from following You. Amen.
—MELODY BONNETTE SWANG

Digging Deeper: PSALM 56:3, LUKE 7:50

Mon 15

"Now I commit you to God and to the word of his grace...."
—ACTS 20:32 (NIV)

My sister Susan called me with the news that Uncle Bob, the last surviving family friend of our parents' generation, was in hospice care in North Carolina. "He'd like to see us girls one last time," she said. "I'm driving up this weekend."

"I have obligations I can't cancel," I answered. I returned to my chores, thinking, *I guess I could call Uncle Bob on the phone, but what would I say?*

Under a stack of photo albums, I unearthed a yellowed guest book that had been my mother's. Bittersweet memories filled me as I read the signatures of deceased family friends. Then I discovered that Mom had copied a poem onto the inside leaf of the guest book: "May the Good Lord bless and keep you/Whether near or far way/May you find that long awaited/Golden day today/May you walk with the sunlight shining/And a bluebird in every tree/May there be a silver lining/Back of every cloud you see/Fill your dreams with sweet tomorrows/Never mind what might have been/May the Good Lord bless and keep you/Till we meet again."

I didn't recognize the poem, so I checked it out online and discovered it was a Perry Como song. As I listened to it, all of the deep connections of family and friends formed a sweet harmony of thankfulness for dear ones like Uncle Bob.

I picked up the phone and called him, saying, "Do you remember the Perry Como song...?" And as I shared the beautiful words with him as a prayer of tender parting, I felt reassured that we would, indeed, meet again in God's eternal sweet tomorrows.

Dear Father, help my farewells be times of placing my loved ones into Your tender care until we meet again. Amen. —KAREN BARBER

Digging Deeper: NUMBERS 6:24, 1 CORINTHIANS 16:23–24

Tue 16

Behold, what I have seen to be good and fitting is to eat and drink and find enjoyment in all the toil with which one toils under the sun.... —ECCLESIASTES 5:18 (ESV)

Before we had left for vacation, I promised myself I'd check my work e-mail only once after we arrived. So when I turned on my computer and couldn't connect to the wireless network, I moaned. I closed the laptop, reopened it, and cringed when the error message flashed again.

Grumbling, I went to find the instructions that came with the vacation lease. I typed in the username and password. *Urghh!* I tried again.

Henry came in still dressed in his pajamas. "So, Mom, are we going to the beach with the big waves today or stay here?"

"Not now," I said. "I've got to do a little work."

"Work on vacation?" Henry said. "That's like me going to school in the summer."

"Just for a minute!" I snapped. Tony decided to take the boys out.

A half hour later I was still on hold with the technical support number that was included with the instructions. I looked out the window at the ocean. Tony, Solomon, and Henry were building a huge seahorse out of sand. The hold music piped away through the receiver. *What am I doing?* I thought.

Just then, the music stopped and a person came on the line. "Hello, how may I help you today?"

"I give up," I said.

"How may I help you?" the technician asked again.

"This is my vacation," I replied. "Thanks, but I give up." I closed the laptop and went down to the water just in time to help the boys find shells for the seahorse's eye and seaweed for its mane.

Dear Lord, thank You for this absolutely beautiful vacation and the insight to enjoy it.
—SABRA CIANCANELLI

Digging Deeper: MARK 6:30, LUKE 5:16

Wed 17

"Give us this day our daily bread."
—MATTHEW 6:11 (NAS)

Nineteen new graduates from Mercer University flew to northern Thailand and will teach conversational English there. One of the most lush and beautiful environs, Thailand is also blessed with lovely and gracious people. Yet, for these young Americans, their new home is on the other side of the world and, for the first time, they are far away from family and security. Exotic novelty is now wearing off, and some write to me of loneliness and fear and second thoughts about leaving home. The reality of a brave new venture is seeping in.

So it is in life. A new job moves us to another state. A wonderful wedding flings us into adulthood, and we realize: *We can't go home again.* The retirement we have longed for casts us into uncharted waters, and we fear the future.

A friend once told me that when life quits changing and fear is conquered, there is a good chance you are dead. I think she is right. A rich life is always seasoned by the spices of apprehension, anxiety, and adjustment. Such painful emotions sing a rich duet with peace, security, and intimacy. Life is filled with paradox, and we must learn to dance amid the dissonance.

Father, give me the courage to weather those times of apprehension with confidence. Amen.
—Scott Walker

Digging Deeper: Isaiah 26:3

Thu 18

"Say not, I will do so to him as he hath done to me...."
—Proverbs 24:29 (KJV)

I was helping our church youth at a weeklong work camp in a poverty-stricken community of Appalachia. By day, we hammered, sawed, and painted homes. The evenings, on the other hand, were filled with fun, games, and getting to know one another from across the country. A few days in, we were like family and having a mighty good time.

But not everyone shared our enthusiasm. The leader of another group had made a long list of rules for his kids. It was my fault that our worlds collided because I was there when my kids decided that it would be a good idea to sneak into his cabin and paint smiley faces on the bathroom mirror.

The next morning at breakfast, the man stormed up to our table and called my kids wild, rude . . . until finally I'd had it. "How do you have the nerve to talk that way!" I said. "After all, there's not a single kid in this camp who likes you!"

The room froze. If I had stabbed the poor man with a knife, he couldn't have been more deeply wounded. His hurt reflected back to me, and I was devastated. No wonder God turned His most important advice into gold and declared it the number-one rule!

"Oh . . . I'm sorry . . ." I stammered, but it was too late. Even now, I see that man's eyes and recognize God there, telling me that when I wound another, I not only hurt myself, I do it to God as well.

Father, I see Your hurt in the eyes of those
I've wronged. Help me think of
You before I speak.
—PAM KIDD

Digging Deeper: LEVITICUS 19:18, PROVERBS 12:18,
TITUS 3:2

Fri 19

"And the king will answer them, 'Truly I tell you, just as you did it to one of the least of these who are members of my family, you did it to me.'" —MATTHEW 25:40 (NRSV)

On Friday afternoons Kenny sits on the fire-plug outside the pharmacy near my office. He's there on Fridays, I've learned, because the deli nearby provides him with a free dinner at 4:00 PM, giving away food that would otherwise go bad over the weekend.

I guess you could call Kenny homeless, but he doesn't act like he's down on his luck. He's a sharp dresser, wearing a coat and tie and a navy-blue over-coat in the winter. He leans on a cane and has a wide toothy grin. He has a chronic condition that requires frequent doctor visits and regular medica-tion, hence the spot near the pharmacy. He has a room in a shelter somewhere up in Harlem.

When I first got to know him, I figured I was performing an act of charity. After all, Jesus tells us to look out for "the least of these." But Kenny has become more than that. He's a friend. Often as not, when I've promised to pray for him, he's stood up from his fireplug and given me a hug.

The other day he was missing something. "Where's your Bible?" I asked.

He grinned and pointed to his head. "I keep it right up here."

"You know, I try to memorize Bible verses, but as soon as I learn them, I forget them."

"Don't worry," he said. "You've got Jesus in the right place." He gestured to my chest. "You've got Him in your heart and that's just where He should be." Then he gave me a big hug.

I walked back to the office, thinking that I'd just lived out a parable of Jesus's. Who was helping whom? One of "the least of these" had just blessed me.

Let me give, Lord, as You have extravagantly given to me. —RICK HAMLIN

Digging Deeper: 1 JOHN 3:18

Sat 20

Fear thou not; for I am with thee: be not dismayed; for I am thy God: I will strengthen thee; yea, I will help thee; yea, I will uphold thee with the right hand of my righteousness.
—ISAIAH 41:10 (KJV)

Sitting across the table from my father, I stare at him. *You have always oozed such confidence,* I think admiringly. When I was a child, my father was always present, always providing, always reaching for the stars. He seemed invincible. I wanted to be just like him. Now, this silver-haired, eighty-two-year-old man with a pacemaker and an oxygen compressor as constant companions is still trying new things, like completing educational requirements to become a mediator.

"You never seem afraid," I say to him. "I wish I had your confidence."

"I was afraid sometimes," he replies, and I am startled. This is a side of my father I've never known. I've seen him face down much bigger men, situations that seemed larger than he was. He's never once discussed his fears.

"Like when?"

"When I first went to work at the Pentagon," he says. My mouth drops open. My memories of him going to work are images of a confident man in a suit and tie, reading the newspaper before heading out in the early morning, his ubiquitous cowboy boots clicking down the sidewalk. "The Pentagon was so big," he continues. "There was so much responsibility."

I think of things that have frightened me: raising a daughter and son alone; eventually leaving my own government job and starting a new career. I smile at my father and reach across the table to touch his hand. Though this revelation comes late in life, that he has wrangled with fear, it is a wonderful gift that he has given me.

Lord, thank You for a father who set a fine example of courage in the face of fear. Indeed, You were courageous even unto death —SHARON FOSTER

Digging Deeper: JOSHUA 1:9, LUKE 12:32, HEBREWS 11:6

Sun 21

"I know every bird in the mountains, and the insects in the fields are mine." —PSALM 50:11 (NIV)

Millie woke me up in the wee hours with a demure little whine at the back door. This usually signals a rare midnight emergency, so I threw on a T-shirt, trotted downstairs, and let her out into the warm, earthy night. I went to the kitchen and tracked her through the dark from the window above the sink while I got myself a glass of water. She briefly disappeared in the shadows of the woods and then reappeared in the middle of the yard. There she sat, very still, ghostly white in the luminosity of a crystal-clear night, head tilted up, staring at the sky.

What on earth was she doing? What was she seeing? It seemed to me she was looking at the stars, at the silvery heavens above, the Milky Way smeared across the firmament. I didn't call her in. I let her stay that way for a spell, just gazing up at the sky. I remembered then that it was the summer solstice.

Who knows what goes through a dog's mind? What powers God has imbued dogs with that we can only imagine? What they see that we don't see? What they feel and sense about nature that is sealed off from our mortal senses, dimensions only they can know? The moonlight was illuminated in her fur. She was out there for a reason, and not the one I thought or was ever likely to know.

After awhile Millie rose and headed back toward the house. I heard a little scratch at the door and let her in. Her tail was swishing. She took a quick drink of water, padded upstairs, and put herself back to bed. I almost followed, but instead I wrote down what I had witnessed. I didn't want to wake up in the morning and think it was only a dream.

We are given the beauty of the seasons and the mysteries of life as gifts to ponder. Father, wake me up anytime to see Your hand at work.
—EDWARD GRINNAN

Digging Deeper: PSALMS 19:1, 148:7–10

Mon 22

"He is wooing you from the jaws of distress to a spacious place free from restriction...."—JOB 36:16 (NIV)

I went to get a tooth pulled today at a dental school and ended up with a fractured upper jaw. As I lay in the chair, absorbing the news, the Lidocaine still flowing through my system helped me accept that my jaw would heal.

The student-dentist who tried to do the extraction didn't look nearly as composed as I convinced myself I could be. I'd worked with her before; she'd always done an excellent job, though she lacked confidence. This freak accident (partly due to an oddly placed root in my molar) shook her up badly. I wondered if she'd drop out of dental school.

While a professor wired my teeth together, I prayed. There wasn't much I could do about my situation besides accepting it. Flitting on the edge of my mind was the realization that there was something I could do for the student.

When she returned, I took a deep breath. Using words that surely weren't my own, I said, "I know you wish there was something you could do for me, and there is. I want you to find a way to grow stronger through this. You will be a fine dentist someday but not if you're scared."

The woman gazed into my pain-glazed eyes and slowly began to smile. I wanted to tell her not to be grateful to me but to God. He's the One Who can turn even disaster into something good.

Jesus, help me to use my pain to transform the lives of others. —JULIA ATTAWAY

Digging Deeper: PHILIPPIANS 2:1–3

Tue 23

"Our Father who art in heaven...."
—MATTHEW 6:9 (RSV)

My dad was diagnosed with lung cancer last Thanksgiving and struggled reluctantly with spiritual matters. We had delicate conversations over the phone and when I flew out to visit. In the midst of our conversations, he composed a spiritual autobiography of sorts and e-mailed it to me.

It was a strangely cheery account, more about his capers as an altar boy and the hearty debates between Jesuits and rabbis at his college fraternity than about his current situation or anything that he believed. We were in opposite places: Dad struggled with faith itself; I with the value of attending church.

I offered feedback on his manuscript, and he sent it back, revised and expanded to include some sentences about his hurt feelings when he'd sought his pastor's counsel during our family's troubles and the pastor had merely said an "Our Father" with him and sent him home.

By my last trip, Dad was barely conscious, alternating between agitated and listless. My stepmom called their new pastor to administer the last rites. We gathered around his bed. The pastor first anointed my father on the forehead and then, to my alarm, began reciting the "Our Father."

Oh well, I thought as I joined in, *Dad's too out of it to notice.*

At that moment, though, Dad's eyes jerked open. He looked right at the pastor and prayed the words fervently.

Finally, the church's role in a believer's life revealed itself to me. Through its habits, its words, and its prayers, the church comes alongside us on our disparate journeys Godward.

Heavenly Father, thank You for giving us prayers and rituals that light our path home. —PATTY KIRK

Digging Deeper: MATTHEW 18:18–20, HEBREWS 10:24–25

Wed 24

Where no oxen are, the trough is clean; but much increase comes by the strength of an ox.
—PROVERBS 14:4 (NKJV)

No," I shouted, "turn here! Go farther before you turn!"

"What? I don't understand." My son, age ten, was mastering the art of mowing the lawn on a garden tractor and was making a mess.

There are few sights more beautiful to me than a manicured lawn. It convinces me that all is well in the world, which is why I spoke sharply to my son.

I saw it in his eyes: the hurt of knowing he'd let me down when there should have been joy. After all, what kid doesn't love driving a riding mower?

God's Spirit convicted me: *Your son's heart is more important than the straightness of the lines on your lawn.*

I caught myself. "Hey, you know what? You're doing great! Just keep going."

Too late. He was already throttling down the mower. "Dad, may I go inside?"

"I'm sorry, Son. I shouldn't have yelled like that."

He climbed off the machine. I repeated my apology. We hugged. For that day, however, he was finished.

There I stood, feeling horrible, when out the door bounded a chance at mini-redemption. "My turn now, Dad?" my twelve-year-old daughter asked.

"You bet, honey. Mow anywhere you like. Just have fun."

Because crooked mowing lines sometimes offer beauty of a better kind.

Teach me the wisdom, Lord, that everything that
brings joy also brings complications, and that
I cannot embrace the joy without
accepting the complications.
—BILL GIOVANNETTI

Digging Deeper: PSALM 6:2, 2 CORINTHIANS 12:10

I SURRENDER ALL

Thu 25

You ... are intimately acquainted with all my ways.
—Psalm 139:3 (NAS)

SAYING YES

Surrender came jaggedly, in broken bits and pieces. Though I'd decreased my work schedule and resumed my quiet times, I hadn't made a decision about volunteering at the pregnancy resource center where my cousin Laura works.

I trekked through the woods behind our house with Clyde, our yellow Labrador. Discovering a wild dogwood tree in full bloom, I remembered a certain Sunday morning in 1969. Right before my ninth birthday, I walked down the aisle to the front of the church with a pounding heart and gave my life to Jesus. Recalling the somber organ music, Mother's perfume, and my clammy hands clutching the gleaming church pew, I realized I was doing the same thing now: hanging on tight, clinging to my way of life.

No one around but Clyde and God, I sensed God speaking to me. Beneath the canopy of trees, I raised my hands and prayed out loud: "Lord, show me what to do about my time and I'll do it. I promise."

Music from so many years ago, "I Surrender All" by Judson W. Van DeVenter, resounded in my heart. I began singing, "All to Jesus I surrender, all to Him I freely give . . . "

I haven't given to You freely, have I, Lord?

"I will ever love and trust Him, in His presence daily live . . . "

I haven't always loved and trusted You. I'm sorry.

I belted out the chorus: "All to Thee, my blessed Savior, I surrender all."

Yes! Yes! Yes! I'd love to volunteer. I couldn't wait to call Laura.

Lord, I can't fool You. You know my hardheaded ways and yet You wait so patiently for me to surrender.
—JULIE GARMON

Digging Deeper: ISAIAH 43:1, MATTHEW 10:30

Fri 26

Give to the one who begs from you, and do not refuse the one who would borrow from you.
—MATTHEW 5:42 (ESV)

After a day on the beach, enjoying the sun and the waves, my friends and I were walking through the vibrant, unfamiliar streets of Barcelona, Spain, making our way back to our hostel under the moonlight. We were studying abroad, and it was my first time traveling around Europe, so I was constantly looking around, taking everything in and hoping not to get lost.

A woman approached us from behind. "Please! I need money to eat and to pay for a place to sleep. I lost everything: my wallet, my passport. My country's embassy is closed, and I don't know what to do. Please help me!"

I looked at my friend and rolled my eyes. Nevertheless, I said to the woman, "I'm sorry to hear about your troubles," and handed her the change from my pocket, a little less than two euros.

She studied the coins in her hand. "That's all?" she asked.

I nodded and walked off.

"She was definitely lying," one of my friends said.

"Who knows?" I responded.

I didn't think about it too much at the time, but now I look back at how quick I was to dismiss her claims and brand her a liar. What if she was telling the truth?

Dear Father, I can't afford to help every beggar, but it doesn't cost me anything to empathize. Open my heart and remove the negativity I hold in my soul about people who ask for help. —Erik Cruz

Digging Deeper: Luke 6:37–38, John 7:24

Sat 27

And he saw also a certain poor widow casting in thither two mites.
—Luke 21:2 (KJV)

Tara Sharma, MD, was a beloved urologist at the Veterans Affairs Medical Center, where I'm a nurse. Last year he passed away. Those who worked closely with him were particularly devastated.

On a quiet Saturday, I attended Dr. Sharma's estate sale. *I would love to purchase a wonderful keepsake for Tara Porter,* I thought. Tara was a nurse who'd worked with him. "My namesake," Dr. Sharma, who was originally from India, often observed.

Money had been short lately, thanks to some trees that had fallen on my property during a storm. But I spotted a crystal bowl on the Sharmas' dining room table in the Star of David pattern. One of the neighbors remarked that it was always filled with something delicious at the parties the Sharmas were known for. I bought the bowl for four dollars.

When I handed it to Tara, she couldn't contain her joy. "That was so loving of you," she said. "It's perfect. And did you know, in India, the name *Tara* means *star*?"

Lord Jesus, in Your economy, the smallest amount of money can work miracles. Thank You.
—Roberta Messner

Sun 28

"What happiness there is for you who weep, for the time will come when you shall laugh with joy!"
—LUKE 6:21 (TLB)

My husband and I were both weary as we sniffled our way into week three of head and chest colds. I wanted to cheer him up but couldn't figure out how to do it. Then I received an e-mail from Joan, who heard me speak at a retreat about the importance of putting laughter into our lives. I'd hauled out a couple of rubber chickens from my collection to use as show-and-tell.

Joan wrote that she'd purchased five rubber chickens after my talk. She hid one inside her friend's suitcase when she took her to the airport. The second one she mailed to a friend in New York. The third was going to find a home inside her daughter's freezer, and the fourth was going in a gift bag to her attorney. She kept the fifth one for future fun.

Inspired by Joan's note, I took my favorite rubber chicken and placed it under the mattress on Jack's side of the bed, so when he flopped down he'd hear a loud squawk. Trouble was, when he sat on the bed to pull on his pajamas, he heard the squawk, got up, and snuck it under the mattress on my side of the bed. When I hit the sheets, I got quite a surprise.

We both felt better that night after proving that laughter is truly the best medicine.

Dear Lord, thank You for the gift of laughter and the way it eases so many of life's little pitfalls.
—PATRICIA LORENZ

Digging Deeper: JOB 29:24, PSALM 126:2

Mon 29

Give thanks to the Lord, for he is good; his love endures forever.
—PSALM 107:1 (NIV)

Every morning at Beacon of Hope, a ministry on the outskirts of Nairobi, a man with a smile a mile wide would spread his hands and declare, "God is good!"

His Kenyan brothers and sisters in Christ would respond with an exuberant "All the time!"

Then he'd raise his arms higher and repeat back to them, "All the time!"

And they would exclaim, "God is good!"

It's a memory that came to mind recently, six years after my trip to Kenya, when I saw three updates on the Internet from people who were celebrating good news and had tacked "God is so good!" on the end of their posts.

They made me pause, reflect, and even question: *What about when bad things happen? What about when life feels disappointing or hurtful? Isn't God good then too?*

Perhaps it's in the valleys when our declaration of God's goodness means the most. Not just to the outside world looking in, but to ourselves. Maybe it's in the low times when we need to cling to the truth of God's goodness all the more fiercely. Maybe that's the key to rejoicing always, even in the trials.

Because God is good! All the time!

Lord Jesus, thank You for being a good God, no matter what the season, no matter what the circumstances.
—KATIE GANSHERT

Digging Deeper: PSALMS 31:19, 86:15;
1 THESSALONIANS 5:18

Tue 30   *Let brotherly love continue.*
—HEBREWS 13:1 (ESV)

Another joyous fabric I think maybe we take for granted a lot is brothers. Most of you who are reading this have a brother or three. And I think we ought to stay in the present tense even if their bodies are grass and clay now, as four of my brothers' bodies are. Because the joy of brothers does not cease with death. And while I miss my brothers' shouldery heft and barrellish bodies, their deep amused voices, and their wry wits, they are always with me. In the kitchen I feel their big hands gentle on my neck; watching basketball I hear their grunts of pleasure as a play is executed perfectly. I feel them grinning and glancing at each other saying without unnecessary words—*Did you see that?*

Yes, brothers, I did. Yes, brothers, I see you also, every day, brothers. Sure I weep that you will never open my headlong letters again. Nor will I laugh to find your spidery scrawls on silly postcards. Nor will we stand in a laughing line at the front door as our tiny bent mother glares up at us and makes sure that we have brushed our teeth and have clean handkerchiefs without which no son of hers will ever appear in public.

But I feel you around me like huge gentle holy birds, brothers. I feel you in my speech and thoughts and songs and dreams. I speak to you aloud in stories and embrace you in my prayers. And I know, I *know* it, brothers, that there will come a day, somehow, when you will lean down your holy wild heads to me—I the shortest of all of us brothers— and I will kiss your foreheads. Yes I will, and be filled with joy inarticulate, inexplicable, inarguable, unending. And never will we part again, brothers. Never.

Dear Lord, You know and I know there are worlds beyond the world I can see. With all my heart, I beg You to let me be with all my brothers together at once when I return to Your Light. Maybe at the far end of heaven where the basketball courts are? If possible?
—Brian Doyle

Digging Deeper: Proverbs 3

DAILY JOYS

1 _____

2 _____

3 _____

4 _____

5 _____

6 _____

7 _____

8 _____

9 _____

10 _____

11 _____

12 _____

13 _____

14 _____

15 _____

16 _____

17 _____

18 _____

19 _____

20 _____

21 _____

22 _____

23 _____

24 _____

25 _____

26 _____

27 _____

28 _____

29 _____

30 _____

JULY

*"For you shall go out in joy
and be led forth in peace;
the mountains and the hills before you
shall break forth into singing,
and all the trees of the field shall clap their hands."*

—ISAIAH 55:12 (ESV)

Wed 1
And the Word became flesh and dwelt among us. . . . —JOHN 1:14 (NKJV)

Years ago, I was called to Zimbabwe on assignment to write about the street children. I didn't plan on becoming involved beyond that, but it became abundantly clear that God's call was for my family to get involved, and soon the children of this AIDS-ravaged country became our passion. Village Hope was born.

Now, standing amid pots boiling on open fires and the delicious smell of bread baking in cast-iron ovens, I see children, once orphaned and alone, working alongside the local couple we partnered with, Alice and Paddington. They've been up since dawn, preparing for guests. Today is the dedication of their new church.

But for me, the anticipated visit by an important official of Zimbabwe's presbytery touches the day with apprehension. Church executives can be stuffy and self-important, and I didn't want to see the enthusiasm over this happy event dampened.

At the appointed hour, a big black car drove through the gates and an immaculately dressed man emerged. I kept my distance, waiting for Alice and Paddington to meet the dignitary and take him on a tour of the little farm. Finally, they appeared in the cooking hut, and I was surprised to see tears in the man's eyes. He looked at us and what he said melted our worries, clarified our struggles, and opened our eyes: "The Word made flesh."

Father, I see You clearly, without doubt,
when I seek to serve. —PAM KIDD

Digging Deeper: JAMES 1:1–22, 2:18;
REVELATION 21:3

Thu 2

Let us run with patience the race that is set before us. —HEBREWS 12:1 (KJV)

I've been dealing with a stress-related illness for the past couple of years that has zapped my energy levels. This was especially frustrating to me because I had harbored hopes of writing a second book and perhaps many others. But now the idea was inconceivable.

I was sharing these laments with a friend who asked, "Josh, do you know how to eat an elephant?"

"No," I said, "but what does that have to do with my life?"

"Well, do you?"

"No. How do you eat an elephant?"

"One bite at a time."

The metaphor was apt. When I wrote my first manuscript, I would wake up in the morning and keep typing until I got dizzy some eight hours later. At that pace, I completed it with great speed. I wasn't capable of that anymore, but I was still able to do a little bit each day that would eventually add up to a lot. So I started working just ten minutes a day, then thirty, sixty, ninety.... Finishing that second manuscript has reframed the way I think about my life. Now I see that God can accomplish big things in and through me with just a little bite each day.

Lord, give me the patience and endurance to take one bite at a time. —JOSHUA SUNDQUIST

Digging Deeper: ISAIAH 40:31

GOD OF JOYFUL SURPRISES

Fri 3   *Let the weak say, I am strong.*
—JOEL 3:10 (KJV)

MAKING MUSIC

My husband and I had never heard Itzhak Perlman perform in person till that evening at Avery Fisher Hall in New York City. We knew from record liner-notes that he was crippled by polio at age four, but nothing prepared us for his awkward, lurching walk across the stage, supported on crutches. He reached the chair beside the conductor's platform, lowered himself onto it, laid down the crutches, unhooked the brace-clasps on his legs, and picked up the violin from its case on the floor.

A moment of tuning, a nod to the conductor, and the orchestra launched into the opening movement of Beethoven's violin concerto. Perlman lifted his bow; the high, sweet solo line soared above the rest. And then there was an ear-piercing *ping!*

The conductor signaled the orchestra to stop. Silence ensued as Perlman lowered the violin and stared at the broken string. Would the performance be canceled or could a new string be found and attached? Would the virtuoso play on an unfamiliar instrument?

Perlman nodded again to the conductor and put the violin back beneath his chin. The orchestra resumed playing; the solo voice sang out, plaintive and angelic. You can't play a violin on three strings! What kind of transposition, invention, substitution did it take to produce that perfect sound?

At the final note, all of us were on our feet, cheering, clapping, shouting for the sheer joy of the performance we'd witnessed. When the pandemonium died down, Perlman fastened his leg clasps, picked up his crutches, stood up, and said with a bow to the audience and a smile, "Sometimes we have to make music with what we have left."

God of joyful surprises, as I grow older, help me make music to You with all my strength.
—ELIZABETH SHERRILL

Digging Deeper: PSALMS 57:7, 92:1

Sat 4   *"I will celebrate before the Lord."*
—2 Samuel 6:21 (niv)

Growing up, our family always spent Independence Day on the Florida Gulf. I believed there was no place as enchanting—sugar-white sand, a swimming pool right outside our small rented apartment, and the thrill of watching fireworks on the beach.

Two years ago, my son-in-law suggested we stay on Fripp Island, South Carolina, for the Fourth of July. I wasn't too sure. South Carolina instead of Florida? Could the Atlantic Ocean replace the Gulf of Mexico? Would the fireworks be as magnificent as those I remembered?

As our caravan of cars pulled up to the rental home on Fripp Island, a pair of does grazing nearby glanced at us and kept eating. "Wow," I said to my husband, "everything's so different here! We never saw deer at the Gulf."

"Look behind the house," he said. "See the channels of water? People probably go kayaking back there."

"We sure didn't kayak in Florida," I mused.

Early the next morning, we walked down the quaint streets toward the dock. Hardwood trees formed a canopy overhead, offering cool shade. Being a fair-skinned redhead, I appreciated the break from the sun. "This is nice. Not much shade where we stayed in Florida. And look at the palm trees growing in the woods. Never seen that before."

On the night of the Fourth, our family gathered on the gray weathered dock outside the house. From there, we saw something I'd never experienced: fireworks bursting into vivid colors overlooking narrow channels of water that led to the Atlantic Ocean. The sparkly explosions raised a new prayer in my heart.

Lord, thank You. Because so many have defended our freedom, all of us can celebrate tonight from sea to shining sea. Maybe one day we'll watch fireworks on the Pacific coast.
—JULIE GARMON

Digging Deeper: PSALMS 18:46, 118:15-17

Sun 5

"Let your light shine before others, so that they may see your good works and give glory to your Father who is in heaven." —MATTHEW 5:16 (ESV)

I have not, as yet, been to every country on this round and amazing rock. But I have been to other continents and to another hemisphere, and I have seen new stars and birds and trees, and I have tried to swim in various other languages and gaped at the glories and machinations of other tribes and nations, and I feel informed and experienced and seasoned enough now to be able to say this: I do not think we sing the miracle and joy of Americanness enough.

We complain and argue and accuse and debate and snarl and roar and insult, and there are endless good reasons for our intemperate burble. But we ought not to forget we are free to speak, free to worship as we please, free to gather and shout and caper, free to call a spade a spade. We take this for granted. We forget the joy of the American idea. We forget that even as we make endless mistakes, we have done brave and glorious things like outlaw selling Americans of other colors and saving millions of people from imperial slavery and facing down every squirming sort of bully there is.

There never was an idea like America before to live free, and it's still a wild and courageous idea that's not dead yet. And there are seeds of great peace and creativity and justice and mercy in the American idea, seeds that might flower in other forms all over this round and amazing rock if we drop our weapons and quash our squabbles. Even as I gnash my teeth at our violence and greed and xenophobia, I take pride in who we are, who we might still be. And bigger than mere pride is joy that we are a country yet of the most amazing possibility ever. What a gift. What sweet work.

Dear Lord, as if it wasn't enough that I was born into this miraculous world, You also made me an American. Grant me the courage and creativity to help my country put violence and greed out of business, and show the world the world we still can be.
—BRIAN DOYLE

Digging Deeper: 1 TIMOTHY 2:1–3

Mon 6 *Let us throw off everything that hinders and the sin that so easily entangles....* —HEBREWS 12:1 (NIV)

I woke up at 3:00 AM today with a sharp stomach pain, a familiar reminder that I'm susceptible to intestinal blockages due to scar tissue from my cancer surgery. I know the drill. Best-case scenario: the blockage resolves itself in a few hours. Worst-case scenario: I'm headed to the emergency room for treatment.

Usually the painful problem is my own fault because I know what I should not eat to prevent these episodes. Immediately I knew the culprit: popcorn.

I quickly reviewed my responsibilities for the day. I was in charge of two meetings, which had been hard to schedule and would be even harder to reschedule. I had to make it to them.

In spite of my pain, I wondered if God might be giving me an opportunity to apply the message of

Sunday's sermon. The pastor had used the passage about "running the race and throwing off everything that hinders" and focused on the meaning of "everything that hinders": things that aren't mentioned as sins in the Bible but impede our progress. Like late-night television that hinders one's ability to get up early to pray before rushing into a busy day. Or excessive use of social media that hinders one from focusing on more important things. Or food that makes one feel sluggish or sick.

So I lay there in the dark and silence of the early morning, praying for God's grace to help me feel better, not worse, by 7:00 AM.

Lord, may I keep learning to throw off whatever hinders me from the ability to respond to my responsibilities. —CAROL KUYKENDALL

Digging Deeper: PSALM 63:6–8, JAMES 1:22

Tue 7

It is for freedom that Christ has set us free. . . . —GALATIANS 5:1 (NIV)

My grandmother Gaia fell at Emily's and my wedding rehearsal dinner. The X-rays showed Gaia's pelvis was cracked, but she wouldn't require surgery, just a stay in rehab for a while.

Gaia is one of the most amazing women I have ever met. She never liked receiving help, always cherishing her independence and freedom. She and my dad fought every summer as he tried to hold her arm when she walked along treacherous Maine beaches. So how would she cope now?

You can imagine my surprise when I saw her one month later with her new walker and letting my dad guide her, but smiling as brightly as ever. She told me that her rehab was going well, and she looked better than I'd anticipated.

"I have learned so much," she said. "Your father and I have fought these last few weeks. But I'm starting to learn that I can't do everything myself anymore and I'm letting him take over for me. And you know what? The more I let him take over and trust him, the more free I feel."

I know, dear Lord, that we are only free when
we submit ourselves to something higher—to You.
—SAM ADRIANCE

Digging Deeper: PSALM 13:5–6

Wed 8   *Glory in his holy name; let the hearts*
of those who seek the Lord rejoice.
Look to the Lord and his strength;
seek his face always.
—1 CHRONICLES 16:10–11 (NIV)

I've never met Katie. I don't know where she lives, who her kids are, what she believes. But

I do know that she doesn't like me. She disagrees with my approach to disciplining. She hates the recipes on my blog. Her theology and mine don't match up. And she's sure to let me know.

She comments on my blog, writing things like "dumb" and "ridiculous." She reviews my books: "incompetent" and "damaging." She follows my Facebook page just so she can let me know when I say or do something that she doesn't agree with. Discouragement sets in; her words hurt my heart.

I start to perform for Katie, instead of the One Who called me. I hold back from saying what I truly believe because Katie might read it and take it the wrong way. I hesitate before sharing my hopes and dreams because Katie might step in and shatter them. What power I've given her, this woman I do not know. What power I've stolen from the One Who chose me, Who sent me, Who loves me.

Today, it stops. It has to. My heart is too fragile to strive for approval from someone who will never approve but fragile enough to be comforted by the One Who needs me to say, "It's You, Lord. I'm doing this for You."

Lord, steel my mind to the echoes of this world and turn my eyes toward You. Amen.
—ERIN MACPHERSON

Digging Deeper: PSALM 27:3–5, LUKE 21:25–28

Thu 9

The human spirit can endure in sickness.... —PROVERBS 18:14 (NIV)

Erika, this has been your home for nineteen years," Bruce, the ranch owner, told me. "You can stay here as long as you want, even if you never heal. But we can't afford to keep your cattle. They have to be sold."

I'd ruptured a disc in my back while fighting a fire on the ranch, and now my greatest fear, losing my ability to ranch, was being realized. But as I stood on the slippery slope of depression, I saw that God had sent comfort.

Within a week of my injury, my friend Lori flew in to Oregon from Georgia and got me through the first series of tests. She called daily to see that I was okay. She believed in me, even when I didn't believe in myself.

My boyfriend, Randy, was by my side too. I was limping through the hospital lobby when another patient eyed me with pity. Randy told him excitedly, "It's a miracle! She was in a wheelchair!" That triggered helpless laughter, and for that moment pain lost its power.

Healing happens when I can make myself see past the pain. It's hard to do, but when mocked, pain weakens. Not a lot, but enough that it's noticeable. I was able to continue on because of my family and friends. They looked after me, supported me.

I know how much I've lost, but I've started to see what I've gained. Leaning on others isn't about my weakness. It's about God's strength.

Lord, whenever I think You've forgotten me, You send encouragement from friends and strangers. These daily miracles are proof that You are with me always.
—Erika Bentsen

Digging Deeper: Proverbs 17:17, Philippians 2:1, 1 John 1:7

Fri 10

They devoted themselves to the apostles' teaching and to fellowship, to the breaking of bread and to prayer.
—Acts 2:42 (NIV)

When my mother-in-law died this past spring, the whole town mourned. Mamaw, as we called her, had taught for over forty years and been everyone's first-grade teacher.

Having grown up in Southern California, where my family barely knew our neighbors, I was surprised by how involved a community can be in the passing of one of its own. In fact, I wasn't sure what a visitation was until I got to the funeral home. My husband told my daughters and me to meet him there after my morning class and said we'd be there "a while." That was all I knew.

On the way, the girls reported that a woman from church they hardly knew had called to arrange delivery of a meal in our absence. "I didn't know what to say, so I said okay," Charlotte told me.

"It was awkward," Lulu added, echoing my own lack of ease with such country rituals.

At the visitation, strangers hugged us and told us stories about Mamaw. She'd visited one old man in the hospital when he'd had his tonsils out and given him candy in a little treasure chest he still kept. Several told of how she could discipline with just a look, and we all laughed.

It was getting dark by the time we got home. Although the day had gone remarkably quickly, we were tired and hungry. What a welcome surprise it was to find a homemade feast on the kitchen table! Lasagna, salad, rolls, sweet tea, a pineapple pie. It was enough for three families, but we sat down and dug in, eating every bit and feeling uncommonly loved.

Father, help me love my neighbors as
I have been loved. —PATTY KIRK

Digging Deeper: MATTHEW 7:12, GALATIANS 5:14

Sat 11

Behold, I have given you every herb bearing seed....
—GENESIS 1:29 (KJV)

Grampy wasted nothing. In fact, he used words as frugally as he used bits of string, aluminum foil, and paper scraps. When we played checkers, he didn't chat. Nor do I remember him reading stories to me or speaking much at all besides saying, "Yup" and "Nope." But even with our very limited telegraph-style conversation, Grampy gave me a gift that has lasted all my life: he taught me to appreciate and identify wild plants.

While I was growing up in New Hampshire, Grampy lived with us, so when he rambled on walks along woodland paths, he often let me join him. I don't remember his holding my hand, but I do remember his pointing out various plants like a professional tour guide: "Lady's slipper." We'd squat down close, so I could touch the bulbous pink flowers. "Checkerberry." He'd snap off a leathery leaf and chew it; I'd follow his example.

"It tastes like gum, Grampy."

"Yup. Wintergreen."

He pointed to tiny flowers with four pale petals: "Bluet"; to the vibrant red, "Indian paintbrush." He carefully pulled aside serrated leaves to reveal where wild strawberries hid. He grasped a long cluster of wine-red berries dangling by a stone wall: "Chokeberry."

Choke? "Will I die if I taste, Grampy?"

"Nope."

Though Grampy was custodian of our church for years before I was born, I never saw him there. He once told me he didn't want to dress up to go. Perhaps he felt closer to God in the woodlands than around a lot of people. Grampy died when I was only twelve, but in those few years I spent with him, he taught me forever to cherish God's creation.

Creator God, in the tranquil beauty of growing things, I feel You are near. —GAIL THORELL SCHILLING

Digging Deeper: DEUTERONOMY 32:2, ISAIAH 55:12

Sun 12

You have said, "Seek my face." My heart says to you, "Your face, Lord, do I seek." —PSALM 27:8 (ESV)

"You'll never guess what my daughter has done," my friend Marcy said.

Her daughter was an aspiring actress, and I knew that Marcy worried about her going into such a tough profession.

Marcy took a deep breath. "She's joined a church."

I suppressed a smile. Marcy had grown up in a secular family and had never made a secret of her skeptical feelings toward religion. I didn't think her kids had ever seen the inside of a church. I wasn't sure what to say.

"Where did you go wrong?" I finally asked with a smile.

Marcy laughed and said that Sasha had been going to a hip new church for almost a year but had just recently confided in her about it. "She thought I wouldn't understand," Marcy said.

"Well, do you?"

"You know," she said, "I'd noticed a change in her lately. I thought she might have fallen in love or something and just wasn't ready to talk about it. But it was this church thing. I never would have guessed. She's become so much more . . . grateful. She's doing volunteer work and is not so obsessed with her career. She says there's a plan for her life, and it may not include acting. I'm kind of glad to hear that."

Relieved, I would say, from the look on my friend's face.

"Maybe you should try going with her sometime," I said. "Just to check it out. You might like it."

"I'll probably draw the line there," she said. "But you never know. Sasha said the same thing."

> *God, there are many paths that lead to*
> *You and many pilgrims. I'm happy to*
> *hear another has made it. Who knows?*
> *Her mother might be right behind her.*
> —EDWARD GRINNAN

Digging Deeper: PSALMS 14:2, 63:1; LUKE 11:9

Mon 13

[Jesus] replied, "When evening comes, you say, 'It will be fair weather, for the sky is red,' and in the morning, 'Today it will be stormy, for the sky is red and overcast'. . . ."
—MATTHEW 16:2–3 (NIV)

Half-awake one morning, I assessed the upcoming week: a stormy forecast, a slow work season, evening commitments beyond my comfort zone. I let trepidation overcome anticipation and wallowed a few minutes. Finally I trudged to the kitchen, looking for fortitude in my coffee pot.

As part of my first-things-first routine, I opened the front blinds and there was a sight worthy of a biblical *Behold!* A mottled eastern sky: miniature cream-puff clouds surrounded by pinks, lavenders, mauves, and blues.

I immediately recalled an inauspicious omen I'd learned as a child from my dad: "Red sky at morning, sailors take warning." *Oh dear,* I thought, *will the week's challenges be more ominous than I'm expecting?*

Still mesmerized, I stepped out and knocked on my neighbor's door. "Look!" I said, pointing to the sky. Her delight drew my mind to a different rhyme in a hymn that my dad sang frequently:

When morning gilds the skies,
My heart awakening cries
May Jesus Christ be praised.

One lavishly colored horizon; two different messages—which should I reach for? Bane or blessing?

Lord, help me today to praise Your name and all
Your glorious wonders. —EVELYN BENCE

Digging Deeper: PSALM 121

Tue 14   *The Lord sustains the humble....*
—PSALM 147:6 (NIV)

My son Mark was a four-day *Jeopardy* champion. I'm simply amazed at the preternatural ability of people like him "to answer in the form of a question" and to be so incredibly quick about it. It's not a gift I have.

Nor, apparently, is it one shared by a man named Johnny Gilbert, even though he has appeared on every episode of *Jeopardy* since its inception in 1984. I'm sure you know his voice, though, and the three words he is most famous for saying: "This is— *Jeopardy!*"

"No, no, I couldn't answer most of these questions," Gilbert said, talking to the studio audience, which included me, before one of the tapings began. "But what I can do is make the contestants who *can* answer these questions feel welcome and comfortable, and make everyone watching at home feel included. And that's pretty important, don't you think?"

I was impressed with the way Gilbert made all of us feel welcome. In doing so, he embodied a simple but awfully important life-lesson: that every one of us has a gift and a calling to use that gift well, in service to others, even if that work never makes our name famous beyond our own household.

I learned a lot from watching my son on *Jeopardy* but nothing more important than this, phrased, of course, in the form of a question:

How can I use the gift You have given me, God, to serve others? —JEFF JAPINGA

Digging Deeper: LUKE 14:10, ROMANS 8:28

Wed 15

I prayed to the Lord my God and made confession . . . .
—DANIEL 9:4 (NRSV)

B less me, Father, for I have sinned."
I make a practice of going to confession every year. I was raised a Catholic and maintain this

discipline because I think it's important to humble myself before another person and to publicly acknowledge my sins and ask God's forgiveness.

"I feel that my faith is not strong enough," I said haltingly, "because sometimes I let fear overwhelm it."

"And you think that's a sin?" the priest asked.

"I do."

"You know," he said, "faith and fear are not opposites."

I looked surprised.

"Think about it," he said. "Fear is natural to us, part of our survival instinct. Fear is often a physical sensation: the hair rises on our arms, our pulse races, we get a metallic taste in our mouth. Faith is not physical. By being afraid, you don't displace faith. Fear can drive you toward your faith, for comfort and understanding. Not only can they coexist, fear can strengthen faith."

I didn't say a word, but the priest watched my expression closely. He smiled. "I can tell you're going to work on this, but no hurry. It can take a lifetime."

Merciful God, help me to remember that the only
thing I have to fear is not fear itself but
the loss of my perspective in You.
—MARCI ALBORGHETTI

Digging Deeper: PSALM 42:11

Thu 16

*"Her branches will spread out, as
beautiful as olive trees, fragrant as
the forests of Lebanon."*
—HOSEA 14:6 (TLB)

Just think, Jack, we'll be able to see five or six
national parks!" I was over the moon about our
honeymoon trip to Arizona and Utah, while Jack,
whose only travel experience was cruising on huge
ships to the Caribbean, was not so sure about my
dream trip. But being generous of heart, he agreed
to my plan.

We flew to Tucson, Arizona, stayed with Jack's
cousins for a few days, and then the two of us rented
a car and drove to Sedona where we took a bumpy
tour in a pink jeep through the gorgeous red rock
mountains. We drove on to Williams, a quaint little town that still celebrates old Route 66 that runs
through it, then on to what was a jaw-dropping experience: seeing the Grand Canyon. I'd been there
three times before and was still awestruck.

We also toured Glen Canyon, Zion, Bryce,
Arches, and Canyonlands national parks. Jack and I
took turns driving but also hopped on buses, something my husband's knees and hips appreciated beyond measure.

I needn't have worried about whether my
cruise-minded hubby would enjoy my idea of a

honeymoon. As we stood hand in hand at one breathtaking overlook after another, we understood the enormity of what we were seeing. We felt closer to our Creator and to each other after seeing the extraordinary scenery God has bestowed upon the United States of America.

> *Heavenly Father, I am in awe of*
> *what You have created in this*
> *country of ours. Thank You.*
> —PATRICIA LORENZ

Digging Deeper: PSALM 50:1–2, HOSEA 14:4–7

Fri 17   *...In the comfort of the Holy Spirit....* —ACTS 9:31 (NAS)

I sat in my rheumatologist's office. Not only did my joints hurt, but the pain seemed to go way down into my soul. I try not to whine to physicians. I suppose I learned that from taking my mother to her appointments.

Doctors smiled when they saw my mother and made comments like, "Well, well, well, look at you!" Dressed to the nines, she would beam and begin a delightful conversation as though at a social function. I longed to be like her. The nurse called and had me fill out a new form about emotions.

Mother would probably have filled it out differently. My rheumatologist is a marvelous man. He never rushes with patients, and we often discuss matters besides my health.

I tried with everything in me to meet his enormous smile. As always, he sat down and held out his hands for mine. I placed my small, cold, skinny hands in his. His kind eyes held mine. "What's wrong, Marion?"

I didn't know exactly what was wrong. Looking into my lap, I said, "Your hands feel so large and caring!" He leaned forward and gave me a hug. On that particular visit, I wasn't like my mother. But I received the care I needed, nonetheless, and more.

Father, thank You for physicians with warm,
caring eyes and comfort from above.
—MARION BOND WEST

Digging Deeper: PSALM 147:3, 1 CORINTHIANS 12:9

Sat 18   *For God gave us a spirit not of fear but of power and love and self-control.* —2 TIMOTHY 1:7 (ESV)

One of the great things about living in New York City are the odd celebrations that happen here. Where else, for example, could you find

a commemoration of the Burr-Hamilton duel of
July 11, 1804? In fact, you can find two: one at
the Hamilton Grange National Memorial and one
at the Morris-Jumel Mansion, where Aaron Burr
lived for a few months during his short-lived marriage to Madame Jumel.

Both my son John and I are history buffs, and
both events were appealing. We chose the second
because it was in the afternoon and gave us the luxury of sleeping in. So we headed for the subway and
the short ride to Jumel Terrace in Harlem, where
an advocate for Alexander Hamilton and one for
Burr made the case for their hero. We learned a
lot about the two men: their foibles, their accom-
plishments, and the disputes between them. And
when the moderator opened the meeting to questions from the floor, John surprised me by raising
his hand. He asked a thoughtful question about
Hamilton's hostility to John Adams in the presi-
dential election of 1800 and how that may have
affected Hamilton's career.

We've been through a lot together, John and I
and the rest of our family: years of troubles and
heartache; years when we prayed and worried and
at times almost despaired for the future of our son;
when a day like this seemed very far away. But now
here he was, almost seventeen, a keen student of
history with the poise and confidence to stand up
and ask a question.

Lord, help all of our young people grow into the people You have called them to be. —ANDREW ATTAWAY

Digging Deeper: ACTS 2:39

Sun 19

Like a snow-cooled drink at harvest time is a trustworthy messenger to the one who sends him....
—PROVERBS 25:13 (NIV)

My husband was home from the hospital but still had trouble breathing when engaged in any activity, so I was taking on many of the things he used to do. By the time of the synagogue's interfaith weekend, I had become compulsive about not leaving Keith alone for very long, in case he needed me.

The weekend was something I'd committed to months in advance, however, and Keith urged me not to cancel. "You always enjoy the interfaith work so much," he said. "Give yourself a treat and go."

The Friday night service at the synagogue, where a local pastor shared the bimah with our rabbi, was fine, but I couldn't enjoy it because I was worried about what was going on at home. I kept glancing at my watch, and feeling my cell phone to see if it was vibrating. I told myself that I could have learned about this and future activities just by reading the newsletter; I didn't need to be there.

I figured the same thing would happen on Sunday morning at the pastor's church, where our rabbi was returning the visit by sharing the chancel. However, there was no telling how many members of our congregation would be there and I wanted to support the rabbi.

At first, I was just as restless as I had been before. Then the pastor spoke. "There's a Hebrew word, *chesed*. It means the never-failing, steadfast, and enduring love that God gives us."

I thought the pastor must have been speaking directly to me because that was the message I needed to hear at that moment. Suddenly I was calm, sure I'd made the right decision in coming.

Thank You, God, for the beautiful messages
You send me and for the wisdom of Your messengers.
—RHODA BLECKER

Digging Deeper: ECCLESIASTES 11:1, MICAH 4:5

Mon 20

Be joyful in hope, patient in affliction, faithful in prayer.
—ROMANS 12:12 (NIV)

I used to be ashamed of my depression. I'd wonder why I just couldn't pick myself up and show a cheerful face to the world. No such luck. Instead, it has taken electroconvulsive therapy (ECT) and lots of medication.

It was hard to admit to this illness, but the responses from *Daily Guideposts* readers have been breathtaking. I discovered I was in no way alone. All across the country were others embarrassed or ashamed of being clinically depressed. They sent sympathy, understanding, and gratitude. One woman wanted to understand why her friend was so confused by ECT; another told of waiting for years before asking for medication she so badly needed.

Treatments for depression are all too often hit or miss. A medication works for one sufferer but not for another. ECT has some daunting side effects but an amazing 80 percent cure rate. Now that I feel supported and understood by so many, I pray for those who haven't yet recognized their own illness or are afraid to ask for help. I'm glad that I finally spoke up. Together we can drive the monster back to its lair.

Lord, thank You for using my pain
to help others who suffer from
chronic depression. We give thanks to
You for the medical advances that help us.
—BRIGITTE WEEKS

Digging Deeper: PSALM 138:6

Tue 21

Let every thing that hath breath praise the Lord. Praise ye the Lord.
—Psalm 150:6 (KJV)

A friend was grieving the death of her mother. An observant Jew, she was following the practice of saying kaddish, the traditional Jewish prayer of mourning.

"Is it something you just pray at home?" I asked.

"On the contrary," she said. "You're only supposed to say the mourners' kaddish in community." Every morning on her way to work, she stops by her synagogue to gather with a small group who say this ancient prayer together.

"Why in a group?" I asked. "Wouldn't it be easier to say it on your own?"

"That's one of the important principles of saying kaddish. If you're grieving, you should be with others. You shouldn't be alone."

"What are the words of the prayer?" I assumed the language would be something like Lamentations, full of chest-pounding agony. "It must be comforting to express your sorrow in a group."

"The words aren't about sorrow or loss," she explained. "They're full of praise." She quoted the opening text, inspired by Ezekiel 38:23: "May his great name be blessed forever and to all eternity."

"How long do you do this?" I asked.

"For a year."

A year of praise during a year of grieving. It took a while for it to sink in. I thought of those times when I was struggling over loss and how an uplifting song could pull me out of myself. Here it was, a spiritual practice that demonstrated the same healing truth.

Today and every day, I praise You, O Lord!
—RICK HAMLIN

Digging Deeper: 1 CHRONICLES 29:13

Wed 22

Boast not thyself of tomorrow;
for thou knowest not what a day
may bring forth.
—PROVERBS 27:1 (KJV)

Since I was a boy puttering around the lake in the decrepit little boat we called *Thunder,* I had dreamed of this day. I gave the horn of the brand-new gleaming red speedboat a long blast as I pulled alongside the pier. I couldn't have been prouder than I was at this moment, presenting the boat to my family.

Within minutes we were all in our swimsuits, raring to take our boat on its maiden voyage. As I turned the key, the engine rumbled to life and we were off. I couldn't help but think how nice my boat was compared to others. As we passed a modest ski boat that had seen better days, I slowed down to avoid rocking it with our powerful wake.

We were pulling the kids on blow-up tubes, and they were having a blast. "Boy, Brock, this boat rides really smooth," my sister said, making my head swell.

It was then that I turned the boat too quickly. The engine made a terrible groan. I had run over the ski rope, which wrapped around the prop, locking it up. We were stranded in the middle of the lake. As we debated our options, the sun got hotter and the kids got hungrier, thirstier, grumpier.

It was then that the old ski boat puttered up beside us. "Everything okay?" the young driver called out. Explaining what I had done was humbling enough but then he said, "We'll tow you back." Slowly but surely the little boat chugged, pulling us toward our pier.

An hour later we were safe on our dock, waving good-bye to our new friend. He had refused any gesture of repayment and had unknowingly gifted me with a much-needed dose of humility.

Father, help me remember that the only way is down when I start thinking too highly of myself.
—BROCK KIDD

Digging Deeper: PROVERBS 25:27,
1 CORINTHIANS 10:12

Thu 23

I forget what is behind, and I struggle for what is ahead.
—Philippians 3:13 (CEV)

My friend Anne and I were having lunch at an outdoor café framed by a wrought-iron fence covered in wisteria. Anne confided that she struggled over letting go of past failures and actions. "They still haunt me sometimes," she said.

"I know how you feel," I admitted. "Sometimes I think about things I've said and done and wonder, *What was I thinking?* They're things I've apologized and made amends for, yet I still feel guilty." I shook my head. "I wonder if the remorse will ever go away."

"Last week my pastor shared a story that I think might help us both," Anne said. "'The Culver Military Academy in Indiana has a marvelous tradition,' he'd said. 'During their graduation ceremony the cadets shake hands with the headmaster and then walk through an arch with a gate.'"

"Like walking into their future," I said.

"Yes," she replied, "but it's about their past too. As the graduates walk through the gate a marshal tells them, 'Don't forget to close the gate!' Seems that throughout their schooling, they were encouraged to close the gate on mistakes and start fresh."

"Wow!" I exclaimed. "It's such a tangible way to begin again."

Lunch ended with both of us promising to work on letting go of our past mistakes.

"Look!" I exclaimed as we turned to leave through the gate on the patio. The sign hanging on the fence read: "Don't forget to close the gate." Laughing, we both reached out and shut it firmly behind us.

Lord, through Your mercy I am forgiven. Help me to accept Your grace and shut the gate on the past, so I can embrace the glorious new life You've promised.
—MELODY BONNETTE SWANG

Digging Deeper: ISAIAH 43:18, 1 JOHN 3:20

Fri 24

Better a poor but wise youth than an old but foolish king who no longer knows how to heed a warning.
—ECCLESIASTES 4:13 (NIV)

I saw the highway patrolman too late. I was coming into Jefferson City, Missouri, where the speed limit suddenly changes from seventy to forty-five miles per hour, and I didn't notice the sign. There he was, waiting for me.

As I pulled over, I felt irritated with myself. *This is so humiliating*, I thought. I haven't had a ticket in thirty years, but that's long enough to get sloppy in driving habits.

At my age, authority figures often appear younger than my own children. This officer looked to be at most sixteen years old.

"May I see your operator's license?" he asked politely.

I felt like saying, "May I see *your* operator's license? I mean, does your mother know you are out here on the highway? And where did you get that police cruiser anyhow?"

Instead I said, "Yes, sir" a lot.

The young officer was a true gentleman—soft-spoken, gracious, respectful. He even pronounced my name right. He gave me the minimum fine and made it mail-in, so I didn't have to appear in court. And then he reminded me of the purpose of speed limits. "This is a dangerous intersection, Mr. Schantz. I know you would not want to hurt anyone."

I nodded my agreement. "Yes, sir. You are right about that, for sure."

It was good for me to be reminded that wisdom knows no age. Not all old people are wise and not all young people are ignorant. I need to be ready to listen to anyone, including my students, my children, even my grandchildren. It was a lot of valuable wisdom for just ninety dollars.

Thank You, Father, for those who care enough to correct us when we drift off course.
—DANIEL SCHANTZ

Sat 25

And they began to speak against God and Moses. "Why have you brought us out of Egypt to die here in the wilderness?" they complained. "There is nothing to eat here and nothing to drink. And we hate this horrible manna!"
—Numbers 21:5 (NLT)

The digital map told me our drive would last eight hours. Disneyland, here we come! With two kids in the back seat and my wife by my side, we left in the predawn darkness.

What the map didn't tell me was how tedious the drive would be: flat, straight countryside with very few good stops and not a lot to see. My wife and I quickly got bored. Our kids did too. Around hour three, "Are we there yet?" began.

"Yes," I said, "get out now." The kids laughed.

Two hours later, I could no longer find the humor. Every whiny syllable ratcheted up my blood pressure. My normally delightful children transmogrified before my rearview mirror into demanding little gremlins, gnawing on my last nerve. I thought of Moses in the wilderness. Two million followers delivering forty years of grousing. His frustration level had to have been off the charts.

As the "Happiest Place on Earth" drew closer, I was about to lay into the urchins, when the Holy Spirit exercised impeccable timing: *Bill, what if you sound like that to God?*

I thought of my boatload of unanswered prayers. Had I turned them into occasions for whining? The trials I thought I didn't deserve. *Lord, have You brought me here just to torment me?* Had my prayers devolved into a litany of complaints, a sanctimonious equivalent of "Are we there yet?"

I whispered my apology to God.

"Are we there yet?" the kids asked again.

I swallowed my planned rebuke. "Two more hours," I said. "But who wants ice cream?"

Lord, teach me to enjoy the journey and trust Your map, no matter how long, painful, twisty, or boring the road may be. —BILL GIOVANNETTI

Digging Deeper: PHILIPPIANS 2:14

Sun 26   *"I will sustain you and I will rescue you."* —ISAIAH 46:4 (NIV)

"What do you want for your birthday?" my husband, Tony, asked.

I shrugged my shoulders and went back to searching the Internet for a used trumpet for our son Solomon. One link led to another, and soon I found myself staring at a blurry picture of a sickly looking white kitten and the words *Needs a Home.*

I've wanted a white kitten ever since I was ten years old and read about Snowdrop in the sequel to *Alice's Adventures in Wonderland, Through the Looking-Glass.* I called the number on the listing. An hour later Tony and I were on our way to pick up my birthday present, two counties away. As we got closer to the destination, I worried about the way the kitten looked in the picture. "What if he's sick?" I asked. "Maybe this is a silly idea." With each passing mile my fears grew deeper.

Finally, we were on the street and counting down the mailboxes. At the end of a long driveway, a woman cradled the kitten in her arms. I got out of the car. "Sorry we're late. It was farther than we thought," I said.

She nodded. Without a word, she handed the kitten to me. "Okay?" she asked. I drew him close to me.

On the way home, we tried out names and settled on Kirby. As I held Kirby in my lap, I began to inspect him. His ears were filled with black gunk; fleas scurried all over his body. *What have I done?*

Within hours, we were at the animal hospital where the vet cleaned Kirby's ears. "He's one lucky cat," the vet said. "He'll be fine. And he'll probably be hearing for the first time in his life."

In a few days Kirby was a fur ball of joy, scampering around the house, climbing the curtains, and falling asleep in his favorite spot on Solomon's top bunk.

Dear God, thank You for leading me to Kirby,
so I could give him a healthy future. Please lead others
to Your creatures that need care.
—SABRA CIANCANELLI

Digging Deeper: PSALM 126:3, JOHN 15:11

Mon 27

Let us run with perseverance the race that is set before us.
—HEBREWS 12:1 (NRSV)

I was tired. I wanted to stop. It was the last leg of the San Francisco Marathon. I'd never run one before. I'd felt exhilarated crossing the Golden Gate Bridge, running foggy, hilly streets. Now I slogged through a landscape of warehouses and vacant lots.

I'm not much of a runner. I'm slow. I don't have an athlete's drive to win. My wife is the runner in our family. Kate's medals hang on one side of our dresser mirror. My side is empty. I was tired of replying, "No," whenever someone asked, "So, Jim, do you run marathons too?"

With one mile to go, the San Francisco Bay appeared. A family stood beside the route, waving: a mom and two kids. *What a lonely place for them.* The crowds were at the finish line, not here. I drew closer. It was Kate and our children, Frances and Benjamin! "You can do it!" they shouted as I staggered past. Kate beamed at me, her sweet face radiant. I waved and picked up my pace. Ahead I saw the finish. I closed my eyes and imagined my wife running beside me. With God's love shining through her, I knew I would make it.

Because You strengthen me,
Lord, today I will do what
I thought I couldn't do.
—Jim Hinch

Digging Deeper: Proverbs 5:18,
2 Corinthians 5:9

Tue 28   *"But I tell you, love your enemies*
and pray for those who persecute
you." —Matthew 5:44 (NIV)

My coworker has a habit of commenting on everything. "Oh, I've seen this one before," I imagine her whispering into my ear before each trick in a magic show. "Here's how he does it." She also points out mistakes people make. "Did you see that?" she says to whoever is close enough to hear. "Pastor was supposed to tell the congregation to stand, but he missed the beginning of the verse so he just waited for the chorus. That was smooth."

Once I tried spending some time with her to get to know her better and found out that she disregarded my request to keep our conversation private. I felt betrayed and couldn't trust her, and I was sure she was judging my every move. I began to flat out dislike her and talked about her behind her back, which made me feel better *and* worse at the same time.

"I'm not sure what to do," I finally complained to a friend.

"Have you tried praying for blessings for her?" he asked.

"*Nooo...*" I didn't want to pray for her and found it difficult to begin. But the minute the words started to come out of my mouth, the negative feelings toward her lifted.

It's impossible for me to dislike those I pray for, and it gave me the space in my heart to talk *with* her about my concerns instead of *about* her.

Father, help me to choose right every time—
even when I don't want to. —NATALIE PERKINS

Digging Deeper: MATTHEW 7:12, 18:15

Wed 29

"Do not be anxious about tomorrow...."
—MATTHEW 6:34 (RSV)

My dermatologist removed a skin lesion from my arm and sent it to a lab to be tested. He was worried about its appearance, and the fact that he was worried scared me.

Through the fog of deep sleep, I heard my phone ring this morning. Grabbing it, I saw that the call was from my doctor. My heart lurched and my blood pressure soared. I croaked a weak hello. "Scott, I've got good news. Lab report says it's a pre-skin cancer. Nothing to worry about. Glad we got right on it and things look good."

Now, several hours later, I am taking it all in, profoundly grateful for life. But I am sixty-two years old and no one lives forever. I will face a day when the news is not good, when my fears are real, when health breaks down, when mortality grasps my hand and will not let go. So I ask, "What has this new lease on life taught me?"

Above all, I affirm that each day I live will be acknowledged as a pure gift, a moment of time that is unique, unrepeatable, and must be savored. Second, I resolve to live each day with one primary purpose: to show love to at least one other child of God, animals included! And, finally, the greatest gift I can offer to God is my heartfelt thanksgiving. For it is simple gratitude that is the most healing medicine known to humankind, and it is thanksgiving that transcends all time and death.

Father, fill this day with love and gratitude. Amen.
—SCOTT WALKER

Digging Deeper: PROVERBS 17:22, COLOSSIANS 3:15

Thu 30

For you know the grace of our Lord Jesus Christ, that though He was rich, yet for your sake He became poor, so that you through His poverty might become rich.
—2 CORINTHIANS 8:9 (NAS)

Our son Phil, who works for a coin company, has taken up numismatics, the study of coins. I called him the other day when I read about a family who for years had kept an inherited coin in a shoebox in a closet. It turned out their Liberty Head Nickel was the lost coin in a set of only five minted in 1912 but erroneously stamped 1913. They wound up selling it for three million dollars!

Phil said the story was the talk of his office. Who doesn't dream of finding treasure somewhere or another?

The Bible tells of a hidden coin in Matthew 17:24–27. Tax collectors wanted Jesus to pay the temple tax. Jesus told Peter to "go to the sea and throw in a hook, and take the first fish that comes up; and when you open its mouth, you will find a shekel. Take that and give it to them for you and Me."

If coinage and property are what make one rich, then Jesus lived a very poor life. From a humble beginning in a cow shed to soldiers gambling over His only tunic at His Crucifixion, Jesus never had much in the way of earthly possessions. What He did have, He gave away—wisdom and joy, peace and love. He said, "I came that they may have life, and have it abundantly" (John 10:10, NAS). Turns out, every day we wake up with treasure all around us.

Jesus, how rich I am with You in my life!
—CAROL KNAPP

Digging Deeper: MATTHEW 13:44, LUKE 15:8–10

Fri 31   *"So do not fear, for I am with you; do not be dismayed, for I am your God...."* —ISAIAH 41:10 (NIV)

I was in pain, so I went to the emergency room. It wasn't an easy decision because without health insurance, I knew this visit was going to cost me.

I waited in line to register, and the woman in front of me was in obvious pain as well. The receptionist took her insurance cards as the woman explained in tears that her doctors were going to meet her there. Sure enough, they did. One of the doctors rubbed her back and said, "It's okay, Carol. We're going to take care of you."

I craved that kind of attention and urgency, but all I got was "Next!" I had no insurance cards to give the receptionist so I was told to fill out some papers and have a seat with everyone else. I waited for hours to be seen, only to wait some more in another overcrowded room. I wanted nothing more than to be scooped up as my parents had done when I was a child, to feel like I mattered.

I called my sister in tears. "It's bad enough I'm in pain," I cried, "but this place makes me feel worthless." She proceeded to text me Scripture, reminding me that God cared for me, loved me, would comfort and heal me. Finally, I was given a bed and snuggled into the soft mattress. I felt God's presence and was reminded that I'm worth everything to Him.

> *Lord, help me to remember You love and*
> *care for me, even when I don't feel*
> *cared for by this world.*
> —KAREN VALENTIN

Digging Deeper: PSALM 34:4

DAILY JOYS

1 _____

2 _____

3 _____

4 _____

5 _____

6 _____

7 _____

8 _____

9 _____

10 _____

11 _____

12 _____

13 _____

14 _____

15 _____

July

16 _____

17 _____

18 _____

19 _____

20 _____

21 _____

22 _____

23 _____

24 _____

25 _____

26 _____

27 _____

28 _____

29 _____

30 _____

31 _____

AUGUST

*For the kingdom of God is not a matter
of eating and drinking but of righteousness
and peace and joy in the Holy Spirit.*

—ROMANS 14:17 (ESV)

GOD OF JOYFUL SURPRISES

Sat 1   *The world is established, firm and secure.* —PSALM 93:1 (NIV)

SECURE IN GOD

It was one of those frustrating dreams where one vague scene dissolves into another and nothing makes sense. People I couldn't identify wanted me to do something—what it was, I couldn't discover. Indefiniteness—that was the nightmare part. *Where am I? Why do rooms keep changing? Why can't I stop one of these faceless people long enough to ask?*

Then the phone rang and I woke up. The floor was firm beneath my feet as I crossed my bedroom, the furniture reassuringly stationary.

"I'm sorry to call so early," my daughter began. She needed an address for a meeting that morning. She started to apologize again, but I was so glad for an actual conversation that I wouldn't have cared if it was 3:00 AM instead of 7:00 AM. After the call, I walked around the apartment, grateful for the real world of stable places and predictable sequences.

Dreams may express unrecognized anxieties: dread of old age as I enter my late eighties; fear of no longer being able to live up to the expectations of family and friends; a feeling that old people are ignored, that everything's moving too fast. What this dream gave me, though, was something more important: a joy I hadn't known existed. Joy in the real world: its solidness and reliability. Joy for God's orderly, beautiful, coherent creation.

God of joyful surprises, amid all the changes in my life, let me cling to Your unchangingness.
—ELIZABETH SHERRILL

Digging Deeper: HEBREWS 6:17–20

Sun 2

And He said to me, "My grace is sufficient for you, for My strength is made perfect in weakness"....
—2 CORINTHIANS 12:9 (NKJV)

Today I visited a Nazarene church in town to hear a popular guest speaker. Nothing much had changed since I was last there, when the congregation hosted a renowned Southern Gospel singing group, the Speer Family. Nothing, that is, except the upholstery on the pews... which had a little something to do with me.

On one scorching summer evening back in 1966, I never would have guessed that I would be gifted with one of the most powerful lessons on grace in my life. All day, I'd been working my door-to-door sales route selling cosmetics. I'd made a delivery to one of the cheerleaders at my junior high. Linda had ordered a tube of leg makeup.

Well, I reasoned, if I couldn't be a cheerleader, I could at least have nice-looking tan legs like Linda. So on our front porch steps, my friend Karen and I massaged some makeup into our chubby legs and then hightailed it to the service. Somewhere between Brock Speer taking the lead on "What a Day That Will Be" and the invitation hymn "There's Room at the Cross for You," I noticed glistening bronze makeup running down my legs and onto the brand-new, textured white upholstery.

When I realized my predicament, I panicked, wanting to bolt from the building. That's when my eyes locked with an usher's. "Everything will be okay," he said. "The main thing is, you're here."

In a heartbeat, grace.

Thank You, God, for Your grace so freely given, so undeserved. —ROBERTA MESSNER

Digging Deeper: ACTS 4:33; HEBREWS 4:16, 12:15

Mon 3

"You shall serve the Lord your God, and I will bless your bread and your water...." —EXODUS 23:25 (RSV)

Four generations of the family are gathered at a beach rental house for a summer vacation. Not everyone is here at once. Some are coming for the day; some arrive for a few days and then have to go back to work.

We never know exactly how many are going to be here for dinner. Getting a head count can be difficult. Carol or Mom or my sister or I make calls before going to the market: "Are you coming tonight?"

Beach time proves elusive for many, but everybody tries to make dinner. My niece has dished up Rice Krispie Treats topped with chocolate for dessert; my brother-in-law brings tomatoes he's grown in his garden; my sister-in-law has made a hummus dip. We come in from the sand, take a shower, change clothes, and gather as the sun slips into the ocean. The conversation bounces from subject to subject: what the kids are doing in school, the new dog, how work is going, baseball scores. Someone's making a salad, burgers are on the grill, zucchini is almost finished.

Dinner is on the counter and we serve ourselves, complimenting the chefs. There are so many of us tonight that we can't all fit at the table. How did our family grow so large? Everybody's ready and the call goes out, "Who says grace tonight?" Mike volunteers, and in a voice so loud it can be heard down the beach, he begins, "Dear God..." We grab hands.

I feel my eighty-something-year-old mom's grip in one hand and my teenage niece's in the other, the words of Mike's prayer ringing in my ears. Should we be surprised that Jesus first offered the gift of Himself to His disciples at a meal? In a beach rental, the generations linked, we give thanks for all we've been given. Soon we will leave this place, return to our homes. But for now we hold on to what is important: each other. "Amen," we say. "Amen."

Lord, thank You for large families where generations can join hands and pray: Bless this food to our use and us to Your service. Amen. —RICK HAMLIN

Digging Deeper: MATTHEW 26:26

Tue 4

Every good and perfect gift is from above, coming down from the Father of the heavenly lights, who does not change like shifting shadows.
—JAMES 1:17 (NIV)

As my new wife, Emily, and I have started to get used to living together, we have developed lots of little routines. We try to go to bed together every night around the same time. We go out to brunch on Saturday mornings. We see movies on Tuesday nights. We wake up together in the mornings, even if I don't have class until later or Emily has a late start at work. I make the coffee while she gets our vitamins. We mix things up every now and then by going on a special day trip or a picnic, but we have settled into a fairly domestic lifestyle.

That can make our lives sound boring, and I can't count the number of times I've groaned at getting up and making the coffee. The truth is, though, that I love our routines. I have always resisted having structure in my life, but I find that this order allows me to focus on more important things, like the earthy aroma of the coffee beans when I grind them, the way Emily smiles at me when I hand her a mug, or the warmth of her hand when I hold it in the theater.

And as I focus more on these special details, my mind uncluttered by extraneous worries and plans, I feel closer to God, as if I am, in this small manner, living life the way He intended it.

Thank You, Lord, for showing me perfection in the smallest things. —SAM ADRIANCE

Digging Deeper: 2 PETER 3:8

Wed 5   *In the same way, the Spirit helps us in our weakness. We do not know what we ought to pray for, but the Spirit himself intercedes for us through wordless groans.*
—ROMANS 8:26 (NIV)

This morning as I was getting ready for a meeting that had the potential to be contentious, I didn't even realize I was sighing.

"*Hssshh! Hssshh!*" My eleven-year-old, Solomon, imitated me by hissing like a snake.

"I can't help it," I said.

I come from a long line of sighers. I remember my sister Maria telling me that when she was taking her college entrance exams, the guy in front of her turned around and asked, "Do you have to do that?"

"Do what?" she whispered.

"Sigh!" he answered.

She nodded. "If I don't, I'll explode."

I used to think sighing was a form of weakness, but ever since I found the verse Romans 8:26, where the Holy Spirit helps us when we have "wordless groans," I've thought of sighing as prayer. I love how God offers love when I don't even have the words to ask, that God responds and sends comfort, strength, and joy when I'm too stressed or preoccupied to seek Him.

> *Dear God, thank You for these natural responses
> You've given me that lead me to joy and
> comfort, that lead me to You.*
> —SABRA CIANCANELLI

Digging Deeper: PSALM 32:11,
COLOSSIANS 3:15

Thu 6   *"And the life which I now live in the flesh I live by faith in the Son of God...."* —GALATIANS 2:20 (NKJV)

I may never fully recover from rupturing a disc while fighting a fire on the ranch where I've worked for nineteen years. Questions flood my mind: *What's my future? Will I ever be pain-free? Will I ever ride a horse again? Can I ever ranch again?*

"I've been waiting a year for God's direction and there's no reply," I complained to my friend Lori.

"Look," she said, "maybe He's waiting for you. A compass won't budge if you're standing still. God will lead you, but maybe He wants you to begin."

In the darkness of this last year, I've had to confront my future without ranching. And, oh, has that been hard! But as I've walked this tough road, understanding that my life will never be the same, I've finally been able to surrender my ranching to God. It took time, hard prayers, hours of weeping, but joy is starting to come in the mornings. New opportunities have flooded in: the ranch offered to buy my cows, hoping I can buy them back one day. Doctors have come up with new theories for making me well again.

Walking in faith doesn't always lead me to where I want to go, but to where God wants me. And I know I'm better off for it. However my life turns out, I am finally at peace knowing God will be there to guide me.

> *Lord, lead me. I'm ready now.*
> —ERIKA BENTSEN

Digging Deeper: MALACHI 4:2, JAMES 4:7

Fri 7

He who finds a wife finds what is good and receives favor from the Lord.
—PROVERBS 18:22 (NIV)

I moved surreptitiously through our apartment, trying not to make it obvious that I was looking for something. I was very casual, rearranging some pillows on the couch, moving some magazines around—no big deal.

"You lost something, didn't you?" my wife finally said.

Reluctantly I confessed. I couldn't find the TV remote. I hate losing stuff, especially when I know it's probably right under my nose. And I hate admitting it because Julee gets exasperated with my so-called absentmindedness. In this case, I had been switching channels while talking on the phone and checking my e-mail.

"Take Millie out for a walk," Julee said with a sigh. "I'll look."

When we returned a little later she greeted us, brandishing the remote like she wanted to hit me over the noggin with it.

"Where?"

"Bathroom."

I hung my head, took the errant device, and mumbled a thanks.

Not a day later I came home from work to find Julee in a frenzy. The apartment looked as if a cyclone had hit it. She couldn't find her sunglasses. "I just got them!" she cried. "The lenses cost a fortune! I've looked all over."

I poked around a bit. It took me about three minutes. I unearthed them from Millie's box by the door where we keep her leash.

"You found them!"

"Simple deduction. You walked Millie, came rushing in to do something, and *absentmindedly* threw them in her box."

"Funny, isn't it," mused Julee. "You can always find what I've lost, and I can always find what you're looking for."

> *Funny indeed, Lord, that*
> *You let us find each other.*
> —EDWARD GRINNAN

Digging Deeper: PSALM 84:12

Sat 8

"You keep him in perfect peace whose mind is stayed on you, because he trusts in you." —ISAIAH 26:3 (ESV)

My husband, Lonny, and I are raising our five boys near the Illinois banks of the Mississippi River. Our town is quiet until the second weekend in August, when it's Tug Fest. For nearly thirty years people have come from miles to witness a mighty tug of war across the river.

"Mom, I'd like to hang out with my friends at Tug Fest tonight," my preteen, Samuel, says.

"You know the deal, Sam," I answer. "You're not running around through the crowds by the river at night."

I can't deny that Sam's at the age of being entitled to earn some freedoms, but Tug Fest weekend seems a poor time to initiate them. Sam eventually concedes, but the freedom issue has caused a battle of the wills.

Two months later, I was in our home-school classroom with my boys, listening to a professor on the radio tell a short regional story. He shared how an engineer discovered that the banks are pulling down, and according to his measurements, if the site of Tug Fest doesn't change, in a number of years the banks will meet in the middle.

That won't happen; the tug will cease or the pull will move downriver. But it makes me wonder:

Does Tug Fest have to bring a struggle to our home each year? Or can I trust God with my fears, loosen my grip, and allow Samuel a few freedoms?

Maybe my son and I can meet in the middle.

Lord, help me to release my fears and my children to You. Amen. —SHAWNELLE ELIASEN

Digging Deeper: PSALMS 37:3, 115:11

Sun 9 *"The eyes of the Lord are in every place...."* —PROVERBS 15:3 (KJV)

My husband and I are visiting Istanbul, Turkey. We expect mystery and intrigue in this place where calls to prayer ring out over the city five times a day and a stone pillar called Million is, in simple terms, the center of the world.

Every morning we sit at the same table, enjoying a breakfast of lentil soup as we plan our itinerary. Overlooking the street, we're captivated by the activities of a man stationed just across the way.

Arriving early, he opens a street locker, stores his jacket, and pulls out a broom. He sweeps the sidewalk, then waters a plant sitting on a windowsill. All day he tends the area between the locker and a corner cabstand. After a while he pulls a teapot from the locker. Cups appear on a wooden-box table. Friends gather to drink tea at his makeshift café. Later, he disappears, then comes back with a bucket of soapy water. He washes the locker and the window ledges. He scrubs the sidewalk. All the while he moves back and forth to the corner, greeting cabs, then waving them off.

We grow fond of this man, as he performs his duties and creates a hospitable space for others. He has no idea that we are watching him, and I can't help but make a comparison: Is this how God watches us? There is no way we can grasp God's magnitude; we are mere mortals. Yet God's eyes are on us, and in some inexplicable fashion, each of us is at His center.

Father, we rest, knowing that as surely as we remember the man in Istanbul, we know that You will never lose sight of us. —PAM KIDD

Digging Deeper: JOB 28:10, PSALM 127:4, MATTHEW 10:29

Mon 10   *"Do not worry about tomorrow, for tomorrow will worry about itself...."*
—MATTHEW 6:34 (NIV)

A forest fire that had been raging several miles away for days had jumped two parallel canyons and now threatened countless neighborhood homes.

From our patio, I stood with the neck of my T-shirt pulled over my mouth in an attempt to filter the smoke in the air and stared at the tall, angry flames in the distance as they licked their way toward the sky.

My husband had declared it go-time, asking me to pack our bags and get ready to load up, but as I scurried through every room of our home, I reached for surprisingly few things: a stack of my old journals; my favorite sweater; my purse; Prisca's favorite stuffed dog, Ike; Perry's beloved baseball cap; a few changes of clothes; our toothbrushes; some pajamas; and books and snacks. What else did we need, really? What else made our life *life*?

I wandered back through the rooms before heading to the car, snapping photos of each space. There was artwork I treasured, clothing I adored, cookbooks whose recipes I'd made for years. That handmade afghan from Nana, the angel figurine from my mom, decades' worth of scrapbooked scenes. But these things proved ancillary to life that is truly life. If our house was to be consumed by fire, these things would go up in flames. And so I went ahead and said good-bye to all my stuff that's just stuff in the end.

Father, help me to hold my stuff loosely today.
—ASHLEY WIERSMA

Digging Deeper: ROMANS 8:32

Tue 11

"What good is it for someone to gain the whole world, and yet lose or forfeit their very self?"
—LUKE 9:25 (NIV)

My girlfriend ran up to me and kissed me, and while we were standing on the sidewalk embracing, we got hit by a car. A pizza delivery SUV had been backing out of a loading bay en route to the street. The driver had not bothered to look in her rearview mirror. After she hit us, she ran out of the vehicle, visibly upset. Upon seeing that I had one leg and crutches, she almost had a complete meltdown.

In retrospect, I realized I had missed the chance to get some financial compensation since she was clearly liable for the accident. Instead, we told her we were fine. Afterward, though, it kind of irked me that I hadn't at least asked for a few free pizzas. I had missed an opportunity to throw an awesome party for my girlfriend and me!

Then I saw that this was an example of something God has been showing me recently. When I indulge selfish ambitions like this, I am missing the point of life, which isn't to get what's mine, to get what I deserve, or to accumulate stuff (pizza or otherwise). The deeper point is to know God. Nothing else is real; nothing else matters. So now, whenever I walk by that pizza place, I let it be a reminder about what truly matters.

Lord, do not let my ambitions or material desires get in the way of my true priorities. —JOSHUA SUNDQUIST

Digging Deeper: MATTHEW 6:33, 1 JOHN 2:16

Wed 12

My heart rejoiced in all my labour....
—ECCLESIASTES 2:10 (KJV)

It had been a long day. After dropping off my son, Harrison, at school, I had rushed to an early meeting, then back to my office to a daunting pile of paperwork. Before I knew it, the office had cleared out and I was late for dinner.

As I powered down my computer, the years fell away and I was a little guy holding a trash bag that was bigger than I was and my grandfather, Pa, was towering over me with a mischievous grin spread across his face. "Okay, buddy," he was saying, "as soon as you fill this bag up with pinecones, I'll take you over to Mr. Tillery's store for some ice cream."

I picked up one pinecone and then another. They were awfully prickly. I peeped down inside the bag, just to make sure it had a bottom. I remember gazing across the lake, wishing I was fishing or skipping rocks, anything other than picking up those creepy pinecones! It seemed like the bag would never be full.

Finally, I dragged it to the front porch and placed it at Pa's feet. "Way to go, son! Let's get going to the store." An ice-cream cone never tasted better.

Now I walked to my car with that same thrill of accomplishment. The joy that comes with working hard and seeing every task to its end swept over me. Like that long-ago ice cream cone, it was sweet all the way down to the tip of my soul.

Father, thank You for the opportunity
to do good work. —BROCK KIDD

Digging Deeper: PROVERBS 14:23,
ECCLESIASTES 9:10

Thu 13   *"I will send an angel before you...."* —EXODUS 33:2 (NRSV)

It was Frances's first day of kindergarten. I was full of mixed feelings. Amazement that Kate and I were now parents of a kindergartner. Sadness at how fast children grow. Nervousness for our daughter. *What will her teacher be like? Will she make friends? Is she ready?*

A gathering bustled as we neared the school: cars dropping off kids; older kids sailing by on bikes; a happy chatter of voices, laughter. Frances held my hand tight. "This school is big," she said.

"You'll do great," I responded. But I agreed. The school looked big compared to her preschool.

We walked to the playground, where children were lining up for class. Suddenly, Frances's hand tore from mine and she raced across the playground. "Charlotte!" she cried. It was a friend from summer camp. "You're in Mrs. Gates's class too?"

Moments later the teacher led the kids to the classroom. Parents hovered taking pictures. My last glimpse of Frances found her comparing lunches with Charlotte.

Kate, our toddler Benjamin, and I walked home. "I think Frances is going to be okay," I said, half to Kate, half to myself. Actually, I knew she would be. And knowing that, I was okay too.

God, You are always ahead of us. Help me
to walk in trust. —JIM HINCH

Digging Deeper: PSALMS 37:25–26, 127:3

Fri 14   *The end of a matter is better than its*
           beginning, and patience is better than
           pride. —ECCLESIASTES 7:8 (NIV)

When my husband and I brought our pup home, we proudly showed him his crate. Lined with blankets, toys, and a few treats, this crate, we thought, was sure to be Colby's version of heaven.

Colby, though, eyed the crate warily and avoided it. We pressed on, sure that we knew better. We lifted him into it each night, but after weeks of bribery and begging, Colby had no more interest in the crate than I had in driving during rush-hour traffic.

So Brian and I gave up. Colby gained free rein of the house, and we were no worse for the wear.

Then, months later, Colby's annual exam turned up heartworms that he'd contracted before we adopted him. Heartworm treatment is hard for a dog and involves confinement, so we limited Colby to the basement and his crate. Imagine our surprise when, day after day, we came home to find him complacently there.

As I watched him snuggle into the crate, I wondered how many other things I'd tried to make happen before their time: relationships I'd attempted to accelerate, jobs I'd struggled to attain, and moments I'd forced with God. It was as if creating mountaintops on my own would result in the same spirit-filled feeling I so coveted.

God, remind me that all things come in Your time and that You aren't bound by any deadlines.
—ASHLEY KAPPEL

Digging Deeper: ECCLESIASTES 3:1–14, 1 TIMOTHY 1:16

Sat 15

They see the works of the Lord, and His wonders in the deep.
—Psalm 107:24 (nkjv)

It was a once-in-a-lifetime opportunity, so our family took the leap: a trip to Hawaii!

As we settled into our friend's Oahu townhouse, I noticed the stress fade from my wife's face. The kids played in the yard, and we packed for the beach. A short drive, perfect sand, crystal-blue waters, refreshing trade winds, the scent of plumeria, and a happy family—days melted into each other and added up to heaven.

Too bad we don't live here, I thought.

Our trip then brought us to Maui. We embraced our inner tourists and visited a pineapple plantation, shared a luau, and even rode a submarine. We saw the teeming life on a coral reef thirty feet beneath the surface.

I wish I could see this every day, I thought.

That afternoon, my daughter and I rented snorkeling gear and headed toward the beach. We had only two days left and hadn't yet tried snorkeling. Our condo sat beside a coral reef, filled with beauties beyond compare: fish every color of the rainbow, large and small; urchins; anemones; and spectacular creatures whose names I didn't know.

Too bad we put off snorkeling till the end of our trip, I thought.

But later I embraced a simple truth: From my wife's smile to my kids' laughter to my dogs' wiggling welcome—wherever life brought me, I just had to open my eyes to the wonders of God right outside my door.

Gracious God, grant me wisdom to feel more deeply Your ever-present joy in everyday life.
—BILL GIOVANNETTI

Digging Deeper: PSALM 119:18

Sun 16

And we know that all things work together for good to those who love God, to those who are the called according to His purpose.
—ROMANS 8:28 (NKJV)

You won't believe it." It was Lemuel, a Guideposts Outreach staff member, calling me at home.

"Believe what?" I asked.

"This morning when I arrived at church, I was informed that this was the last Sunday service for the congregation." The interim pastor had resigned, and the congregation was unable to find another one. In addition, attendance and the church's financial stability had declined significantly. A decision was made that it was best to close the doors.

"How are the members?" I asked.

"Some are emotional, but most understand the practicality of this decision. How are you feeling?" Lemuel asked me. I'd left the church years ago as the pastor.

"I'm sad, disappointed, but to some extent I understand. My hope was that the church would continue its ministry for many years."

"Pablo, all things work for God's glory," Lemuel said to me. I struggled to accept the idea that closing our church would work together for God's glory. Yet I knew that God could turn difficult moments into opportunities for blessings.

"I think you are right," I said to Lemuel. "Although the church's ministry was brief, the impact of God's love on the people will live on."

Lord, You help us get through the unexpected and changing things. Thank You. —PABLO DIAZ

Digging Deeper: ISAIAH 55:8, 1 THESSALONIANS 5:18

Mon 17

Which of you by taking thought can add one cubit unto his stature?
—MATTHEW 6:27 (KJV)

O*ne, two, three, breathe.* I stepped into the warm water of the hotel pool, put my face underwater, and began to swim. I was in Logan, Utah, planning the funeral of my father and praying that the swim would relax and distract me.

When I stopped swimming, a little Latino boy was staring at me. "Where are your kids?" he asked me.

"They're coming soon," I told him.

"When they get here, can I play with them?"

"I guess so, but they're grown," I said, smiling.

He cocked his head. "So if you go under the water, will you turn white?"

I chuckled to myself. I was praying for distraction, and there he was! "No, black is my color."

My new acquaintance looked me over. "So when will your hair turn white?" he asked.

"You mean, when will my hair be straight?" He nodded. "Never." I laughed. "This is my hair and this is my skin."

He looked perplexed. "Don't you want to be white like me?"

His mother informed him he was brown. He was incredulous! It was, in fact, hard to worry when my new friend was so comically perplexed.

"What if all the flowers were the same color? Wouldn't it be boring? All the different colors make flowers—and people—beautiful," I said. His mother nodded, smiled, and relaxed. My new friend mulled it over. "God did it on purpose," I told the boy.

There were more questions. In between them, I swam. Before he left the pool with his family, my new friend turned and blew me a kiss.

Thank You, Lord, for providing exactly what we need when we're dealing with the death of a loved one. Your comfort is perfect. —SHARON FOSTER

Digging Deeper: ISAIAH 54:10–12, LUKE 18:15–17

Tue 18

Even before a word is on my tongue, behold, O Lord, you know it altogether. —PSALM 139:4 (ESV)

Several phone conversations got me thinking about different levels of intimacy in relationships. Around nine o'clock I called the garage. "Hello. This is Evelyn Bence," I said. "I'd like to make an appointment for an oil change." The man on the other end of the line, whose name is Matt, scheduled me in and asked for the model and year of my car.

Then I called a close friend. "Good morning, Sandra. Evelyn here. You know that garlic-potato dish you make? I'd really like the recipe." We chatted for five minutes. I told her about my dinner guests; she told me about her recent museum visit.

I was hardly off the line when the phone rang. "Hello," I said.

"Hi, it's me." It was my sister, who doesn't bother to introduce herself. She knows I'll recognize her voice. Having known each other our whole lives, I picked up on her clipped tone. "I'm at an estate sale," she explained. "There's a ceramic flower pot here. I think it's what you're looking for. Shall I buy it?"

Those three conversations remind me that it's time for a fourth. I quiet myself and attune my spirit to the Shepherd who has known me longer and knows me even better than an older sibling. He whispers, "I know my sheep and my sheep know me" (John 10:14, NIV)—my name, my voice, my situation, my thoughts.

Good morning, Good Shepherd. You've known me since before I was born. Draw me now into a prayerful conversation. You with me; me with You; we two, bound fast, closer than kin. —EVELYN BENCE

Digging Deeper: PSALMS 23, 139:1–15; JOHN 10:1–14

Wed 19

"Continue earnestly in prayer, being vigilant in it with thanksgiving."
—COLOSSIANS 4:2 (NKJV)

I was worried. My cat Prince was terribly sick. I felt like a meanie dragging him to the vet but prayed for the strength to get Prince into his carrier without my needing a doctor, too, for bites and scratches.

I accomplished my goal, and the vet said Prince sounded and looked a lot worse than he was. She called in a prescription anyway that would speed his recovery.

Still I worried. *God, she only examined Prince for a few minutes. I've been hearing his hacking cough for days. Please make sure he is all right.* My worry was in overdrive and gave me a headache, but before I could buy aspirin, I needed to settle Prince back at home.

Finally, I headed over to pick up his prescription. The pharmacist checked the shelf and said, "There is nothing here, Linda." I was annoyed. My vet was usually super-reliable, which was why I'd chosen her.

I turned to go, then had a thought. "By any chance, is there a prescription for Prince Neukrug?" And, of course, there was. I explained to the pharmacist that Prince could not come in to pick up his prescription, so he sent his courier.

Both of us had a good laugh, and when I left the store—without aspirin—my headache was gone.

Laughter is good medicine, Lord. Thank You for letting me find it in the middle of worrying.
—LINDA NEUKRUG

Digging Deeper: PSALM 126:2, ECCLESIASTES 3:4

Thu 20

"For I will satisfy the weary soul, and every languishing soul I will replenish."
—JEREMIAH 31:25 (ESV)

My wife and I were having a discussion about the way I'd been feeling: sad, anxious, irritable, and withdrawn. "I want you to call your doctor and tell him you're depressed," Julia said. I wanted to shrug off her suggestion, but I knew she was right.

For most of my life I've lived in the shadows. There have been periods, sometimes long ones, when the sun has peeked through the clouds, but the darkness has always come back. During the last few years I've spent a lot of time in the dark.

For a while I told myself I was just extremely introverted or having a normal reaction to difficult circumstances. But whether I'd admit it or not, in the back of my mind I knew I was depressed. When I became a Christian, I thought it would go away. For a while, it did. When I got married, became a father, and began working at Guideposts, the clouds dispersed. But in the end, they returned.

The day after that conversation with Julia, I called my doctor. Eventually I was referred to a psychiatrist and began a regimen of therapy and medication. My progress is slow, but it is there. Little by little, the clouds are parting.

When I hear people talk about joy, my first reaction is often to question myself. *Am I denying the Spirit? Do I have real faith?* I have to keep reminding myself that faith—and joy—is more than feelings. Faith is trusting that God will keep His promises. And beneath the surface, joy is bubbling like an underground spring.

Lord, I know You're with me as I struggle toward the light. —ANDREW ATTAWAY

Digging Deeper: NEHEMIAH 8:10

Fri 21

So teach us to count our days that we may gain a wise heart. —PSALM 90:12 (NRSV)

Ding-dong. Reluctantly, I pushed my chair away from the desk and opened the door. Rachel, my four-year-old neighbor, stood on the porch. "Can you go to the pool?" she asked, her big brown eyes hopeful.

"Not today, sweetie. I have things to do," I said. Her mom waved from the sidewalk, and they headed toward the neighborhood swimming pool.

This wasn't the first time Rachel had come over. She'd asked to play with my dog and to help in my flowerbed. Despite my explanations, Rachel didn't understand I had errands and chores. She just wanted to spend time with me.

The next day, I walked to the mailbox and spotted Rachel wearing a bright blue bathing suit. She and her mom were loading a wagon with inflatable rafts. "Going swimming?" I asked.

Rachel's dark blonde ringlets bobbed up and down as she ran to meet me. Scooping her up in my arms, I felt her warm hug. "Can you go?" she whispered.

I thought about the e-mails to return, housework that needed to be done, appointments I wanted to schedule. Next summer Rachel might find friends her own age.

"You bet!" I said, knowing that work could wait, but a child's favor, like the summer days, fades all too quickly.

Lord, help me balance my play with my work.
—STEPHANIE THOMPSON

Digging Deeper: ECCLESIASTES 2:10-11, MARK 10:14

Sat 22

Woe to us, for we have sinned!
—LAMENTATIONS 5:16 (NIV)

During our usual Saturday phone call, my sister Sharon launched immediately into the "terrible thing that happened at work." She and a coworker were discussing a woman who'd just begun working with them, and Sharon used the word *midget* in reference to her. At that moment, another coworker happened by and heatedly corrected her. "She's not a midget. She's really nice!" she said, stomping off.

"I feel so bad," Sharon lamented. "I wish I could undo it."

I could certainly identify. I'd once joked about a student's mispronunciation of an unfamiliar word in class. And I'd disparaged graduate degrees obtained from programs abroad—"degree mills," I'd called them—in the presence of a coworker who had gotten a diploma from such a school.

We discussed praying about the blunder and how the experience might make Sharon a better person. "I'll never use the word *midget* again. That's for sure," she said. Eventually, we got to how she might repair the damage she'd done and her fear that apologizing to the coworker might backfire.

"It might, but it probably won't," I said, drawing on my long experience. "Sometimes apologizing is the beginning of a real relationship with someone."

My Rock and my Redeemer, teach me to honor each of Your children. Help me to learn and grow from my mistakes. —PATTY KIRK

Digging Deeper: PSALMS 19:14, 141; PROVERBS 18:6–8

Sun 23

Pray in the Spirit at all times in every prayer and supplication. To that end keep alert and always persevere in supplication for all the saints. —Ephesians 6:18 (nrsv)

Well, I thought to myself, *maybe I can just tell her I already have plans.* Suddenly, I became aware that I had just zoned out at church during prayer. I quickly snapped back into the service. It surely wasn't the first time; I just happened to catch myself.

I struggle with how to keep myself engaged in corporate prayer. I know there is power in praying together as a church. I start off strong, praying along with whoever is praying, until at some point I get distracted. "Yes, Lord," I'll be praying, "give a special blessing for that lady's sick cousin. I should probably add a blessing for my own cousins. I haven't talked to them in a while. I'll call them this week. Mental note: Add *call cousins* to my to-do list . . . like there's not enough already on that list. I should probably start tomorrow with the laundry because I'm running out of underwear. Oh, shoot! But I promised I'd meet my friend for coffee and I've been so busy I haven't seen her recently. I really shouldn't back out. . . ."

Since this has become a habit, I decided to come up with a game plan. During corporate prayer, I give myself the freedom to pray along with the prayer or to say my own. I still have moments when I allow distractions to interrupt my time with God, but my mind wanders less frequently. Maybe this is because I'm holding myself more accountable or perhaps it keeps me from "flipping through the channels." Whatever the reason, this game plan keeps me firmly aware—in prayer.

Lord, the spirit is willing, but the flesh is weak. Have mercy. —NATALIE PERKINS

Digging Deeper: ACTS 1:14

Mon 24

For it is by grace you have been saved, through faith—and this is not from yourselves, it is the gift of God. —EPHESIANS 2:8 (NIV)

It should have been a touching good-bye. Instead, I was arguing with my three-year-old over his refusal to give my parents a hug. It seemed ridiculous to try to force my son into a warm, affectionate embrace, but I did it anyway. "Give Grandma and Papa a hug right now or you're in big trouble!" His scowl didn't melt into sweetness, which only made my scowl even worse. "Fine! Get in the car!" I scolded. "That is so mean!"

Hours later when we arrived home, I was still hurt. My parents had done nothing but shower my son with love, kindness, gifts, and tons of candy. There was no reason for him to be so cold. I called my mother to apologize again for his behavior.

"Oh, Karen, don't be upset," my mother said. "I know he loves me. He will always be my little baby."

I felt the weight come off me, knowing that her unconditional love for my son was even greater than mine at that point. It not only made me rethink my anger, but it brought to mind God's grace. Hadn't I sometimes withheld my affection and appreciation from Him like a grouchy child? Yet God's unconditional love always prevailed.

Thank You, Lord, for giving us a place in Your heart, not by our works, but by Your mercy and grace.
—KAREN VALENTIN

Digging Deeper: ROMANS 11:6

Tue 25

In building the temple, only blocks dressed at the quarry were used, and no hammer, chisel or any other iron tool was heard at the temple site while it was being built.
—1 KINGS 6:7 (NIV)

My husband and I were sitting on rockers on the back porch of a small cottage in the mountains of north Georgia, enjoying an overnight getaway from our busy lives. As we read the newspaper, I became aware of the amazing silence of the forest, interrupted only by the sweet whisper of the wind ruffling the leaves of the trees. I savored the rich quiet and heard a faint trickling sound coming from the deep ravine below, hinting that there was a hidden mountain creek somewhere nearby.

When we returned home, I came across an article that said noise can be a stressor without our knowledge, leading to chronic health issues like heart disease and high blood pressure. I learned that the National Park Service is taking steps to prevent noise pollution in our parks by limiting nearby industry, highways, and the encroaching modern racket that would overpower the sounds of nature.

I became aware of the refrigerator whining away in the kitchen and the clothes thumping in the dryer. *Hmm,* I thought, *it's raining outside, but I can't hear it over the noise.* I went to the bedroom, closed the door, and pulled up a chair to the window. As I heard the gentle pitter-patter of raindrops falling on the windowpane, I felt my breathing relax and sat for several minutes being renewed by God's glorious music.

Dear Creator of the Universe, help me to separate myself frequently from all things electronic and mechanical, so I can enter Your gentle presence to be healed. Amen. —KAREN BARBER

Digging Deeper: HABAKKUK 2:20, LUKE 4:35

August

Wed 26

Observe how the lilies of the field grow; they do not toil nor do they spin. —MATTHEW 6:28 (NAS)

I hadn't had a very good workout at the YMCA that morning. Everyone looked younger than I am—and more athletic. I dreaded going home. I'd just drop into a chair, exhausted. My body was weary, but so was my soul. God seemed so far away.

The sun was Georgia hot, even at eleven in the morning, as I exited the building. Discouragement tagged along with me. A woman passed me, walking briskly to the parking area. She stopped a few steps in front of me and took out a bottle of water. I slowed down. It didn't appear she was going to drink it. I pretended to rummage through my gym bag in order to observe her. She leaned way over, after removing the cap to the water bottle, and singled out one red zinnia in the garden that grew beside the iron fence. Carefully, even lovingly, she allowed the flower to drink.

An amazing thing happened. It felt as though someone had poured joy directly into my soul. One flower in all the hundreds had been tended to with such deliberate care. The woman straightened up and walked to her car. I lingered by the red zinnia. Somehow, I felt refreshed, as though God had reached down to Earth and touched me. "I see you, Marion. I love you."

Father, You find such tender ways to show me Yourself when I need You most. —MARION BOND WEST

Digging Deeper: GENESIS 50:25, I PETER 5:7

Thu 27

My eyes stay open through the watches of the night, that I may meditate on your promises.
—PSALM 119:148 (NIV)

I had to wake my four-year-old son, Brogan, early to get us both ready and out the door, so we could be at church in time to pray with the other leaders before the beginning of our women's Bible study. This morning, however, we were having a hard time getting going.

My son really wanted to go to the park. For whatever reason, that was the desire of his heart. As he begged while I dug his shoes out of our messy closet, I glanced out the window, taking note of the blue sky and the bright sun. I looked him in his face and said, "Brogan, we're going to church first. But after, we'll go to the park."

That's all it took. He was ecstatic, jumping up and down with a big smile on his face, filled with confident expectation.

His mommy said he was going to the park after church, so to the park we would go. He didn't question me. He didn't doubt me. He took me completely at my word, believing that what I said would really happen.

And it hit me: That's how we are called to respond. Scripture is jam-packed with God's promises. Yet when was the last time I responded to them in the same way my son responded to mine? Without doubt. Without question. With a confident expectation that if God promises it, it will happen.

Lord Jesus, instill an excitement in my heart over Your amazing promises. May You find me bouncing on my toes, bubbling over with joyful anticipation and unshakable confidence. — KATIE GANSHERT

Digging Deeper: ROMANS 8:37, PHILIPPIANS 4:19, 1 PETER 1:14

Fri 28

Let the peace of Christ rule in your hearts, since as members of one body you were called to peace. And be thankful. —COLOSSIANS 3:15 (NIV)

I sprawled out in the hammock, hung from two giant oaks just steps from the lake, and closed my eyes, soaking in the glory of the day. Crickets chirped. A woodpecker rattled. Tiny butterflies floated by on the breeze.

Okay, they were moths. But they were still pretty. And the breeze was a bit chilly for my taste. And fleas bit my legs, reminding me that the great out-doors is called "outdoors" for a reason.

Yet still, this city girl who loves things like climate control and pest control was finding something akin to—was it peace? Closing my eyes and tak-ing in a deep breath of the country air, my heart cried out to God. *Why is it so hard for me to just "be"? To let You fill my spirit with Your Word, life, hope, and peace? To listen to the quiet, still voice and know that You are God?*

It came like a whisper from one of the moth's wings: *You don't let Me.*

I had let my own thoughts interfere. I had let those pesky fleas interrupt. I had let the chilly breeze steal my peace, the peace that God so des-perately wants to give me.

Speak to me, Lord, not through the noise and clutter,
but through the silence. Amen.
—Erin MacPherson

Digging Deeper: Psalm 26:2–3, Philippians 4:6–7

Sat 29

Whatever you have learned or received or heard from me, or seen in me—put into practice. And the God of peace will be with you.
—Philippians 4:9 (NIV)

I attended a funeral for a friend who died of ovarian cancer. She was diagnosed a year after I was with the same cancer. I was Stage 4; she was Stage 3. Yet she died, and I am living.

As my husband, Lynn, and I left the church, I felt angry about the unfairness of it all . . . until I saw our car and stopped in disbelief. The passenger side was badly dented with paint scraped off. Someone had hit it while we were inside the church but left no note of identification or apology. That elevated my anger.

We headed to a body shop where an employee estimated the cost of the repair and advised us to call our insurance company, verify our deductible, file a hit-and-run accident report, schedule the repair, and make arrangements for a rental car while ours would be at the body shop. "It's unfair," I fumed. "We have to pay for someone else's actions."

Lynn said nothing, which helped me to hear an internal whisper—a combination of my mother's voice and the clear promises I know from the Bible: Life's not fair. Cancer's not fair. Paying for another's mistakes isn't fair. But Someone already did that. He understands your struggles and gives you strength and hope and perspective, especially when life's not fair.

Lord, when I don't understand life's realities, I desperately need Your presence and promises.
—CAROL KUYKENDALL

Digging Deeper: LUKE 4:18–19, PHILIPPIANS 4:8

Sun 30

But the fruit of the Spirit is love, joy, peace, patience, kindness, goodness, faithfulness, gentleness, self-control....
—GALATIANS 5:22–23 (NAS)

Last night, I uncovered several old cigar boxes filled with fading, yellowed photographs. Some were from my high school years; others were of Beth and me during our early years of marriage. Then I found a crinkled envelope amid the pictures. It was a card from a friend who has been dead for more than fifteen years. He was a young man when he died, successful, talented, and full of promise. Then cancer riddled his body.

The card states: "Some people come into our lives and quickly go... some stay for a while and leave footprints on our hearts, and we are never, ever the same." On the back of the envelope is a note he had scrawled: "This small card expresses my feelings and thankfulness for what you have done for me this past year."

In the midnight dimness of my study, I swallowed hard as my eyes brimmed with tears. A memory reached across the years and touched me. I became intensely aware that at the end of our short day, all that really matters is human touch . . . those whom we have loved and who have loved us.

I look at my to-do list. Ironically, it is scratched on the back of an envelope too. Most of my day will be focused on errands; very little is directed toward caring for the needs of God's children. Maybe I need to listen to the voice from my past who is softly saying, "Use tomorrow to walk into someone's life and leave footprints on her heart."

Father, shape my day to achieve Your priorities
of love and mercy. Amen.
—SCOTT WALKER

Digging Deeper: PSALM 26:3

Mon 31 *"A word of encouragement does wonders!"*
—PROVERBS 12:25 (TLB)

When Kincaid, a young man in our church, entered Air Force basic training, his parents distributed information so the congregation could write to him. I put the paper on my desk but didn't write. What could I say that would interest a guy right out of high school? It would be easier to just pray for him, so I added him to my list.

A few days later, a *Daily Guideposts* reader phoned. "I told my husband I appreciated the way you shared your faith struggles," she said, "and he suggested I look up your number and let you know. I hope you don't mind." Of course I didn't mind! I was delighted she took the time to call. Then I got a text from my grandson David: "How r u? Ok I hope. Luv U!" It was short and sweet but warmed my heart.

Were these nudges from God? If I was cheered by knowing others were thinking of me, wouldn't Kincaid be as well? So I wrote to him, giving scores from the high school basketball games, a weather update, and telling him I prayed for him daily.

Prayer is still the most important thing I can do for others. But when Kincaid's dad reported that the letters he received provided encouragement during an exhausting and difficult boot camp, I realized that there were also times when my prayers needed to be signed, stamped, and delivered.

Thank You, Jesus for reminding me that prayer accompanied by action is often the most powerful prayer of all. —PENNEY SCHWAB

Digging Deeper: PHILIPPIANS 4:21, JAMES 2:20, 1 JOHN 3:11

DAILY JOYS

1 _____

2 _____

3 _____

4 _____

5 _____

6 _____

7 _____

8 _____

9 _____

10 _____

11 _____

12 _____

13 _____

14 _____

15 _____

16 _____

17 _____

18 _____

19 _____

20 _____

21 _____

22 _____

23 _____

24 _____

25 _____

26 _____

27 _____

28 _____

29 _____

30 _____

31 _____

SEPTEMBER

A joyful heart is good medicine....

—PROVERBS 17:22 (ESV)

GOD OF JOYFUL SURPRISES

Tue 1

And after the fire came a gentle whisper. —1 KINGS 19:12 (NIV)

LISTENING IN THE EVERYDAYNESS

What made Corrie ten Boom risk her life to save Jewish people living in occupied Holland? *It must have been some great event,* I thought, *some dramatic soul-stirring call from God.*

"No," she said, "it was a simple, very ordinary moment."

By 1942, it was dangerous for Jews to appear in the streets of Haarlem. So Corrie, a watchmaker and repairer, started going to the homes of her Jewish customers to pick up and deliver work. One evening this took her to the house of a doctor and his wife. They were chatting over cups of rationed tea stretched with rose leaves, when from upstairs a child's voice piped, "Daddy, you didn't tuck us in!"

Excusing himself, the doctor hurried upstairs. Corrie and her hostess kept chatting. Nothing had changed. Everything had changed. At any minute, Corrie realized, there could be a knock at the door of *this* house. *This* mother, *this* father, *these* children could be herded into the back of a truck.

Still carrying on their conversation, still sipping tea, Corrie silently dedicated her life to the Jewish inhabitants of Holland. "Lord Jesus, I offer myself for Your people in any way, any place, any time."

Out of a daily domestic moment grew a heroine of the Dutch resistance, whose story of loss, suffering, and unstoppable joy inspires even today.

God of joyful surprises, help me listen for Your voice in the everydayness of my life. —ELIZABETH SHERRILL

Digging Deeper: DEUTERONOMY 30:20, PROVERBS 8:34

Wed 2

"Come to me, all you who are weary and burdened, and I will give you rest." —MATTHEW 11:28 (NIV)

A new e-mail blipped on my laptop screen. It was an attachment for the "Picture of the Day" from my friend Edel. I clicked on it, and sunlight glinted off an expanse of snowcapped mountains that rimmed the grassy meadow where a rickety and weathered homestead barn stood. There were gaping holes in the sagging moss-covered roof. The door stood ajar and was canted at an angle, as if the burdens of the last hundred years rested on it. Many of the boards, which had served as siding, were missing.

That barn looks exactly like I feel—empty and weary, I thought. Although it was still early in the morning, I was exhausted. Everything that could go wrong had gone wrong.

In the stillness as I sat there looking, I heard, *When you're run-down, that's when you're open to the winds of the Holy Spirit. Invite Me in.*

I'm such an independent person that oftentimes I hammer away at life, trying to fix things myself. But when I wilt from life's troubles, come to the end of myself, and earnestly seek God, that's the beginning of the journey with Him.

I prayed the following prayer and, amazingly, the rest of the day passed without any more calamities.

Lord, the door to my heart is wide open. Fill me with Your Counselor, the Holy Spirit of peace, comfort, and wisdom. Amen. —REBECCA ONDOV

Digging Deeper: JOHN 14:26

Thu 3

Lord, you alone can heal me, you alone can save, and my praises are for you alone. —JEREMIAH 17:14 (TLB)

A number of my close friends and family members were experiencing lost jobs, marriages on the brink, homes going into foreclosure. My heart ached because I could not solve their problems.

Then I had hand surgery that left a five-inch wound in the shape of a Y on my left palm. As I went through occupational therapy to get the feeling back in my hand and fingers, I was absolutely amazed at how my body healed itself. Each day I could see a noticeable improvement from the day before. After day eleven when the stitches came out, my hand seemed to heal even faster.

I thought about my loved ones' problems as I watched my hand heal. I learned what an absolutely perfect engineer God is. If God could create a body that heals itself, there was no doubt that God could heal the problems of my friends and family who were hurting. At that moment, my heart started to heal, knowing they were in the hands of a creative genius. All it took to get things started was prayer and faith.

Master of all creation, how brilliant You are for giving me the ability to grow new skin, heal my wounds, regenerate my body, and solve life's problems over and over and over again. —PATRICIA LORENZ

Digging Deeper: MARK 3:1–5, HEBREWS 12:12

Fri 4

"I, wisdom, dwell together with prudence; I possess knowledge and discretion." —PROVERBS 8:12 (NIV)

You did what?" said my wife, aghast at the news I had given her. "What were you thinking?" We were on the subway—she taking Maggie, twelve, to an art supply store; me taking Stephen, ten, on an outing to Governors Island.

Just what was I thinking? A couple of weeks earlier, I'd offered to put up a friend for a few days. We had no room, our daughter Elizabeth was about to pay us a visit from college, and Maggie was having a difficult time. My offer was impulsive; I'd wanted to help a friend, but I hadn't considered the circumstances at home when I invited him.

Now I don't think I'm entirely lacking in common sense. My problem is the anxiety that comes with my depression. Even a relatively small decision becomes fraught and worrisome, and I short-circuit the worry by doing the first thing that comes to mind. As you can imagine, that leads to a lot of bad decisions.

What am I doing about it? Working with a counselor to control my anxious thoughts and remembering to pray when I feel the anxiety coming on. As for my friend? Forty-five minutes later I was sitting on the steps of the old customs house in lower Manhattan with my cell phone, straightening things out with him.

Father, Your Spirit is peace and Your every decision is wise. Help me to think carefully and act wisely.
—ANDREW ATTAWAY

Digging Deeper: I CORINTHIANS 14:33

September

Sat 5

One person gives freely, yet gains even more; another withholds unduly, but comes to poverty.
—Proverbs 11:24 (NIV)

My five-year-old daughter stood in wait, tightly clutching her sack and inching closer to the piñata with every *whack* of the stick.

With a loud crack, the unicorn broke open and piles of candy poured onto the ground. Kate dove right in, scooping up piles of treats and grinning as she filled her bag. She caught my eye and waved. "They have my favorite kinds, Mom!"

Then she turned and noticed two of the younger kids standing off to the edge, scared to break into the fray. Their bags were empty. And before I could snatch some candy for myself, Kate turned to the two children and dumped her entire bagful into theirs.

"Wait," I wanted to say, "don't give it all away!" But her smile stilled my heart as she tossed her bag into the garbage and joined the other girls as they played.

Kate already understood what I too often forget: Generosity is joyous.

Lord, help me to be generous as You are with me. Amen. —Erin MacPherson

Digging Deeper: Proverbs 19:17,
2 Corinthians 9:7

Sun 6

"Whenever I am afraid, I will trust in You."—PSALM 56:3 (NKJV)

Recovery International is a free self-help group for people with anxiety or depression (or both) and was started decades ago in Chicago by the late Abraham Low, MD, a neuropsychiatrist who wanted to help his patients help themselves.

I sometimes pray for help with my anxiety and depression, so when a friend found a mention of Recovery International in *Dear Abby*, I went with her as moral support. I related, too, so I kept going back.

One of the group's tools for dealing with misplaced feelings is something called "spots," from the phrase "to throw a spotlight on." If I start to feel fearful about something, I can interrupt that thought with a spot. For example, "If you can't change a situation, you can change your attitude toward it."

I like to remind myself that I am not transparent. No one can see my inner feelings when I am shaky, like when I substitute teach in a noisy high school classroom. Another helpful spot is "Feelings are distressing, but they are not dangerous." A favorite of mine: "Don't take your own dear self too seriously." The spots help stop the worry when it grows and starts to spiral downward.

One thing that hinders people from getting the help they need is being ashamed of their feelings, of not being perfect. I know what that's like, so I decided to pray that I would "not take my own dear self too seriously."

God, if there is something that has helped me and might help another today, please give me the strength to share it.
—LINDA NEUKRUG

Digging Deeper: GENESIS 21:6, JOB 8:21, 1 JOHN 4:18

Mon 7

"Yea, their children shall see it, and be glad; their heart shall rejoice in the Lord." —ZECHARIAH 10:7 (KJV)

Labor Day. The end of summer. And for one whole day, rest from work that I love on the family cattle ranch where I live in Sprague River, Oregon. But the best part is heading to the Lake County Fair.

In the years when we showed our purebred Salers cattle, Lake County Fair didn't set a limit on a bull's age. That meant we could keep bringing Brute. At 2,600 pounds, Brute was too big to be a range bull, but we kept him anyway. He was the perfect ambassador of goodwill for our ranch and the breed. A giant black teddy bear, Brute genuinely loved people and kids loved him back. When our trailers rolled into the fairgrounds, children lined up, eagerly waiting their turn on Brute's massive back. At times there'd be as many as six kids piled atop him while their grandmas snapped pictures. Even city kids would overcome their fear of Brute's size and be won over by his kind brown eyes. So many times I'd hear them say, "I've never been this close to an animal this big before!"

I delight in sharing my world with these children, watching them fall in love with an animal and returning to see Brute year after year. And I enjoy teaching them that ranching isn't just about meat and markets, but it's also about living life among the animals in the wide-open country. I cherish kindling in these kids the love of cattle and nature that burns within me.

Dear Lord, this Labor Day, help me to rejoice in the opportunities You provide to share my love of Your creation with others.
—ERIKA BENTSEN

Digging Deeper: MARK 10:14, LUKE 18:16

Tue 8   *For he will command his angels concerning you to guard you in all your ways.* —PSALM 91:11 (NIV)

A few minutes before the school bus was about to come down the road, Henry ran to the desk and came back with a piece of paper and a pen. "Write it, Mom," he said. "Write it small, so I can put it in my pocket and keep it there."

Following his instructions, I penned in tiny print, "It's all okay, Hen," and drew a smiley face. I tore off the scrap and handed it to him. "What's going on? Why do you need this?"

Henry folded the tiny note into a tinier square. "Sometimes I feel a little bit sad at school and I want to have it with me."

"Why do you feel sad?" I asked.

He bit his lip. "Sometimes I don't finish my work. And if I don't finish my work, I miss free time."

I looked into his deep brown eyes. "That's okay if you need more time."

"I know," he said, "but sometimes I forget. That's why I need the note. It helps me remember."

"Hold on, Hen." I ran upstairs to my dresser drawer and came down with a pewter angel, the size of a dime. My sister had given it to me years ago as a stocking stuffer. I gave Henry the angel. "For you," I said, "to remind you that your guardian angel is always with you."

Henry inspected the tiny angel, turning it around before putting it in his pocket. He patted his pants to make sure it was there.

As the bus came down the road, I whispered, "You're going to have a great day."

Dear Lord, send Your love and angels when Henry needs comfort. Help him find joy in Your promise that everything will be okay. —SABRA CIANCANELLI

Digging Deeper: PSALMS 27:1–3, 61:2

Wed 9

For when I am weak, then I am strong.
—2 CORINTHIANS 12:10 (NIV)

I absolutely dread being in charge, but there I was, chairperson of the board and managing director of Prayer Igniters International, a Web site offering practical prayer ideas.

I presented my plan to the board to hire a part-time program director, and one board member began, "You've written down way too many duties for a part-time person. Identify your top priorities." Another board member added, "You need to set up measurable performance expectations."

After the meeting I thought in dismay, *They're right. I should have thought about these things. I'm just not equal to this task.* Then I remembered a film I'd recently watched on the life of Saint Philip Neri. At one point he humbly prayed, "Jesus, I feel I am destined to fail at this task, but I will do it because You have asked me to."

Saint Philip Neri's prayer was powerful because of his honest assessment of his own skills. That allowed him to trust strongly and solely in a very different sort of confidence—confidence in God's call. All that God asked of him was humility, obedience, and trust. That's all God is asking of me too.

Father, I'm not sure that I have what it takes to succeed in the task You have called me to do, but I will do it simply because You asked, confident that the outcome is in Your hands. Amen.
—KAREN BARBER

Digging Deeper: 1 CORINTHIANS 1:26–31, 2 CORINTHIANS 4:7–12

Thu 10

She seeketh wool, and flax, and worketh willingly with her hands.
—PROVERBS 31:13 (KJV)

One of the recent blessings of my life is Janice, a woman who runs an alterations shop in her living room near the hospital where I work. When my eyes are giving me trouble, I take my sewing to her. Janice is usually bent over her trusty Singer, sacred music playing in the background. If I'm picking up something after work and she's not at home, it's fine to come in and leave money on her ironing board. Janice, choosing to believe the best about others, works on the honor system.

Janice knows I admire and appreciate her, but I've never told her what an incredible source of joy she is. You see, my beloved grandmother ran an alterations shop out of her cottage. Mamaw's treadle sewing machine was in her back bedroom, and she hung finished garments from sconces in her dining room. It was at my grandmother's that I learned to sew and garnered the confidence that comes with being able to say, "I made it myself!" It was also where I first experienced unconditional love, when I unknowingly made a coat of many colors for my doll from fabric Mamaw had been reserving for a special quilt.

It's been years since my grandmother passed away, on a Labor Day weekend at 4:30 PM. But each time September rolls around, my heart remembers and I miss her fiercely. Every time I enter Janice's shop at 4:30 PM after work and see the loose red and green threads on her beige carpet, it's as if I'm in my grandmother's loving presence again.

Lord, thank You for bringing people into our lives who remind us of those we have loved and lost.
—ROBERTA MESSNER

Digging Deeper: PSALMS 33:5, 59:16

Fri 11

For I am persuaded, that neither death, nor life, nor angels, nor principalities, nor powers . . . shall be able to separate us from the love of God. . . . —ROMANS 8:38–39 (KJV)

The school nurse gasped. "They just crashed into the Pentagon!" I had no time to learn more, but I grabbed a first-aid kit and hurried to the school bus where the other fifth-grade teacher loaded our forty students. We were on our way to study Wyoming wildlife in the Continental Divide, elevation 7,500 feet.

During the forty-five-minute ride, we told the children nothing as we could confirm nothing. Instead, high above the tumult of the world, God's serenity reigned in the pristine sky, the minty air, the pond surrounded by beaver tracks (both feet and tail), and to the joy of David, a new student from California, his first snow. The driver listened to his radio and whispered to me, "Another plane crashed in Pennsylvania." Still, we did not tell the children. Instead, under the lulling pines, we enjoyed our picnic lunches.

Back at school, the children used the last thirty minutes of class to write their discoveries in their journals. For them, September 11, 2001, records a day of discovering nature: red-tailed hawks, a beaver dam, bearberry plants, and snow. I like to think that this experience gave forty children an extra day of innocence. Only after they had left did we teachers crowd into a classroom and watch the TV images in numbed horror.

My day with my dear fifth graders reminds me that though catastrophe happens, so much of our world is still very good, serene, and beautiful.

Heavenly Father, You hold me in the palm of Your hand. I shall not fear. —GAIL THORELL SCHILLING

Digging Deeper: PSALMS 23:4, 91:10–11

Sat 12

Give, and it will be given to you.... —LUKE 6:38 (ESV)

My parents had their twenty-fifth wedding anniversary. They called my brother, Ned, and me and said they wanted to celebrate with the family. I was excited but thought, *Why don't they want to go off somewhere together, just the two of them?* I felt like I would be intruding on something that should have been private.

We all went out to a nice dinner at our favorite restaurant, the Tewksbury Inn. After we ordered, my mom said, "This is a very special day for us. Matt, you have been my partner for twenty-five years now, and I knew from our first week together that you would be the best thing in my life.

Marriage hasn't always been easy, but it has always been worth it."

My dad kissed her and held her hand. He said to us, "I wish for you all that we have."

I now understand a little better what has made their marriage successful. They never wanted to keep their love private, had never focused themselves entirely on the other. They have something wonderful, so they have to share it, spread it to others, like a gospel.

Thank You, Lord, for making life better when it is shared. —SAM ADRIANCE

Digging Deeper: MARK 16:15

Sun 13

"You have put gladness in my heart...." —PSALM 4:7 (NRSV)

My grandfather was a complicated man. Stern and serious by day, he was a Baptist pastor with a wide range of responsibilities. But in the evenings, he would make jokes, offer up belly laughs, and pinch me with his toes (they were like fingers!) when I wasn't looking. I loved him.

I remember one Saturday afternoon, sitting in his living room, drinking iced tea and watching a ball game on television. I didn't pay much attention as he walked out the door, but a few minutes later

I glanced out of the window to see him pushing the mower across the lawn, wearing the same white button-down dress shirt, black slacks, and black wingtips he'd just worn to the hospital to visit his sick congregants.

"*Yessir*, what can I do for you?" he said playfully.

"Grandpa, are you okay? Why are you wearing those clothes to cut the grass?" I asked.

"I hadn't even noticed," he said, looking at himself. And then I spotted a piece of paper in his pocket. It was a bulletin for a funeral he'd performed the weekend before. "Anyway, this is what I always wear." And he started the mower back up.

I watched him for the next half hour and saw a man completely comfortable in his own skin, singing hymns with joy while mowing the lawn.

Thank You, Lord, for grandparents and the special quality of time and love they give us when we're young. —JON SWEENEY

Digging Deeper: PSALM 16:8–9

Mon 14 *Sons are indeed a heritage from the Lord, the fruit of the womb a reward.* —PSALM 127:3 (NRSV)

Our son Will was going to give a business presentation one morning at a New York City hotel and invited us to come and watch. "What if I don't understand what he's talking about?" I asked my wife.

"You'll ask him later."

We arrived early to be sure to get a seat. It was like going to see him perform in the class play in fifth grade. "Hi, Mom. Hi, Dad." He found us in the lobby. He looked so grown up and professional. He hugged us and introduced us to his boss. "Just like meeting one of his teachers," Carol whispered.

We found seats in the back and studied the crowd; they looked even more intimidating in their business suits, checking phones and laptops before the program began.

The lights dimmed. The screen was illuminated. Will made a few disarming jokes, then guided the audience through the presentation. I looked around. Were people still checking their phones? No, they were listening to Will, rapt. I wanted to stand up and shout, "That's my boy!" I restrained myself. I even understood most of what he said.

He clicked the last slide, then thanked the audience. They applauded. Carol and I rose and let ourselves out but not without first sending him a text: "Wow, that was great! Proud of you. xo Dad."

Does anyone ever tell you when you first have kids that you will be surprised and amazed, time and again? You work hard and hope some of it rubs off on them. You worry a lot and pray even more.

You have big dreams, and yet who they become is so much bigger and better than you could have ever guessed. But then, you weren't really in charge, were you?

> *Father in heaven, we are all Your offspring.*
> *May we make You proud!* —RICK HAMLIN

> *Digging Deeper:* ISAIAH 54:13

Tue 15

Also I heard the voice of the Lord, saying, Whom shall I send, and who will go for us? Then said I, Here am I; send me. —ISAIAH 6:8 (KJV)

You're going where? To...how is that spelled? G-n-o-m-e?"

My son, Chase, laughs. "No, Mom. N-o-m-e."

There is no great demand for operatic tenors in Nome, Alaska, but there is opportunity for him to work with a crew mining for gold in the Bering Sea. Chase has always loved adventure. In fact, he has been to Oman and Israel recently, shining his light around the world.

Despite his sister Lanea's protestations ("It's so far away and so-so-so cold, Chase!"), he has packed extra-heavy coats and boots that will help him survive the frigid weather. He is a grown man; it is his life, so I try not to crowd him. Besides, the excitement in his voice is contagious.

When Chase arrives, he texts pictures of Nome. It's frozen, solitary, wide open white space. He calls to say he is settling in well. He is cooking for the crews. There is no Internet, no running water, and no indoor toilet. Luckily, his cell phone works, so we are able to pray together. One member of the mining team has died in a recent tragedy, and Chase asks us to pray for the crew. They are disheartened. He tries to encourage them, though some don't believe in God.

Over the phone, Lanea and I hear his roommate come into the cabin. I open my mouth to end the prayer, but Chase speaks first. There is no hesitation, no arrogance, no agenda in his voice—just welcome. "Hey! Want to join us?" he asks his roommate.

"Sure."

And then there we are, the four of us, breaking spiritual bread together over the miles. Suddenly, it all makes sense why Chase is where he is.

As You, dear Jesus, call the hearts of our sons and daughters to Your purpose, give us the courage to release them to You.
—SHARON FOSTER

Digging Deeper: NUMBERS 9:23, MATTHEW 10:9–11

Wed 16

"Your labour is not in vain...."
—1 Corinthians 15:58 (KJV)

A friend of mine just lost her job. Reasons like budget cuts and downsizing were offered, but to her she'd been fired. "Did I ever really matter?" she asked.

This is a haunting question. And because we seldom get positive feedback as we travel through life, we rarely get the question answered. "Hey, God, my friend needs a sign," I pray.

The next morning I wake from dreams of Deanna. Deanna had been dear to both my friend and me. The three of us gave parties for brides, organized meals for young mothers, and kept an eye on older church members. While Deanna created the acolyte program at church and started a children's choir, my friend was running what was known as the best youth group in Nashville, Tennessee. Deanna's influence on our children remains profound.

As I make breakfast, I touch a silver triangle hanging in the window, a gift from Deanna. She has been gone almost ten years, but still the acolytes light the church candles, the children's choir sings, and the triangle rings her message to me. Not only did her life matter while she was here, but it still does.

My friend, like the rest of us, isn't going to get an award to acknowledge how much she's given the world. But with God's prompting, I can remind her of Deanna, who still tells us that while we are here—and after we're gone—we do matter.

Father, we know we are always important to You. Help us let others know that they matter, not just to us but to You. —PAM KIDD

Digging Deeper: PSALM 37:18, PROVERBS 13:21, HEBREWS 10:35

Thu 17

Then the Lord called Samuel. Samuel answered, "Here I am."
—1 SAMUEL 3:4 (NIV)

I went over to the chapel around the corner this afternoon. It had been an overwhelming day, and a bit of quiet seemed like a good idea.

A woman who was acting a little strange followed me in. She wandered around, touching things: books, flowers, a lamp. My mind wandered alongside her to make sure she didn't knock over a lit candle or something valuable. After a while, she pulled out a bottle of vodka in front of the altar and took a swig. I went in search of help. When she was escorted out, I knelt to pray.

"Lord, I came here to be with You," I began with irritation and a sigh and then stopped. I was talking as if handling an alcoholic in the sanctuary was an inconvenience to me instead of a service to Him. I have a tendency to interpret things that don't go according to *my* plan as a burden. God had already shown me His plan: He wanted me to pay attention to someone else before considering my own needs.

I started my prayer again. "Lord, I ask You to bless the woman who was here. Whatever her suffering is, comfort her. Whatever help she needs, provide it to her. Let those she meets today be filled with grace." And as an admission of my own weakness, I added...

And however You want me to serve You today, Lord, I am here. —JULIA ATTAWAY

Digging Deeper: GENESIS 22:11, 46:2; EXODUS 3:4

Fri 18

"To the thirsty I will give water...."
—REVELATION 21:6 (NRSV)

It had been a dry year in California, and the mountains were parched. I didn't realize how parched until I reached the place I intended to camp and found the creek dry. I was miles from the nearest road, and my water bottles were empty.

I made camp but felt alone, exposed. *Will I find water tomorrow?* It was a long way back to the trailhead. In the wilderness, small mistakes can quickly compound.

I lay in the tent, unable to sleep, reading passages from *Mere Christianity*. The words said something about God being unshakably good. I wanted to believe it. But at that moment, the world God had made felt like a harsh, indifferent place.

At the first sign of light, I ate a quick breakfast and hurried back to the trail. It switchbacked up toward a pass, leveled out, and I was in a meadow. I saw pools in the creek bed. There was water here. Lots of it.

An intense feeling of God's presence enveloped me. It was piercing joy and solemnity and heaviness and lightness all at once. I remembered the words from my book: *God is unshakably good.*

I laughed out loud, tears in my eyes. There, in the green meadow surrounded by granite peaks reflected in pools of water, I felt the goodness of God in this place.

Lord, I will turn to You for everything I need.
—JIM HINCH

Digging Deeper: JOB 5:10, PSALM 65:9

Sat 19   *Of what importance is the human race, that you should notice them? . . .*
—PSALM 8:4 (NET)

After my dad's cancer diagnosis, I visited him several times. We mostly sat at the family room game table, he with his daily crossword and I with my Sudoku. We didn't talk much. Whenever we did, he always ended up asking, "What's the point?" His question resonated ominously in my mind.

After his death, a friend reported the recurrence of an old cancer, treatable but incurable. Gloria is the spiritual opposite of my dad. She's also pain-free, proclaiming with characteristic buoyancy: "I feel great! If I hadn't been told something was wrong, I wouldn't know."

Still, when I asked how to pray for her, she said, "Mornings are hard. As I'm getting dressed, I think, *What's the point?* I need help with that."

Again that horrible question ricocheted inside me. I prayed, as I had for my dad, for God to remove Gloria's despair. This time, though, I needed an answer.

My husband's answer was that only the next world mattered, and I tried to believe it. But *this* world mattered, didn't it? Certainly, to Gloria and my dad it did. And even Jesus begged that the cup be taken from Him.

Somehow, pondering that mystery—Jesus's reluctance to die—convinced me. I wanted to call up Gloria and say, "*We're* the point for everyone we know. And, for me, *you're* the point."

It's in our daily interaction with one another that we encounter You, God. Help us all, seekers among seekers, to find You. —PATTY KIRK

Digging Deeper: MATTHEW 18:20, JOHN 3:21

Sun 20

What, then, shall we say in response to these things? If God is for us, who can be against us? —ROMANS 8:31 (NIV)

My husband took a sip of coffee and turned away from the sermon he was watching on his laptop. "Hey, honey, do you know what command is used the most in the Bible?"

"'Love'?"

"That's what I thought too. But nope."

"'Obedience'?"

He shook his head. "'Fear not.'"

"Really?" I had no idea. But how very apt, especially since a God-sized opportunity had landed in my lap, one that was every bit as terrifying as it was amazing.

I had the chance to travel to Kinshasa, the capital city of the Democratic Republic of Congo. We're adopting from the DRC and had recently accepted a referral for a young child there. I had the opportunity to go, yet fear was holding me back.

I was afraid of stretching ourselves financially. I was afraid that I'd take this precious child in my arms and fall that much more in love, only to discover that we couldn't adopt her. I was afraid for my safety, since there were warnings advising against traveling to Kinshasa. Yet I knew this opportunity was straight from God, that He had been calling me to do something with all I had learned regarding the plight of the orphan.

So who would I listen to: God's voice or my fear?

Thank You, Jesus, that when You are on our side, we have nothing to fear! —KATIE GANSHERT

Digging Deeper: PSALM 27:1, PROVERBS 1:33, 2 TIMOTHY 1:7

Mon 21

For God hath not given us the spirit of fear; but of power, and of love, and of a sound mind.
—2 TIMOTHY 1:7 (KJV)

Hi, Carol!" a woman greeted me enthusiastically in a crowd emerging from a movie theater.

I looked at her and drew a blank. I knew her; I recognized her daughter. But I felt a panic that paralyzed my brain because I had forgotten their names. I was unable to come up with small talk that might cover up my memory lapse, so I just looked at them, speechless.

I was with a friend, which made the moment even more awkward because I would have introduced her if I had remembered their names. Thankfully, my friend sensed my dilemma and introduced herself. "No big deal," she assured me as we walked away.

"But it feels like a big embarrassing deal to me," I confessed.

Early the next morning I sat at my computer, going through e-mails, and the memory of that moment came back to me. Embarrassments have a way of doing that: the more I think about them, the larger they grow until they consume my thoughts.

I was about to delete a Scripture verse that pops up on my screen every day, but I saw the word *consumed* and paused to read it: "Because of the Lord's great love, we are not consumed, for his compassions never fail. They are new every morning" (Lamentations 3:22–23, NIV).

The words made me smile. They seemed a personal, timely reminder from God, Who knows that embarrassments can consume me, making me forget that His great love and compassions wipe my slate clean every day.

Lord, thank You for helping me recall what to forget and what to remember, like Your faithful love and compassion. —CAROL KUYKENDALL

Digging Deeper: PHILIPPIANS 3:13–14

Tue 22

Your love, Lord, reaches to the heavens, your faithfulness to the skies. —PSALM 36:5 (NIV)

One of my oldest friends comes from a Jewish background. "*Culturally* Jewish," Patty is quick to emphasize. Her mother was a sociology professor and didn't talk much about faith. Her father, a brilliant surgeon, openly doubted God. "To my dad, the Holocaust was very real. It happened to his family. He struggled with that. He was a proud Jew, but he could not forgive God for what happened to the Jewish people at the hands of the Nazis."

Still, I remember Dr. W. as a man who took great pains to explain Jewish faith traditions to me. I learned what a dreidel is, a menorah, and the meaning of Purim. I picked up a little Yiddish, too, and sometimes wondered, *If his faith means so little, why does he kvetch about it so much?*

As I grew older, though, I saw where inexplicable tragedy and seemingly unbearable loss could drive a wedge between man and God. In fact, I'd struggled with it myself.

Dr. W. died a few years back. When I finally got a chance to talk to Patty, she said, "You know something? Dad was different toward the end. He softened. He didn't seem so mad at God anymore." As it turned out, he started going to temple and observing the High Holy Days. "I think that he simply knew he couldn't die with this burden on his heart."

Patty said her father couldn't forgive God. I think it was more that it took him many years to let himself trust God again. And when he was ready, I know God was too.

Lord Father, sometimes the most terrible events drive a wedge between You and us that can only be overcome with great struggle. Yet the reward is there. You are always ready to embrace and be embraced.
—EDWARD GRINNAN

Digging Deeper: PSALMS 36:7, 69:13

Wed 23

Grant, then, Your servant an understanding mind. . . .
—1 KINGS 3:9 (JPS)

The clerk at the Department of Licensing took our application for a temporary disabled person's parking hangtag and said, "You get six months on a temporary. Then you'll have to renew it."

"Six months will be enough," I said in a firm voice. "I'm sure my husband will be back to normal by then." Keith didn't say anything to contradict me, and we left with the temporary tag.

But when we reached the five-month mark, he was still unable to walk even a short distance without supplemental oxygen. Sometimes simply sitting taxed his lungs. "I think we'll need to renew the tag," I said.

Keith sighed. "Perhaps I just ought to get a permanent plate."

"No!" I rejected the idea instantly. "You're going to get well." I thought he had to get better; it was just a matter of time. But slowly, it dawned on me that Keith knew what was happening in his body more accurately than I did. And my demanding that he improve was making him feel worse. So when the time came to go back to the Department of Licensing, I told him that I thought he was right and we should apply for a permanent plate.

"Some things are just harder for me to get used to than others," I said apologetically.

Keith grinned at me. "I know," he said. "I have trouble with the new normal too."

Lord, please help me to distinguish between what
I can fight against with hope of success and what
I need to accept without arguing and despair.
—RHODA BLECKER

Digging Deeper: JEREMIAH 29:11

I SURRENDER ALL

Thu 24 *Rejoice with an indescribable and*
glorious joy. —I PETER 1:8 (NRSV)

A NEW PEACE

Are you sure you want to do this?" I asked my daughter Katie. "It's not too late to back out. I bet Laura would understand."

"I'm positive, Mom."

We walked toward the pregnancy resource center together, where my cousin Laura works. When I told Katie about my volunteering, she said she wanted to help too. We'd spent weeks training and were prepared, but my heart ached for my daughter. She'd been dealing with infertility issues. Would she be able to handle working in this atmosphere?

On our first night, Katie and I accompanied new parents to the baby boutique to pick out clothes. As I opened the door, the powdery scent of diapers met me. Surely, Katie noticed the sweet smell too. *Lord, can she handle this?*

The new father gently cradled his infant daughter while the mother *ooh*ed and *aah*ed at the rows of tiny outfits and shoes. "Your baby's beautiful," Katie said. And she was too—dark hair and eyes just like Katie's.

Katie touched the baby's head. "Let's find something really pretty for you," she suggested.

Later, I asked, "Are you okay?"

"It's harder than I thought," Katie responded, "but something amazing happens when I see mamas with their babies. I forget about myself and what I want. All I feel is joy for them."

Father, surrender brings an unexplainable peace all its own. —JULIE GARMON

Digging Deeper: ISAIAH 26:3, PHILIPPIANS 4:7

Fri 25

To every thing there is a season, and a time to every purpose under the heaven: A time to be born, and a time to die...
—ECCLESIASTES 3:1–2 (KJV)

It was picture day at my daughter's preschool, but Jada wasn't as excited about it as I was. She hated the skirt I'd picked out because she wouldn't be able to do cartwheels in it. She didn't like the wavy pigtails I gave her either, worried that her friends would laugh at her hairstyle; she wanted braids instead.

Why is my daughter concerned about her hair at age four? I worried. *What will age fourteen bring?*

We finally compromised on the outfit, adding leggings beneath Jada's skirt. I won out on the hairstyle, insisting that her classmates would love her pigtails.

I drove Jada to school, feeling frazzled and frustrated. "Have fun today," I said, bending down to kiss her cheek. As she walked away, my eyes suddenly welled with tears. My baby girl was growing up so quickly. It felt like just yesterday I'd held her in my arms and caressed her nearly bald head. Where had that mass of red hair come from? And when did she develop an opinion on everything?

Jada was growing up, letting go. *It's time for me to let go too*, I thought, wiping away my tears.

Change is hard. But I was learning that instead of lamenting no longer being home full-time with my daughter, it was time to be grateful for the opportunity—and the freedom—to use my gifts elsewhere.

Lord, help me to embrace this season of life and make the most of the time You give me.
—CARLA HENDRICKS

Digging Deeper: PSALM 139:13–16, DANIEL 2:20–21

Sat 26

"The spirit of the Lord is on me, because he has anointed me to proclaim the good news...."
—LUKE 4:18 (NIV)

This year marks my fortieth anniversary of preaching the Gospel. It was the fall of 1975. I was a member of the youth ministry of my home church on the Lower East Side of New York City. Every Saturday at noon, the group met for prayer before heading out to the streets to hand out literature, visit the sick, and hold what we called a "street service."

On the day that my life changed forever, Sylvia, our fearless leader and a single mom, looked at me, pointed, and said, "Pablo, you are going to preach today. Get ready."

My heart started pounding, my hands got sweaty, and the butterflies in my stomach kicked in. I thought to myself, *What am I going say? What if one of my friends sees me? What if nothing comes out of my mouth?* I had never done public speaking, never mind preaching.

We walked out of the church, headed east, and positioned ourselves on the corner of East Broadway and Clinton Street. A light rain was coming down. We sang a few songs without music until it was my turn. We had no microphone. I opened my mouth, and words began to come out. I raised my voice as loud as possible, so the people there could hear me.

The longer I spoke, the more empowered and confident I felt. It was an incredible feeling, unlike anything else I had ever experienced. When I finished, my heart was filled with great joy.

There is a proverb that says, "A journey of a thousand miles begins with one step." That first step changed the rest of my life.

Lord, thank You for the opportunity to serve You with my gifts and talents. —PABLO DIAZ

Digging Deeper: JEREMIAH 1:4–8, 1 CORINTHIANS 12:4–6

Sun 27

"For as the lifetime of a tree, so will be the days of My people. . . ."
—ISAIAH 65:22 (NAS)

Her ninetieth birthday celebration was just days away. Fun-size Baby Ruth bars were ready for the tables. My mother's name was Ruth, and a single Baby Ruth candy bar had been her fifth birthday gift in 1927. Now I sat next to her on a couch, listening to her memories, so I could write a little something for the party:

"The Depression years were rough . . . I sold my mother's cookies door-to-door; I was about ten. Once I lost a quarter in the snow and cried all the way home—that was a lot to lose back then. I still remember my library card number . . . I loved roller-skating . . . my mother never understood why I wanted to read so much. . . ."

I loved listening to Mom's recollections, mesmerized by all she'd lived through, all she'd done, accomplished, everything about who she is. I could hear in her stories, more than anything else, that she'd lived a life of purpose, a life of determination.

I knew the answer before I asked—about her being widowed, about surviving cancer—"How'd you do it, Mom?"

Her response, invariably: "I always had the Lord."

This day, Lord, what will I do with it? Let me be intentional, building a legacy that honors those who came before me. —CAROL KNAPP

Digging Deeper: GENESIS 25:8, PSALM 90:12, HEBREWS 12:1–2

Mon 28

Be not quick in your spirit to become angry, for anger lodges in the heart of fools.
—ECCLESIASTES 7:9 (ESV)

One of the roughest periods of my life was the year I spent unemployed after college graduation. If I had to choose one emotion to best sum up that time, it wouldn't be frustration, sadness, or worry; it would be anger. I went to college with the expectation that I not only would achieve personal growth, but I also would be set for the rest of my life. Falling short of those goals fueled my bitterness.

"Keep applying. That's all you can really do," my family and friends told me.

The best advice came, as usual, from my mother. "God will give you an opportunity soon that will make all of this worth it," she said.

Eventually, I landed a job at a real-estate company. It wasn't my dream job, but it paid the bills, kept me sane, and, best of all, gave me the experience I needed to get the position I have now at my alma mater, New York University.

Once the anger had subsided, it was easier to view the experience from another perspective. I was able to see how much support I can rely on from my family and friends. And, most important, I achieved a level of personal growth after college that I hadn't attained during those four years as an undergrad.

Life isn't always smooth or fair. But I'm learning not to allow anger to reign when life's difficult, and to trust that God is preparing amazing opportunities for me.

Thank You, Lord, for loving me when I'm foolishly
blind to the opportunities You lay at my feet.
Be patient with me. —ERIK CRUZ

Digging Deeper: PROVERBS 12:15, COLOSSIANS 3:15

Tue 29

If we confess our sins, he is faithful and just and will forgive us our sins and purify us from all unrighteousness. —1 JOHN 1:9 (NIV)

Ever since boyhood, I've taken my showers at night. Part of the reason is my heritage; it's typically a Chinese practice to bathe before bedtime. Part of the reason is also practical; growing up, when I sometimes spent summers in hot and humid Hong Kong, I'd never want to get into bed without washing away the dirt of the day, the accumulated grime.

Recently, as I went through my preslumber ritual, it occurred to me that I should be as vigilant each evening about spiritual cleansing. Yes, I always say my bedtime prayers, but often they're just the adult version of that childhood ditty: "Now I lay me down to sleep. I pray the Lord my soul to keep. . . . "

That's fine, of course, if it's prayed wholeheartedly. But what I want and need most nights is a little time spent in confession and thanksgiving.

Having taken that spiritual bath—having acknowledged what I've done wrong and what, in God's grace and mercy, He's done to make it right—gives new and deeper meaning to the phrase "sleeping easier."

God, grant me the wisdom to come to You daily, seeking forgiveness for what I've done wrong and offering thanksgiving for Your grace and guidance for the days to come. —JEFF CHU

Digging Deeper: ROMANS 8:26–30, HEBREWS 10:19–23

September

Wed 30

"The Lord will give her twice as many blessings...."
—ISAIAH 40:2 (TLB)

My daughter dealt with a multitude of serious issues after the abrupt end of her marriage. Along with the pain of a shattered family, Rebecca had to relocate and give up her job of ten years. She found an affordable apartment, a good school for the children, and a supportive church family, but the only openings in her field were part-time with no health insurance. As savings dwindled, discouragement grew.

Distance made it impossible for me to visit Rebecca as often as I'd have liked, but we kept in touch through texting and phone calls. Then one day I walked past the greeting card rack at a discount store and a shiny card caught my eye. On the front was an angel set amid randomly shaped blocks of magenta, orange, and gold. "There's an angel watching over you," the message read. I bought it and sent it to Rebecca with love and prayers.

"You won't believe this!" Rebecca called three days later. "I received a beautiful angel card from you and an identical one from Aunt Amanda! I've been praying for a word from God, and I received double what I asked for."

We knew then and there that God would provide just the right job for Rebecca.

Amazing God, thank You for the miracle of angel cards, answered prayers, just-right jobs, and Your ever-wondrous love and care. —PENNEY SCHWAB

Digging Deeper: PSALM 23:6, MATTHEW 7:7–11

DAILY JOYS

1 _____

2 _____

3 _____

4 _____

5 _____

6 _____

7 _____

8 _____

9 _____

10 _____

11 _____

12 _____

13 _____

September

14 _____

15 _____

16 _____

17 _____

18 _____

19 _____

20 _____

21 _____

22 _____

23 _____

24 _____

25 _____

26 _____

27 _____

28 _____

29 _____

30 _____

OCTOBER

But the fruit of the Spirit is love, joy, peace,
patience, kindness, goodness,
faithfulness, gentleness, self-control;
against such things there is no law.

—GALATIANS 5:22–23 (ESV)

GOD OF JOYFUL SURPRISES

Thu 1

"You shall go out in joy...."
—ISAIAH 55:12 (RSV)

SHARING THE JOY

When a patch of blue sky broke through after five days of nonstop rain, my husband and I got in the car and headed for Nantasket Beach, Massachusetts. How good it felt to stretch our legs after so long indoors! Gulls shrieked; waves thundered; we walked on and on.

Only when the first raindrops began to fall did we notice that the hint of blue sky had vanished. As the rain began in earnest, we dashed to a shelter by the road and huddled there, drenched and shivering. We hadn't brought umbrellas, and the car was probably a mile away.

"Would you like a ride to your car?"

Over the booming surf, the words were so faint I thought I'd imagined them. But an old brown car had pulled up to the shelter. "Do you need a ride?" repeated the woman at the wheel.

Our rescuer's name was Stella, and she often picked up stranded walkers. "You'd be surprised how many people go farther than they plan to. I'm sorry to have no towels for you. The parents never bring them back."

Parents?

"They bring their kids here to play in the sand, but what child can stay out of the water? I buy a stack of towels every spring."

Stella had grown up in the Midwest, she explained, always longing to live near the sea. "Now I do, and the joy of it never fades!"

And the car lifts, the towels? Helping people is her response?

"Of course," Stella went on, "you can't feel joy and not share."

> *God of joyful surprises, remind me today that*
> *sharing is simply the overflow of joy.*
> —ELIZABETH SHERRILL

Digging Deeper: PHILIPPIANS 2:1–3

Fri 2   *"The road the righteous travel is like the*
sunrise, getting brighter and brighter
until the daylight has come."
—PROVERBS 4:18 (GNT)

I'm standing by the dining room table, where my wife is laying out a jigsaw puzzle. "You know, hon, life is like a jigsaw puzzle," I philosophize. "Only you don't have the box lid to show you what it's supposed to look like."

Sharon rolls her eyes. "Well, it does seem rather overwhelming at first. A thousand pieces! Where do I start?"

As I go about my business, I pause from time to time to watch her work. She is very organized, laying out all of the edge pieces first, then sorting pieces into piles according to color. "I'm in no hurry," she admits. "A puzzle is not a speed race. It's something to savor, to enjoy."

I usually snitch one piece and hide it, so I can have the joy of putting the last piece in place. "You bum, you stole a piece, didn't you? Give it to me please. Now!" At last she is done and she walks on air for a couple of days, stopping to admire her work from time to time.

At bedtime I think, *Life really is like a jigsaw puzzle. It becomes clearer as time goes on. One piece added to another adds more light, until finally one's life is fully developed.* Then I reflect on Sharon's words: *It's not a speed race; it's something to enjoy.*

I tend to live in terms of achievement, but from Sharon I am learning to pay more attention to the process: to enjoy a friendly conversation, to linger over a good meal, to drive a little slower and enjoy the scenery. Life will be over all too soon, and I don't want to miss anything along the way.

I thank You, God, for giving life to me one small piece at a time. —DANIEL SCHANTZ

Digging Deeper: DEUTERONOMY 33:25,
2 CORINTHIANS 4:6

Sat 3

"Do not judge, and you will not be judged. Do not condemn, and you will not be condemned. Forgive, and you will be forgiven." —LUKE 6:37 (NIV)

Hoping to experience the benefits of decreased stress, improved flexibility, and association with a trendy fitness fad, I developed a mild addiction to yoga. Recently, I was in class doing my deep breathing and relaxing when I noticed a woman on a mat behind me writing text messages on her phone. I was appalled. Didn't she realize that yoga was about unplugging and being in the moment? I found myself stealing glances at her anytime my head was in an upside-down pose. Several times I saw her pick up the phone again to check for new messages.

Then her behavior got worse. She pulled a can of soda out of her gym bag and started drinking it! I thought, *Okay, not only are you not getting the relaxation of turning off your phone, you're also drinking a less-than-healthy beverage that is probably counteracting any benefits you would otherwise receive from the workout.*

After class, I took one more glance at her, so I could have another opportunity to judge her and congratulate myself on having far superior habits. This time I got a better look at her handheld device and, to my great shock, it was not a phone but a blood-sugar monitor. She was diabetic, I realized, and had been checking her blood sugar during class and needed the soda to keep her levels stable.

As I walked out, I made a note: *Who am I to judge?*

Lord, allow my default offering to strangers to be grace, not judgment. —JOSHUA SUNDQUIST

Digging Deeper: MATTHEW 7:1–5

Sun 4

He did not say anything to them without using a parable....
—MARK 4:34 (NIV)

A couple I'm friends with reported that their son has autism. I have little knowledge of what autism might entail. I couldn't connect the word with much more than the name Ethan and the happy-faced toddler I saw at church. As far as I knew, autism had no medical cure and, as such, nothing to pray for short of a miracle. And miracles, for me, are hard to pray for.

This couple, colleagues of mine, started posting accounts of their son's struggles and progress on the Internet. Ethan was leading his family members by the hand when he wanted to go somewhere, throwing tantrums but recovering, learning to ride a Big Wheel, singing "Twinkle, Twinkle, Little Star." They also posted glimpses of their fears about Ethan's future. Their main prayer was that someday they would be able to converse with their son.

Invariably, I teared up when I read these posts. Through their accounts, I was also learning more about autism.

One day, Ethan's mom explained to me that autism is not always something a child is born with but seemingly acquired in some cases. She told of a child who became autistic after learning to talk, whose last words to her parents were "I can't talk!" When I reported this story to my husband, Kris, who'd had a debilitating speech defect as a child that rendered him impossible to understand, he cried. And soon, we were praying for Ethan and his family every night at dinner.

Stories, I learned, engage the Spirit and fertilize our faith.

Holy Spirit, help us to tell our stories well and,
more important, to hear the stories of others.
—Patty Kirk

Digging Deeper: Mark 4:10–20, 14:3–9

I SURRENDER ALL

Mon 5

So Naaman went down to the Jordan River and dipped himself seven times, as the man of God had instructed him.... —2 KINGS 5:14 (NLT)

RESTING IN GOD

I called my Al-Anon sponsor to ask for advice. She lives in another state but knows me like we're next-door neighbors. "So what do I do? Part of me thinks I should . . ."

"Oh, Julie, you're stuck in stinkin' thinkin'. Aren't you?"

My sponsor was right.

"I've been there plenty of times," she said gently. "Remember, we have to surrender daily, moment by moment. When we hang up, stand beside your sofa. Then fall over onto it, like dead weight. You know the sofa won't drop you. God won't either. Lie there for a few minutes. While you're still and quiet, let go and let God. Whatever decision you make, it'll work out just fine."

But standing beside my sofa, my friend's idea seemed far-fetched. How could collapsing onto it do any good?

Then I considered how well my sponsor knows me and how much alike we are. We laugh together and remind each other of the amazing power of surrender, though at times the concept sounds unlikely.

"Okay, God. I know this looks silly..." I lined up alongside the sofa and dropped over. Lying there, it seemed as though I rested fully in God's strong and mighty hands.

Lord, when I start stressin' and obsessin', I need to do what sounds foolish—and surrender my troubles before they get too heavy. — JULIE GARMON

Digging Deeper: PSALM 55:22, ISAIAH 45:1–7

Tue 6

I lift up my eyes to the mountains—where does my help come from? My help comes from the Lord, the Maker of heaven and earth.
—PSALM 121:1–2 (NIV)

My two-year-old's voice held an edge of desperation as I heard him whine through the monitor: "Mama, hold me out!"

I hopped out of bed and ran to throw on some sweats and brush my teeth before I "held him out" of his crib for breakfast. But Will wasn't feeling patient.

Next he tried Cameron. "Daddy? *Daddy?* Hold me out!" But Daddy was already at work. Then his siblings who were fast asleep: "JoJo? Kate? Hold me out!" Finally, he called in the big guns: *"Oma"* and *"Opa."* When that didn't work, he started to cry. "Mama, *peeze! Jus* hold me out!"

I plucked him out of his crib, and he immediately snuggled close to my chest, staring at me with those big, brown I-need-you eyes.

So often when I seek comfort and help, I may start by saying, "Jesus, help me!" But when His response isn't immediate, I turn to others. I go through the list: my husband, my mom, my dad, my sister, my friends, my neighbors. And only after I've run the gamut, begging and pleading for help, do I come back to the One Who can really comfort me.

"Jesus, help me out!" And then I wait for the only One Who can truly help.

Lord, help me to turn my eyes toward You when I need help and to trust You to respond in the way that I need it most. —ERIN MACPHERSON

Digging Deeper: PSALMS 22:19, 71:12

Wed 7   *Set their hopes on... God who richly provides us with everything for our enjoyment.*
—1 TIMOTHY 6:17 (NRSV)

Frances and I sat on the sofa. She was in her pajamas, hair wet from a bath. Outside, it rained.

Frances held a book. *"It is too hot to play,"* she read slowly. *"Can I have a glass of* . . . what's that word, Daddy?"

"Lemonade." I fought to keep the excitement out of my voice. For years I had dreamed of the moment Frances would begin to read. That moment had arrived.

"I am still too hot," Frances read. The book was *Amanda Pig and the Really Hot Day* by Jean Van Leeuwen and Ann Schweninger. We'd read it countless times when Frances was younger. A measure of sadness leavened my excitement. Once, Frances had insisted that if she learned to read, "You'll stop reading to me." Now the tables were turning. The day would come when cozy moments like these would end.

"What's that word, Daddy?"

"Breeze."

"Amanda felt a cool breeze. 'Ah,' she said. 'Now I am not hot at all.'"

"Okay, Daddy, now you read to me." Frances handed me a book of fairy tales. She nestled closer, eyes shining. I put my arm around her and marveled at the miraculous workings of her mind. *Reading,* I thought, *is a gift.* And now Frances had that gift.

"Once upon a time," I began, savoring the sound of rain pattering on the window. One day Frances would read this book by herself. For now, we would enjoy it together.

You give all gifts at their right time, Lord. Help me to remember that. —JIM HINCH

Digging Deeper: LUKE 11:15

Thu 8

Rejoice always, pray continually, give thanks in all circumstances....
—1 THESSALONIANS 5:16–18 (NIV)

"We have everything we need," she told me. "We don't need more stuff!"

The cash-strapped young couple kept the wedding as simple as they could but still had no funds left for a honeymoon. Someone had the answer to their dilemma: a honeymoon registry!

They wanted to go to Italy, so the registry broke down everything for them into gifts, from the costly to the most economical: $125 for a night in a hotel in Florence; $20 for an admission ticket to the Colosseum. Family and friends were delighted to help fulfill their dream.

Their story reminded me of the often quoted "when two or three are gathered together" (Matthew 18:20). Jesus was telling us that there is power in community.

So imagine a *prayer* registry. At that thought I checked out the Internet and found many such sites, including Guideposts' own OurPrayer.org. Every generation finds new ways to speak to God.

To You, God, Who hears our prayers, we give thanks for the family and friends in our lives, their affection, and Your blessings. —BRIGITTE WEEKS

Digging Deeper: PSALM 55:22

Fri 9

And the God of all grace, who called you to his eternal glory in Christ, after you have suffered a little while, will himself restore you and make you strong, firm, and steadfast. —1 PETER 5:10 (NIV)

We were having a family work day, and all five sons were set loose on the lawn with rakes, shears, spades, and two wheelbarrows. Logan offered to prune the bush. It was sprawling and out of shape, creating a hazard when we backed down the drive.

"I'll Google *pruning* first," he said, "so I know just how to do it."

"Sold!" I said and handed him the electric clippers.

An hour later my husband, Lonny, poked his head through the kitchen door. "Shawnelle," he called, "better come out. Logan's trimming the bush."

"I know," I said, but what I saw made my breath come fast. "The bush," I said, "it's ruined."

Logan stood at the end of the drive, saw buzzing and branches falling. The bush was now a naked claw jutting from the ground. Lush green growth pooled around his ankles and the bush's bony base. For the rest of the summer, each time I saw what remained of the bush, I winced and looked away.

Now it's fall. New green is beginning to appear on the branches. It's evident that the bush will be stronger and healthier in the end.

It's sort of like how the past few months have been for our family. We've had some tough times, a hardship with one of our sons. Lonny and I often felt stripped down, sheared, bare, and exposed. After a long season, however, our family is healing. We're sprouting new growth. In the end, we'll be stronger, lovelier, for it all.

Lord, thank You for healing us, making us stronger when life has broken us down. Amen.
—SHAWNELLE ELIASEN

Digging Deeper: PSALMS 34:6, 116:8, 147:3

Sat 10

Sing to the Lord with grateful praise.... —PSALM 147:7 (NIV)

My husband and I find ourselves in a hotel that misses criteria by a couple of stars. "It's convenient and the price is good," David points out. But the next morning I'm congested and red-eyed, and David says he feels like he's slept on a bed of rocks.

To be sure, no one's going to be bringing us coffee, so as David showers, I set out for salvation. I dash down the stairs, thinking, *Coffee!*—and almost collide with a man pushing a housekeeping cart.

"Good morning," he says. "And isn't it a fine day?" His enthusiasm startles me. There's something in his eyes. Contentment? In his warmth, my bad attitude melts like spring snow.

I squeeze out my first smile of the day. "Do you know where I might find coffee?"

"Oh yes, missy, there's a machine just down the hall."

As he points, I say, "Oh, great, I didn't bring money...."

"Don't you worry," he says, digging in his pocket. "I always carry a little extra to help out folks."

Back in the room with two cups of tepid, watery coffee, I dig through my purse and come up with some cash to leave on a pillow. I scribble out a note of thanks, determined to put an even bigger smile on the man's face when he comes to clean our room.

Later, David and I sit in a trendy restaurant as the waiter serves us a special coffee blend, but I find this cup not half as good as my first one of the day.

Father, I see You in the eyes of a man pushing a cart, content. Let me exude that as well to those I meet along the way. —PAM KIDD

Digging Deeper: PROVERBS 14:14, 16:8

Sun 11

"But a Samaritan, who was on a journey, came upon him . . . and bandaged up his wounds. . . ."
—LUKE 10:33–34 (NAS)

We were late for a wedding. It was drizzling, and I was pushing the speed limit. I noticed a distant car in front of me make a sudden U-turn across the median. As the car drew closer, the driver veered into the median again and lurched to a halt. A woman jumped from the car. Holding up her skirt in one hand, she ran toward us, frantically motioning us to stop. Stomping the brakes, we skidded to a halt.

As I gaped at this wild-eyed woman, my wife glimpsed the real problem thirty feet in front of us. Two Canada geese were escorting their six goslings across the highway. Each mate was on either end of the line like guardian battleships, urging the little birds to hurry. If this woman had not flagged us down, we would have never seen this small feathered family until it was too late. A tragedy had been prevented by someone who took the time and trouble to care.

As the geese waddled off the highway toward a farmer's pond, I rolled down my window and gushed a profoundly felt thank-you.

Life is frequently changed for the better when caution is discarded in order to care for others, and God knows, He'll take all the help He can get.

Father, whether it be geese, goslings, or people, help me to slow down today and help others. Amen.
—SCOTT WALKER

Digging Deeper: GALATIANS 6:2–10

Mon 12

We have not stopped praying for you. We continually ask God to fill you with the knowledge of his will....
—COLOSSIANS 1:9 (NIV)

I felt it was a major answer to prayer when our son John received a job offer with an insurance company during his final semester in college. It wasn't ideal, but with the economy as bad as it was, it seemed wise to say "yes." The day before the deadline to accept the offer, John phoned me saying, "I keep wondering if maybe I went to more interviews, I might find a job that's a better fit for me."

I shook my head. *Just when you think your prayer work is over and everything is all settled, it's time to pray again.* I hung up the phone, got up from my computer, and went to pray all over again about John's decision.

I had been praying for about five minutes when the phone rang again. It was John. "I just received another offer! This one is in telecom."

"I was just praying about your decision," I said.

"Thanks for keeping up the prayers, Mom. It helps."

That second job offer changed John's thinking and encouraged him to keep looking. He went to more interviews and, in the end, accepted the fourth job offer he received, which turned out to be a great match.

As for me, I learned not to stop praying even when a solution appears on the horizon. You never know what other opportunities God might be sending your way if you pray one more time.

Dear Father, help me to keep on praying for Your guidance. Amen. —KAREN BARBER

Digging Deeper: MATTHEW 4:1–11

Tue 13

And so we know and rely on the love God has for us. . . .
—1 JOHN 4:16 (NIV)

I was walking by a colleague's work area this morning when I noticed a little magnetic sign above his desk: Jesus loves you, but I'm His favorite.

Really? Outrageous, maybe even a bit sacrilegious, but I laughed anyway. It was a funny notion, antithetical to Christianity but very human. Of course Jesus loves us all equally. And, of course, we all want to be His favorite, like children vying for parental approval. I tapped my colleague on the shoulder and said, "Everyone knows *I'm* His favorite."

My colleague just smiled, shook his head, and went back to work.

Yet this notion nagged at me; my mind kept drifting back to it throughout the day. Does Jesus have favorites? John was called "beloved," but did Jesus love him more than his brother James or the other apostles? And since John is only referred to as beloved by Jesus in the Book of John, was John himself trying to claim the mantle of Jesus's favorite? Do we all have this problem of wanting to be the one Christ dotes on? Would any good Christian want Jesus to love him or her more than anyone else?

Yes, I decided. In a way, at least. I believe that Christ loves every one of us, even those who do not know Him, as if we are each in fact His favorite. This is the nature of divine love—infinite, limitless, ineffable. In Ephesians, it says that we may not fully understand the breadth and depth of Christ's love. That includes its simultaneity: He loves all of us equally and infinitely. We are each His favorite.

Perhaps the reward of heaven is that we will finally be able to love Jesus the way He loves us, not in our small, imperfect human way. We will love Jesus as He intended us to love Him. We will love eternally. Until then, though, I'm happy to be Jesus's favorite.

Jesus, Your love for us exceeds all human understanding. It is like a light that shines in all directions and is brightest everywhere at once and never fades.
—EDWARD GRINNAN

Digging Deeper: EPHESIANS 3:17–21, 1 JOHN 4:7–8

Wed 14

"Watch out! Don't do your good deeds publicly, to be admired by others, for you will lose the reward from your Father in heaven."
—MATTHEW 6:1 (NLT)

My husband heard the buzzing of my phone and didn't even have to ask who it was. This person had been calling and texting almost nonstop. It was someone who was extraneedy, somebody God had placed in my life to serve.

I was fine with this, as long as people knew just how much I was helping her and understood how much time and energy I was expending to do so.

Why did I need others to know? Because I wanted to be acknowledged and appreciated and, yes, even admired for all of the work I was putting in. I didn't want it to go unnoticed.

But while praying and reading the Bible one morning, I came across Matthew 6:1, which stopped me in my tracks. In this passage, Jesus tells us that when we give of our time and gifts in obscurity, not seeking the approval of others, God sees and rewards us.

After reading that verse, I had to ask myself: Whose reward was I chasing after? The temporary, fickle praise of others or the lasting praise and eternal reward that comes from God? Did I truly believe that God's reward is better?

Lord Jesus, You see everything done in secret. Let me not chase after the consolation prizes of others when You have something so much richer for me.
—KATIE GANSHERT

Digging Deeper: ISAIAH 49:4, LUKE 12:2–3

Thu 15

Count it all joy, my brothers, when you meet trials of various kinds.
—JAMES 1:2 (ESV)

I was in first grade when my teacher pointed to my finger and said, "Look at that! You've got a writer's bump." At the time, I didn't understand that the bump on the tip of my finger was a callus.

I thought it had miraculously appeared to show the world I was going to be a writer.

I remember going home and proudly holding my hand up to my mom's face. "See! I'm a writer." And from then on, whenever someone asked me what I wanted to be when I grew up, I'd answer, "I'm a writer," and show them the bump to prove it.

It isn't lost on me that a weakness in my hand, a small spot on my finger that grew thick to heal itself under pressure, played such a significant role in my life by guiding me to a career that I love. But sometimes when there's a deadline at work, a blank page that can't seem to get filled, a bit of criticism that I take too much to heart, I can get frustrated and become filled with doubt. *Is this really what I'm supposed to be doing?*

And then I need only to feel my finger and remember all the other bumps in life—job changes, money worries, family concerns—that at the time seemed too difficult to manage but, in fact, have prepared me for, and guided me on, this amazing life journey.

Dear Lord, help me to remember that challenges are simply a stepping-stone to joy.
—SABRA CIANCANELLI

Digging Deeper: PSALMS 18:32–34, 23:2; JEREMIAH 29:11

Fri 16

*Jesus looked at him and said, "You are Simon son of John. You will be called Cephas" (which, when translated, is Peter). —*JOHN 1:42 (NIV)

I'd moved into my home years ago on the condition that we'd renovate it as soon as possible. Its worn carpet, faded Formica countertops, and out-of-date brass light fixtures desperately needed upgrading. My husband had owned the house before we were married. We'd agreed that keeping it was the most practical thing to do.

And now, years later, I'd finally finished the work. The new wood floors, granite countertops, rubbed bronze fixtures, and freshly painted walls were beautiful.

"After all these years, I can finally say that I love this house," I declared to a friend who'd stopped by to see the improvements. "You know," I confided to her, "I never liked this house before."

She looked at me surprised. "Really? Well, I think it's just beautiful! But then I've always loved it."

"You have?" I asked. "Even before the renovation?"

She nodded. "I've always looked at your house from the standpoint of what it could become, its potential."

She walked over and touched the new brown slate that framed the fireplace. "It's like Jesus giving Simon the name Peter, which is the Greek word for rock," she said. "In spite of all of his failures and shortcomings, Jesus looked at him and said, 'Here is a piece of rock, a stone that can be polished into something strong and beautiful.'" She turned to look at me and smiled. "Isn't that how Jesus really sees us? He sees our potential and loves who we can become."

Help me, Lord, to see the world with the potential and promise that You see.
—MELODY BONNETTE SWANG

Digging Deeper: LUKE 22:31–34

Sat 17

Let's just go ahead and be what we were made to be, without enviously or pridefully comparing ourselves with each other, or trying to be something we aren't. —ROMANS 12:6 (MSG)

Well, there's always next time," I said, smiling, trying to encourage my nine-year-old daughter, Rachel, whose soccer team had lost yet another game.

"I know," she said, smiling back. "We're going to win soon."

I was relieved that Rachel hadn't given up. Not only had her team not won a game, but they hadn't even scored a goal. They spent too much time clustered around the ball, everybody vying for a chance to kick it. When they did remember to spread out, they often lost focus, shoving the ground with their feet, looking for four-leaf clovers, or sharing secrets with their friends on the field.

When the last game of the season arrived, it looked as if the outcome would be no different than usual. They were behind, 7–0. Then, lo and behold, they scored a goal! The final score was 7–1, but Rachel was ecstatic.

"You guys lost," her sister reminded her as we walked to the car, Rachel skipping beside us. "Why are you so happy?"

Rachel grinned. "We got a goal! We won in our own special way!"

Lord, thank You for the reminder that though our successes may not seem as great as those of others, with Your grace, we are able to win in our own special way.
—KIM HENRY

Digging Deeper: PROVERBS 15:15

Sun 18

Praise the Lord. Praise God in his sanctuary; praise him in his mighty heavens. . . . praise him with timbrel and dancing, praise him with the strings and pipe.
—PSALM 150:1, 4 (NIV)

The summer after college, I went to Ghana to work for a small not-for-profit in rural villages. I learned lessons that were never part of my formal education: how to do laundry in a bucket; how to eat with only my right hand and no utensils; how a beach is used (let's just say it's a place to tread carefully and not where you'd ever want to lie down).

The biggest lesson I learned was one of perspective, and I learned it during offering at church. In the congregations I grew up in, the plate (or sometimes a velvet sack) was passed around. There was always offertory music, as if to distract from the money stuff. Nobody was supposed to see what you put in. There was something almost surreptitious in the act.

In Ghana, offering allowed worshippers to praise not just with their mouths but also with their financial resources. The jar was at the front of the small open-air church. The members danced to the front—full-body, ostentatious, whoop-and-cheer-accompanied dancing—to deposit a few coins, a few wrinkly bills.

I was, of course, a dancing disaster. Nobody cared. What struck me was how they saw this as a time to be loud and celebratory, not sober and silent. Each sang praises as the Holy Spirit led. This wasn't separate from the praise time earlier; it was an extension. These weren't offerings of obligation but of thanksgiving. These were gifts—deposited, sung, danced—given in pure joy.

Forgive me, Father, for forgetting to arm myself with Your love when I'm assaulted by negative thinking.
—JEFF CHU

Digging Deeper: PROVERBS 11:24–25,
2 CORINTHIANS 9:6–15

Mon 19

Wherefore take unto you the whole armour of God, that ye may be able to withstand in the evil day, and having done all, to stand.
—EPHESIANS 6:13 (KJV)

Now *that you're older, you never get anything accomplished anymore,* I thought angrily. *You almost never cook a good meal for your husband. Remember when you used to shop most of the day? Remember when you used to get dressed up for the evening and go out with friends? Remember when you . . .* I couldn't outrun the self-condemnation.

Pulling out of our driveway that morning, something caught my attention—something very fast. A lone deer raced through our neighbor's yard. It ran like the wind, crossing the busy road that led out of our neighborhood. Suddenly, it encountered a tall iron fence. I crept along behind it at a distance, praying it would be safe.

At the fence, unable to jump over it, the deer hesitated only a moment. Then it turned its body around and stood stock-still, as big as possible— brave, it seemed, facing whatever would come. My heart thumped loudly, joyfully, as I, an ordinary-looking woman on a seemingly ordinary day, drove past the courageous animal. But an extraordinary thing happened: my weary soul stopped running— turning around and around—and stood dressed in the full armor of God to face my menacing thoughts and reduce them to nothing.

Forgive me, Father, for forgetting that You've made adequate provisions for me. Remind me of them always. —MARION BOND WEST

Digging Deeper: ROMANS 5:2, 1 CORINTHIANS 16:13

Tue 20

[Love] *always protects, always trusts, always hopes, always perseveres.*
—1 CORINTHIANS 13:7 (NIV)

Melissa had worked in Guideposts' Outreach ministries when she became ill with cancer. Shortly after this diagnosis, my colleague Rhonda and I went to the hospital to meet with Evelyn, Melissa's mother, during Melissa's last days.

Although Evelyn was in emotional turmoil watching her only daughter die, she welcomed us with great love.

During the funeral service, I shared a story about how Melissa loved her ten-year-old son. I turned to him and said, "Jake, your mom loves you. She always bragged about your football practices." Melissa dreaded going to practices, but she endured them to watch her little boy play. She knew the importance of being there for her son.

Two years later, at an Outreach ministries event, Rhonda told me, "Melissa's mom was looking for you but had to go. She asked me to give you this card."

"Dear Pablo," Evelyn wrote, "I will always appreciate the memories of love and compassion you gave to my daughter, Missy. I will also cherish the stories you told and the kind words you gave to Jake."

The irony here was, I was the one who was appreciative. I remembered the love Evelyn had demonstrated to Rhonda and me. How, despite her great loss, Evelyn had the ability to love others. Melissa and Evelyn are inspirations to me, for the love they displayed through their actions, for the love that still lives on.

Lord, teach me to love those around me, even when life is tough. —PABLO DIAZ

Digging Deeper: 1 CORINTHIANS 13:13, 1 JOHN 4:7

October

Wed 21

But I trusted in your steadfast love; my heart shall rejoice in your salvation. —PSALM 13:5 (NRSV)

"You better come look at this." My husband Charlie's voice was tense.

The river on which we live flooded, driving waves into our parking lot. The storm turned docks into tinder. We'd already moved our car to higher ground, but it was a frightening sight. On the top floor, we were safe from flooding, but if the water got into the building, the furnace and utilities would stop functioning. Many people evacuated, but we heard that the city's storm shelter had a broken generator so we stayed.

It was the first crisis in our life together where I saw Charlie anxious and I felt calm.

I had been praying differently, in what I call "Lynn Holm style." Lynn is the only person I know who completely lives his faith. He's been a missionary in Africa, a pastor, a father, a husband, and an all-around adventurer in the Lord. He is never afraid because he is never without God's presence. He once told me that when winter storms threaten his home and life in Minnesota, he simply tells God that it is His home to do with as He will. This kind of prayer initially seemed impossible.

But I realized that I didn't have to be Lynn in order to pray like him. And so I took Charlie's hand.

"Dear Lord, please watch over this, Your home, which You've given us to live in. Please keep us, Your children, safe, protected, and warm. Amen."

Father, let me pray with confidence in Your plan.
—MARCI ALBORGHETTI

Digging Deeper: ISAIAH 25:9

Thu 22   *"I have grown old and advanced in years."*—JOSHUA 23:2 (JPS)

I would rather grow old with you than with anyone else I've ever known." That was a line in a short story I wrote years ago, where a young man asks a young woman to marry him.

I thought of it because this has been a very tough year for my husband, what with a stroke, chronic obstructive pulmonary disease, skin cancer, and a possible blood clot in his leg. "I started out this year about seventeen years old in my head," Keith said to me after the stroke, "and now I guess I've aged to about forty." And when the COPD got exacerbated and the medications that were supposed to work a miracle just plain didn't, he sighed and reflected, "This is the year I got old."

"I'm sorry you didn't get to spend more time being forty," I told him. "I remember it as a good age."

"I guess any age this side of the fence is a good age," he said.

Keith couldn't do things he used to, like grocery shopping or lifting the sacks of cat litter or the bags of birdseed. It was all left to me and he hated that, but I didn't mind taking on the chores. I was just doing what had to be done in the marriage. So every time he said regretfully, "So much is falling on you," I would say, "You'd do the same thing for me."

We've slowly gotten used to how things are now, and it was only after we reached some kind of equilibrium that I realized what I'd written all those years ago had been a basic truth of my life. I married the man that I would rather grow old with than anyone else I've ever known.

Thank You, God, for Your great gift: the right husband. —RHODA BLECKER

Digging Deeper: RUTH 1:17, SONG OF SOLOMON 2:16

Fri 23

O come, let us sing to the Lord; let us make a joyful noise to the rock of our salvation! —PSALM 95:1 (NRSV)

We were at an orphanage in a village in Kenya. We had come with friends from the United States who had raised money through their church to dig a well here.

We sat at a long table in a spare concrete-block room with a group of village dignitaries, waiting for lunch. Their English was good, but after twenty minutes most of the nice-to-meet-you conversation topics were exhausted. Lunch was still heating up in the kitchen.

"Rick," the head of our group turned to me, "why don't you lead us in a song?"

What song will everybody know? "Amazing Grace" was a safe bet. Everyone picked up the tune, some singing in Swahili, some in English.

"Let's do 'What a Friend We Have in Jesus,'" one woman suggested.

"Do you know 'Shall We Gather at the River?'" we asked. Someone fetched hymnbooks, and our repertoire expanded.

Our voices—young, old, Kenyan, American—echoed through the tin roof. The twenty-something Kenyan student sang a beautiful descant; the eighty-three-year-old former principal of the local school sang a baritone harmony. We learned new songs and they learned new songs, but time and again, we discovered we knew the same ones. At one point, the woman sitting next to me asked, "Where did you learn these hymns?"

"Probably the same place you learned them."

"In church?" she asked.

"Yes," I said.

How different our lives were. I lived in a place where fresh water was something we took for granted and flush toilets were hardly considered a luxury. She grew up here where a new well had changed lives dramatically, but our vocabulary of faith was exactly the same.

Music is Your gift to us, Lord. I sing my thanks and praise. —RICK HAMLIN

Digging Deeper: ROMANS 12:4–5

Sat 24

He went there to register with Mary, who was pledged to be married to him and was expecting a child.
—LUKE 2:5 (NIV)

Recently I visited my dear friend Susan's charming cottage in Louisville, Kentucky. When I arrived, there was a *Welcome Home!* sign in her front yard. As I drove up her long driveway, I spotted Susan peeking out of the kitchen window. She'd placed a basket of toiletries and potted pink miniature roses on the dresser in the guest room, and there was a set of new sheets on the bed in a delightful cabbage rose pattern, topped by an exquisite white coverlet.

After I got settled, it was time for dinner in front of the television. Susan had found me a wonderful TV tray featuring a cottage with pots of pink geraniums on each concrete step. For dinner, she'd prepared a delicious chicken salad made with grapes and pecans and served it on buttery croissants. Then there was dessert, a chocolate torte she had spent hours perfecting.

All weekend long I had never felt so cared for in my life. Susan knows I love shopping for antiques, and she'd mapped out a day chock-full of antiques malls and estate sales. She even found a flea market in a nearby town, where I bought a gray graniteware pitcher for my sister and a double wedding ring quilt to add to my collection.

When I left, I couldn't help but think of the soon-approaching Advent season. If Susan could so meticulously prepare for my visit, how much more could I ready my heart for the arrival of Jesus?

I am so ready for Your coming, precious Savior. My heart says, "Welcome Home!" —ROBERTA MESSNER

Digging Deeper: ROMANS 12:13, HEBREWS 13:2, 1 PETER 4:7–11

Sun 25

Many waters cannot quench love; rivers cannot sweep it away.... —SONG OF SOLOMON 8:7 (NIV)

It was two days after Hurricane Sandy had flooded and devastated much of the East Coast. The Upper West Side of Manhattan, where I live, was unaffected. My church downtown, however, didn't get off so easily.

I wanted to help, and since there was no public transportation, I rollerbladed more than a hundred blocks to get there. I skated through a fully functional uptown with undamaged shops open for business, but as I continued downtown I encountered another world: traffic lights were darkened, stores were closed, signs were torn down, trees had fallen, damaged items lined the sidewalks, and people looked tired and defeated.

When I arrived at the church, I saw a similar scene—but one thing was different. There was no look of defeat on the faces of those who busied themselves with the cleanup. I, too, felt positive in the midst of our loss and was overwhelmed by the volunteers who showed up with water, snacks, a generator, and a pump to empty the water from our basement.

In no time, the floors were dry, items were donated, and a new ministry grew to help our neighborhood heal and rebuild. Hurricane Sandy flooded our community, but from it came a flood of love, generosity, and hope.

Lord, thank You for giving us hope, even in the storm.
—KAREN VALENTIN

Digging Deeper: PSALM 85:1

Mon 26

Now faith is confidence in what we hope for and assurance about what we do not see.
—HEBREWS 11:1 (NIV)

My husband, Don, and I had tickets for window and aisle seats, but when standby passengers boarded, it was clear the airplane was going to be full. I moved to the center seat to make way for an exhausted-looking woman with a heavy coat, lunch bag, and carry-on luggage.

"I hate to eat when you don't have anything," the woman said once we were airborne, "but I'm diabetic. I also need to inject my insulin, but I can go to the lavatory if that will bother you."

I assured her I was neither hungry nor squeamish. Her name was Maria, and we discovered we were both Christians. But while I was returning from a vacation, she was returning from a visit to her oncologist. "I have pancreatic cancer as well as diabetes," she said. My eyes filled with tears, but she managed a smile. "I am blessed to be in a clinical trial for a new drug. I hope the medicine will give me more time to spend with my family. I believe that God is with me through every minute of the time I have."

It's been several months since that flight. I don't know whether Maria is still alive, but I pray that she is enjoying time with her family. Her witness of hope and faith strengthened my own.

Jesus, help me to speak words of hope and faith today.
        —PENNEY SCHWAB

Digging Deeper: ISAIAH 12:2, 1 CORINTHIANS 13:13

Tue 27

Therefore be imitators of God, as beloved children; and walk in love, just as Christ also loved you....
—EPHESIANS 5:1–2 (NAS)

Our daughter Brenda's nine-year-old, Sarah, was so excited after reading her first Choose Your Own Adventure book, she decided to write one of her own. Brenda stayed up with her until 1:00 AM.

When Sarah finished, she wanted to read her book to her dad. He, of course, was sound asleep. When she ran in and woke him up, he said sleepily, "Sure, Princess. Read me your story."

I was struck by so many things upon hearing about this incident. Sarah was captivated by a story, enough to try writing one herself. Her mother, with four other children and a million more things to do, supported Sarah's creative urge, patiently staying up late with her. Sarah's father, upon being woken, did not order her off to bed, telling her it could wait until morning, but instead affirmed her accomplishment by listening to her story.

When Jesus spoke with His disciples in the Sermon on the Mount, He taught them, "Or what man is there among you who, when his son asks for a loaf, will give him a stone? Or if he asks for a fish, he will not give him a snake, will he? If you then, being evil, know how to give good gifts to your children, how much more will your Father who is in heaven give what is good to those who ask Him!" (Matthew 7:9–11).

Heavenly Father, You are a loving parent who neither slumbers nor sleeps. How I flourish in Your constant care!
—CAROL KNAPP

Digging Deeper: PSALM 84:11, ISAIAH 49:15–16, JAMES 1:17

Wed 28

Rejoice always, pray continually, give thanks in all circumstances; for this is God's will for you in Christ Jesus.
—1 THESSALONIANS 5:16–18 (NIV)

As I took off my sweater for the fourth time that morning, I tried to give thanks. "Thank You, God, for hot flashes." Oh, He could tell my heart was not in it. I tried again. "Thank You for the changes in my body." *Hmm. Yes. Thank You for these changes.*

I am changing, and it's rather fascinating. The last time I experienced this much physical change I was pregnant; before that it was adolescence. "Hey, God, how cool is being human? We grow over a lifetime. You created an amazing machine!"

Another hot flash surged through me. My face flushed and my back heated up. I pulled off my sweater again. Rather than getting upset, I was intrigued by the wonder of my body. I timed the heat wave—ninety seconds. It was not nearly as long as I had thought. My annoyance faded just a little.

Being thankful in all circumstances does not mean you have to like it. Being thankful means acknowledging the situation and doing your best to give thanks. With that prayer comes a response from God, an offering of peace.

I still have hot flashes and get annoyed with the drastic change in my temperature, but when I remember to give thanks, it is easier.

Dear Father God, saying thank You is a hard discipline. Remind me that all of the circumstances in my life come from You and that I can rejoice over them. Amen. —LISA BOGART

Digging Deeper: PROVERBS 3:5–6, COLOSSIANS 1:11

Thu 29

Thy word is a lamp unto my feet. . . . —PSALM 119:105 (KJV)

A young neighbor knocked on the door, wanting to borrow "a lamp." She speaks better Spanish than English. Sometimes I have to guess her meaning. "With electricity?" No. "A candle?" No. She gestured with a tight fist pointed outward. "A flashlight?" Yes!

Her phrasing came to mind when a violent storm knocked out our electrical service. Being better prepared than some of my neighbors, I lent out three of my four "lamps." For my own use, I kept a hand-crank model gifted to me in the uncertain days after 9/11. In the face of hardship, it promised to be the most reliable. Push, pull, around, again and again— with a little effort on my part, the bulb sustained vibrancy. Our electricity was out for three days, but each evening my personal energy source generated light to guide my way.

Within a few days, the neighbors returned all of my flashlights. "Here's your lamp, Miss Evelyn." As I tucked away the trusty tools that had been our aids through the ordeal, a long row of Bibles reminded me of myriad scriptural phrases I've memorized over the years: God's Word hidden in my heart (Psalm 119:11, 105). The power is mine; no batteries needed. With a little effort to access the source—supplies unlimited—I'm prepared to walk through the dark.

God, I want more of Your Word in my heart. Today, help me to learn a verse, even a phrase, that can enlighten my journey. —EVELYN BENCE

Digging Deeper: JOHN 8:12, 2 TIMOTHY 3:14–17

Fri 30

"Even to your old age and gray hairs I am he, I am he who will sustain you. I have made you and I will carry you; I will sustain you and I will rescue you." —ISAIAH 46:4 (NIV)

My son John and I were talking about our neighborhood dog run. "Amsterdam really enjoyed chasing his ball today," I said.

"Yeah, he had a good time yesterday too. By the way, when I brought him into the run, a woman asked me his name. When I told her, she said, 'Oh, I know him! He's usually here with an elderly man.'"

I was momentarily puzzled, until I realized she'd been talking about me. *Elderly indeed!* I thought.

It's a funny thing about getting older: as you mark each milestone, the point where you're actually a senior citizen seems farther and farther away. With me, though I have my Medicare card, there's a part of me that's still a twenty-year-old, gazing out at a life with endless possibilities. When someone offers me a seat on the subway, I look around for the old guy he really meant to offer it to. *Surely he couldn't have meant me!*

But, of course, he does. I'm sixty-five, not twenty, and for all my fretting, that's not a bad thing. My younger self got one thing right: whether I'm eighteen or eighty, there are endless possibilities in front of me.

Eternal Father, the years past may not have given me enough wisdom, but may the years ahead bring me closer to You.
—ANDREW ATTAWAY

Digging Deeper: JOB 28:28, PROVERBS 16:31

Sat 31

Can a woman forget her nursing child, or show no compassion for the child of her womb? Even these may forget, yet I will not forget you.
—ISAIAH 49:15 (NRSV)

I walked into the special care unit to see my grandmother who suffers from Alzheimer's. "Hi, Grandma Caryle," I said warmly, stooping to hug her.

The outgoing, vivacious woman who used to be the center of attention now sat alone. She looked up when I approached, but there was no recognition in her face. She didn't even hug me back.

"How are you feeling today?" I scooted close to her on the couch, speaking in an exaggerated, enthusiastic tone, attempting to cheer her up—and maybe myself too.

"Oh, fine," she answered automatically.

I made small talk about the weather, our family, and the antics of my daughter, her only great-grandchild. "Remember the time you and I went to California?" I asked, hoping to retrieve a long-ago memory. "It was my first plane ride." Grandma listened with interest as if hearing about the trip for the first time. "Of course, you've traveled all over the world: Spain, Switzerland, Greece. Portugal was your favorite country."

"I don't remember." My heart ached because this woman, who was a major part of my formative years, couldn't remember her life.

Standing to go, I got up my nerve. "Grandma, do you know who I am?" My voice quivered.

Her brown eyes looked hard at my face. "I don't remember your name," she answered, "but I know you're someone I love."

Lord, others may forget, but You always remember.
—STEPHANIE THOMPSON

Digging Deeper: PSALM 71:9, ISAIAH 46:4, ROMANS 8:38–39

DAILY JOYS

1 _____

2 _____

3 _____

4 _____

5 _____

6 _____

7 _____

8 _____

9 _____

10 _____

11 _____

12 _____

13 _____

14 _____

15 _____

October

16 _____

17 _____

18 _____

19 _____

20 _____

21 _____

22 _____

23 _____

24 _____

25 _____

26 _____

27 _____

28 _____

29 _____

30 _____

31 _____

NOVEMBER

Sing for joy, O heavens, and exult, O earth;
break forth, O mountains, into singing!
For the Lord has comforted his people
and will have compassion on his afflicted.

—ISAIAH 49:13 (ESV)

Sun 1

*"The Pharisee stood and was praying
this to himself: 'God, I thank You that I
am not like other people . . . .'"*
—LUKE 18:11 (NAS)

As Jesus dined in the home of a prominent leader,
He told a parable about a wealthy man giving a
big dinner party. His invited guests began to make
excuses for not attending. The wealthy man commanded his servant to "go out into the highways
and along the hedges, and compel them to come
in" so that his house would be full (Luke 14:23).

There is an interesting context to these "highways
and hedges." The hedges are meant to symbolize
the place where "all have sinned and fall short of
the glory of God" (Romans 3:23). It took a major
stumble for me to truly own up to being from the
hedge myself.

Growing up as a pastor's daughter, I harbored
a certain smugness. I believed I was automatically
in God's pocket. The hedge is made up of people
making willful and hurtful choices and in need of
a turnaround. Jesus calls us from the hedge to His
Father's feast, a table replete with things pleasing
to God that bring lasting joy and fulfillment.

Understanding the hedge has opened my heart to
other hedgers. Jesus was moved with compassion
for such people, the sheep in need of a shepherd.

I'm done thinking as the Pharisee in the Scripture verse above who boasted he wasn't like other people.

Jesus, You are the only perfect One who can invite me to Your Father's feast. I accept humbly.
—CAROL KNAPP

Digging Deeper: LUKE 18:9–14, GALATIANS 6:1

GOD OF JOYFUL SURPRISES

Mon 2

Owe no one anything, except to love one another....
—ROMANS 13:8 (RSV)

DOING GOOD

At first, when I saw that Lucille's letter was all about a real estate deal, my mind glazed over. I know nothing about real estate.

Apparently, Lucille had been trying to sell her house in Missouri for a long time. With the bad market, she'd lowered the price again and again. Now, she wrote, it was almost within reach of a young woman who worked in the lab at the local hospital. The would-be buyer, however, was six thousand dollars short of the down payment the bank required.

Since the technician hadn't been able to come up with this amount, Lucille offered her a deal: "I'll make up the difference. I'll give the bank the six thousand dollars, and you can pay me back with good deeds." Lucille would count these deeds as three hundred dollars a month.

"What constitutes a good deed?" the young woman wanted to know.

"Actions," said Lucille, "that help make the world a better place."

"Today I received my buyer's first accounting," Lucille wrote. The technician had worked thirty extra hours to provide time off for a coworker with cancer. She'd taken part in bake sales for a diabetes foundation. She'd bought a coat for a child the lab had adopted for Christmas. She'd gone once a week to visit the elderly at the senior center.

"I sure got my three hundred dollars' worth of joy, hearing about these things," Lucille concluded. "I can't wait for next month's report!"

God of joyful surprises, how many
good deeds would it take to
pay my debt to You?
—Elizabeth Sherrill

Digging Deeper: Matthew 5:16, 1 Timothy 5:10

Tue 3

Would it not be better for you to be wronged? Would it not be better for you to be robbed?
—1 Corinthians 6:7 (GNT)

The barbershop was full, so I counted off and noted that I would be customer number nine. When it was my turn, I stood up and started for the chair, but out of the corner of my eye I could see another man coming toward it.

My face grew warm. *If this man thinks he is going to jump in ahead of me, he needs to think again,* I thought. My plan was to scowl at him with laser eyes until he shrank back to his chair, but when I got a good look at him, I noticed that he was about seven feet tall and three hundred pounds. He was wearing a brown uniform. On his left hip was a pair of handcuffs; on his right hip was a holstered gun. On his shirt pocket was the word *Sheriff.*

Suddenly, I remembered that math was never my best subject and that there was a distinct possibility I had counted wrong and it was really this man's turn for a haircut. I crawled back to my chair and buried my face in a magazine, brooding over the injustice in the world.

Turns out the sheriff was a real firecracker. Soon he had the whole shop laughing at funny stories of inept criminals. When it was finally my turn, I was sorry to see him leave.

I made up my mind that the next time someone gets ahead of me, I will try to look for the sweet spot. After all, there are other values in life besides fairness. If I am willing to be "wronged," I might find that God has something better for me than mere justice.

*Correct me, Lord, when I get to thinking that the whole world revolves around me and my rights. —*DANIEL SCHANTZ

Digging Deeper: PSALM 98:8–9; ECCLESIASTES 8:14, 10:6–7

Wed 4   *"It is the Spirit who gives life; the flesh is no help at all. The words that I have spoken to you are spirit and life."* —JOHN 6:63 (ESV)

Isaiah, my five-year-old son, was learning to read. The whole world began to unfold for him. In the grocery store, he'd move through the aisle, his pointer finger gliding over the smooth surfaces of cereal boxes. In the van, he'd sound out the names of storefront signs. At home, he'd sit in our home-school classroom, sputtering digraphs and diphthongs and stringing sounds into words.

"Dogs. Big dogs. Little dogs. Big and little dogs," he read. He sat on a small wooden chair. His head dipped low and his blond bangs fell in his eyes. When he finished a sentence, he punctuated the ending with a lift of the head and a brighter-than-the-sun smile.

Words. They were changing Isaiah's life. They opened new doors of learning, of self-sufficiency, of pleasure and freedom and bliss. I curled on the sofa beside his chair, nearly as excited as he.

Isaiah finished the page and closed the book. Then he erupted from his chair. His arms wrapped around my neck, and his breath was sweet and warm on my ear. "I'm doing it, Mama!" he said. "See how I've grown?"

I held him tight. Growing and changing by the power of words—that's a precious thing.

Lord, thank You for Your life-changing Word. Amen.
—SHAWNELLE ELIASEN

Digging Deeper: PSALM 119:18, 48; ISAIAH 55:11; HEBREWS 4:12

Thu 5 *Stand firm then, with the belt of truth buckled around your waist. . . .*
—EPHESIANS 6:14 (NIV)

Most mornings I dress without much thought. My day-to-day routine does not require that I wear anything more elaborate than a clean T-shirt with jeans or a blouse and dress pants. And yet I enjoy dolling up for special occasions. A fancy night out requires planning. It takes time to select a dress, coordinate the accessories, do my hair, and figure out the shoes. It's fun to present my prettiest self, and I like seeing my husband in a tuxedo.

Just like dressing up for a party, putting on the armor of God takes effort and each piece is chosen with intention. What if I dressed with such deliberate care every day? I imagine I would feel safe, blessed, privileged.

Today when I dress, I will buckle the belt of truth. I will pick up the sword of the Spirit. I will slip on the shoes of readiness. Today I will use my wardrobe as a reminder of Who my daily companion is.

Dear Father God, today I will dress with You in mind. Thank You for helping me dress for success. Amen. —Lisa Bogart

Digging Deeper: 1 Peter 3:15, 4:11

Fri 6   *"So when he had received food, he was strengthened...."* —Acts 9:19 (nkjv)

While wandering around Oakland, California, one day, I came across a sign that read "Soul Food." It wasn't on a restaurant but on what looked like a triple-wide wooden ladder leaning up against the side of the escalator I'd just come down.

Puzzled, I headed toward the sign, which was festooned with red ribbons, and there were books: a Bible, *I've Got to Talk to Somebody, God* by Marjorie Holmes (one of my favorite authors), and even a well-thumbed copy of *Guideposts* magazine. Under the Soul Food sign was a note: "If you want a book, please take it. If you would like to put a book here, please do so. Any comments? I'd love to hear them. Makaiya."

Well, I just had to contact Makaiya. I pictured a serious religious person—a nun even—but to my surprise Makaiya was a young student at Mills College who had to do an installation for an art class. "I think art and spirituality can blend very nicely," she said when we met. "I've been helped—fed, you might even say—by books when life felt rough. So when I had to do an art installation, I thought, *Why not feed others with food for the soul?* I built that display stand and set up all the helpful books I could find, thinking that someone would take it down quickly. But it's been there for weeks."

"Would you mind if other people borrowed your idea?" I asked.

Her face lit up. "I'd be pleased if they did!"

I went home feeling fed—with a book by Marjorie Holmes in hand and a smile on my face.

God, is there a way that I can give "soul food"
to someone? Maybe it won't be as elaborate as an art
installation, but it may lead me to share a nourishing
title or even the Good Book itself.
—LINDA NEUKRUG

Digging Deeper: JOB 35:10; PSALMS 51:8, 92:4

Sat 7

Whatsoever ye do, do it heartily....
—COLOSSIANS 3:23 (KJV)

Our granddaughter Abby has always loved being in the kitchen. Since age two, she has sifted, stirred, and measured her way into an impressive range of cooking skills. At nine, her favorite task is slicing and chopping.

"Surely you're not going to let her use that knife," David says, horrified as Abby arranges stacks of carrots, celery, tomatoes, and peppers on the counter by the cutting board.

"Big Dad," she says, "Mimi taught me to be careful."

It's true. I have tried to teach Abby the proper way to hold a knife. I've showed her how to handle food to avoid the blade. I even bought her a special knife that's safer than most. But sooner or later, it will be bandage time. I dread that day but think, *I hope nothing ever holds her back from what she loves doing.*

"Mimi," three-year-old Charles calls, "I need scissors. I want to cut." I riffle through a drawer, searching for toddler-friendly scissors with blunt tips.

A little while later, David comes into the kitchen to pick a sliced carrot off the top of Abby's salad. "Surely you haven't given Charles scissors!" he gasps, looking past the mound of paper scraps on the table where Charles works happily.

"Yep," I say. "He says he wants to be a 'cutter' when he grows up."

Pleased, Charles simply smiles.

Father, in our zeal to explore Your world, keep us safe without holding us back. —PAM KIDD

Digging Deeper: 2 KINGS 10:16, JEREMIAH 29:13

Sun 8   *"Neither this man nor his parents sinned," said Jesus, "but this happened so that the works of God might be displayed in him." —*JOHN 9:3 (NIV)

As an amputee, I'm often mistaken for a veteran who lost a leg in combat. Strangers approach me on the street to thank me for my service to my country. Regardless of political views, most people appreciate veterans, which is cool. But not long ago this guy saw my missing leg and said, "That's what you deserve for joining the army."

The notion that someone would deserve to be an amputee was so absurd, so infuriating, that I just stood there speechless as he walked away. The encounter reminded me of when Jesus's disciples saw a blind man and asked Jesus whether he or his parents had sinned because he'd been born that way. The disciples assumed the man deserved the disability. But Jesus told them that the man didn't do anything to warrant blindness; he was born blind so that the works of God could be displayed in him.

That comment from the guy on the sidewalk helped me connect the story of the blind man and me. I didn't do anything to deserve having one leg (I lost it to cancer nearly twenty years ago). But based on Jesus's words, I know at least one reason it happened: so that the works of God can be displayed in me.

When I don't understand why certain adversity has befallen me, Lord, help me to trust that You are displaying Your works in my life.
—JOSHUA SUNDQUIST

Digging Deeper: JOHN 9

Mon 9   *But one thing I do: forgetting what lies behind and straining forward to what lies ahead.*
—PHILIPPIANS 3:13 (ESV)

Hi," a girl who looked six or seven years old said. She sat across from me as I waited for my first piano lesson.

"Hi," I replied.

"Are you new?" she asked.

"Yes, can you tell?" I asked, laughing.

She pointed to my book. "You have a beginner songbook," she replied.

"Oh," I said.

"Are you nervous?" she asked.

"Why, yes, I am," I replied.

"Why?" she asked.

"Well, I guess because I just don't want to mess up." I leaned toward her and said softly, "I don't like making mistakes."

"Oh," she said, "well, you probably will."

"I know," I said, sighing. I'd made a mistake at work earlier in the day that had caused some problems and I was still reeling from the stress it had caused the staff.

"I have to go now," the girl said. "Time for my lesson." She held up her book. "I'm in the intermediate book."

"Yes, I see," I said. "Congratulations."

"Just remember," she said matter-of-factly as she gathered up her things, "mistakes are your friend. Without them we can't learn. That's what my music teacher always says. Bye!"

Lord, please help me to let go of mistakes I make but never the lessons learned from them.
—MELODY BONNETTE SWANG

Digging Deeper: PSALM 37:24, EPHESIANS 5:8

Tue 10

Every good and perfect gift is from above. . . . —JAMES 1:17 (NIV)

My indoor cycling instructor wrote the names of that day's winners in fluorescent orange marker on the mirrored wall of the steamy spin room at my gym: Johanna, Eric, Brad, Amy, Edward, Champion Sr. Div.

Senior Division? When did that happen?

Actually, a few years ago. In the locker room I dressed slowly, pondering this sudden realization that I was definitely, positively, no longer young. It said so in fluorescent orange marker.

Then a guy about half my age came over. "I always sit in the row behind you," he said. He seemed pretty intense, pretty serious, and very athletic. "In the more advanced classes there's always a point where it gets so hard that I tell myself, 'I am never, ever doing this again.' And then I watch you. I keep coming back because one day I'm going to beat you."

I tried to keep myself from laughing. "It won't be long now," I said.

The first time I ever took an indoor cycling class back in my thirties I almost died. And I'm sure I said I was never, ever going to do this again. But I have, practically every day since. You could say I'm addicted, but I like to think I'm dedicated. Probably it's a little of both and a blessing either way.

I zipped up my gym bag and headed out, feeling a lot better about my win. Senior Division—not so shabby after all.

You give us the gift of life, Father. Thank You for letting mine last this long and for giving me the gift of dedication, even when my talents were wanting.
—EDWARD GRINNAN

Digging Deeper: ECCLESIASTES 5:19

Wed 11

"They asked for meat, and he sent them quail and gave them manna—bread from heaven."
—PSALM 105:40 (TLB)

"The person who said 'the way to a man's heart is through his stomach' was right," my mother once grumbled. "Your father sure likes to eat!" Trouble was, Mother didn't like to cook.

Fast-forward forty years. "You're cooking!" my husband, Don, says, surprised.

"Just chili," I respond.

"Your chili is always great. I can hardly wait until supper."

Why is Don excited about chili? I wondered as I added chopped peppers to the pot. I didn't make meals from scratch very often, but he didn't care . . . or did he? What about last week, when he went to a farm sale and didn't buy anything except lunch? "The Mennonite ladies served sour cream-raisin pie," he'd said, "just like you used to make." How long had it been since I made a pie or served a meal that made his eyes light up?

I'm a lot like my mother. I'm not fond of cooking. But Mother cooked because she loved my dad. It was about time I did the same for Don.

I stirred up a pan of his favorite Texas cornbread to go with the chili and made a triple-berry cobbler for dessert. "Like heaven in a bowl," Don said when he tasted it.

Since then I've been spending a bit more time in the kitchen. We've had green chili enchiladas, slow-cooked brisket, sweet-and-sour chicken, and even a sour cream-raisin pie. The way to a man's heart isn't necessarily through his stomach, but a home-cooked meal can definitely be an expression of love.

Thank You, Lord, for good food and good times with the one I love. —PENNEY SCHWAB

Digging Deeper: PROVERBS 31:27-28, JOHN 21:12-13, 1 JOHN 3:18

Thu 12

Do not conform to the pattern of this world, but be transformed by the renewing of your mind....
—ROMANS 12:2 (NIV)

We moved the cups closer to the water, the mugs closer to the coffee maker, and the plates closer to the dishwasher. With a few more tweaks, our cabinet reorganization was finished. It just made sense, though I still kept reaching into the wrong cabinets.

About that time, our family passed around the nastiest bug we'd ever suffered. Chills, fever, aches, and a cough that moved in like noisy neighbors. As sickness set in, misery rose. We tried doctor visits, medicines, home remedies, chicken soup, and gallons of herbal teas. No dice. And the coughing was wearing us down. Nothing stopped it, not even prayer.

"Why can't You heal us, Lord? You don't care about me. You don't answer prayer. What if this stuff about Your presence, Your care, Your healing power isn't true?"

I reached for a mug to make tea but reached into the old cabinet. At that moment, God's Spirit delivered a loving whack upside my head. *Bill, you're reaching into the wrong cabinets for thoughts about your heavenly Father. Those thoughts are the old cabinets. The false ideas. The unreal expectations. You've*

stockpiled new cabinets with better truths, remember?
Reach into those cabinets and find your peace.
  I shut the old door and reached into the new one.

Father, renew my mind by Your Word that I might
stockpile wonderful thoughts about You.
  —BILL GIOVANNETTI

Digging Deeper: ISAIAH 55:8–9, ROMANS 8:28

I SURRENDER ALL

Fri 13
You, God, are awesome in your
sanctuary; the God of Israel gives
power and strength to his people.
Praise be to God!
—PSALM 68:35 (NIV)

WORRY-FREE

A pastor's wife called. "Hi, Julie. Remember two years ago when you spoke at our luncheon?"
  I cringed. *What if Sandra asks me to speak again?* God's always been faithful to help me talk to groups, but I usually dread the event for weeks and worry about a million what-ifs: What if people look at me with blank stares? What if I trip again when I'm walking onto the platform? Or knock over the microphone like I did before? What if…

"Julie, would you consider leading our retreat this fall?"

Maybe she'll ask me to speak about an unfamiliar topic, so I can say no.

"We'd love you to share whatever God's teaching you," she said.

"*Um*, my word for the year is *surrender*. You probably aren't interested in something—"

"That sounds wonderful!"

Jotting "Surrender Retreat" on my calendar, something occurred to me: my fear of public speaking was tied to my desire to control, and I'd just agreed to lead a retreat on surrender.

I sank to my knees beside my prayer chair. "Lord, I can't do this without You. I surrender my fear of speaking. Even if they boo and throw eggs at me, You'll be with me. I give the retreat to You."

Instead of worrying, I began praying for Sandra and her group. For the first time ever, anticipation about speaking replaced all my apprehension.

Lord, I know who I am without
You: a self-centered scaredy-cat.
You are my confidence.
—JULIE GARMON

Digging Deeper: DEUTERONOMY 31:6,
ISAIAH 41:10–13

Sat 14

But if from there you seek the Lord your God, you will find him if you seek him with all your heart....
—DEUTERONOMY 4:29 (NIV)

Another month passed, and I still hadn't found a new board member for Prayer Igniters International. I was tired of trying and seriously thinking of leaving the vacancy unfilled.

Then Gordon and I invited our sons and their families for a weekend at a rented lake house. We planned a series of scavenger hunts and trivia competitions. The family with the highest cumulative score would win a restaurant gift certificate, so the competition was intense.

For the hide-and-seek challenge, Gordon was "it" and easily found family members hiding behind shower curtains and under piles of old blankets. But there were still two left when he completed his sweep of the house. So he went through again. Nothing. Gordon slowly went through the nooks and crannies a third time, then said, "I know they're here, but I can't find them. I give up!"

Once the call went out that the game was over, our daughter-in-law emerged from a kitchen cabinet and our son appeared from a space behind the basement furnace. Gordon hadn't probed deep enough to find them.

When I got home, I sat down and compiled a broader list of people for possible board members because you sometimes have to seek in places you don't think you'll ever find.

Dear Father, help me continue to seek, believing that You will help me find. Amen. —KAREN BARBER

Digging Deeper: JEREMIAH 29:12–14, LUKE 11:9

Sun 15

And they cried with a loud voice to the Lord....
—NEHEMIAH 9:4 (NAS)

My heart was heavy as I entered our church. My son was being released from prison, and he was free to go and do whatever he wanted—no probation. I was greeted on the steps by Burt. He attends our church with a group of other men from a local halfway house for addicts seeking to recover.

"How are you doing?" Burt smiled. He meant it. He knew about both my sons' battling addictions.

"Burt, with Jon getting released, I'm worried he'll make the wrong decisions and..."

Burt's smile was like the sun, and he cut me off lovingly: "He's gonna be all right!"

I smiled, too, realizing that no one else had spoken so optimistically about my son in ages. "Could you say that again?" I asked. Joyful tears blurred my vision. He did—over and over. Hope crept into my heart and rested there.

In church, fear tried to attack again. I went over to Burt during prayer time and asked, "Would you please pray for Jon and me?"

"Let's go to the altar," he said. People do that freely in our church. Burt looked upward with his eyes wide open as though he was looking directly at God. He bellowed out a prayer for Jon and me, passionately and joyfully. We would be all right, just like Burt said.

Oh, Father God, give me faith like Burt's and
watch over Burt and my son and me.
—MARION BOND WEST

Digging Deeper: ROMANS 8:26

Mon 16

Spend your time and energy in the exercise of keeping spiritually fit.
—1 TIMOTHY 4:7 (TLB)

What is it about exercise that makes it hard to get into a daily habit? I do water aerobics for forty-five minutes, six days a week, if the temperature outdoors is at least fifty-eight degrees at 8:30 AM. But even in Florida, in the winter, there are many days when it's just too cold to get into the heated pool, and getting out in the cold air is a killer.

Then I'd tell myself that I'm going to bike ten miles every day, but most days I'm too busy, too tired, or too lazy to be bothered. So I tried walking. That hurt my arthritic knees. Next I tried the machines in the clubhouse across the street. But I really dislike exercising indoors. (I'm an outdoor kind of gal.)

About that same time I started thinking about how hard it is to get into a daily habit of prayer. Oh, I'd pray here and there, usually during grace before meals, but I rarely found the time for longer, more specific prayers.

The answer came one day when I was putting a few social events on my calendar. I thought, *Why don't I schedule my prayers and daily exercise the way I do movies, parties, and lunches?*

Now a simple P and an E remind me to pray and exercise. I may only eke out five minutes of prayer and a couple of miles on the bike, but at least when I see these two little letters on my calendar, I do it.

Father, give me an extra dose of grace and faithfulness every day to pray and to keep my body active.
—Patricia Lorenz

Digging Deeper: Luke 11:1–8, 1 Timothy 4:7–10

Tue 17

Do not be anxious about anything, but in every situation, by prayer and petition, with thanksgiving, present your requests to God. And the peace of God, which transcends all understanding, will guard your hearts and your minds in Christ Jesus. —PHILIPPIANS 4:6–7 (NIV)

Worry is temporary atheism," writes author Randy Alcorn.

Funny how a simple quote could result in an overwhelming flood of conviction. You see, I'd been worrying a lot, especially about adopting a little girl from the Congo. Everything that could go wrong was going wrong. Despite God's many commands not to, I was letting worry reign in my heart.

I knew it was time to wage war on my worry. If I wanted to experience that all-surpassing peace Paul talks about in Philippians 4:7, I had to live out the verse that came before it. So the next day, I started a worry journal.

Every single morning, for four months, I wrote a list of my worries. Then I got on my knees and, out loud, I not only gave each worry to Jesus, but I asked Him to deposit peace and joy in the empty space that my worry left behind.

I wish I'd started this a long time ago. I'm no longer wasting energy and emotions on things I can't control. I'm truly living out Philippians 4:6, and in so doing, I'm reaping the rewards of joy and peace and an ever-increasing trust in God.

Father God, thank You for the truth of Your Word and for the reward that comes when I live out those truths. —KATIE GANSHERT

Digging Deeper: PSALM 55:22, 1 PETER 5:7

Wed 18   *Therefore, if anyone is in Christ, the new creation has come: The old has gone, the new is here!*
—2 CORINTHIANS 5:17 (NIV)

My son Solomon is a grudge-holder. Years ago, his first-grade teacher blamed him for a mishap that he didn't have anything to do with— a small injustice that most kids would have let slide. We still hear about it from him with the same intensity as if it happened yesterday.

I've tried to explain to Solomon that holding on to bad things gives them power. That every time he gets mad about the same thing, it's taking time away from something better that could be happening. But nothing seems to register.

I hate to admit it, but I fear that he gets this personality trait from me. I, too, have struggled with forgiveness. Name any person in my life and I can rattle off disappointments, disagreements, hurt feelings so easily it's as if they're stored on a grudge index card in my soul. Some nights when I can't sleep, something might rise in my memory and there I am, exactly like Solomon, getting angry and upset about one thing or another that happened a long time ago.

So I got to thinking, *What would happen in this month of thanksgiving if I do my best to rip up my resentment score cards and start anew? Replace the bitterness with gratitude? Look for the good, the kind words, the favors, the love, and the laughs we share? What if, in addition to recognizing the good, I let go of the grumblings?*

Dear Lord, wash my spirit clean of rancor. Give me a heart that holds blessings and love. Give me a heart of thanksgiving. —SABRA CIANCANELLI

Digging Deeper: MICAH 7:18–19, PHILIPPIANS 4:8

Thu 19

And that Christ may dwell in your hearts through faith, as you are being rooted and grounded in love. —EPHESIANS 3:17 (NRSV)

I was on the subway, going home from a talk I'd given on prayer. I sat next to a young woman, took out a book to read, and then realized she was crying . . . hard. Should I ignore her? Give her a tissue?

All at once I heard an older woman on her other side ask, "What is it, honey?" Maybe they were friends. Maybe I'd be off the hook. Someone else could do the comforting.

"I got laid off," the young woman said and burst into more tears.

"There, there," the older woman said. From the way she said it, I realized she was a stranger to this young woman too. "You'll be okay. Take it from me—whenever God closes a door, He opens a window."

"It's my second job," she said. "I need the money."

I glanced at the older woman for encouragement; she nodded. "I'll bet they really liked you," I offered. "They probably just had to make some cutbacks."

"I was a temp, but I wanted the job to go on forever."

The older woman put an arm around her shoulder. "I'm going to pray you find something else, and it will be better than that old job."

"Yes," I said, "it'll turn out okay."

Two strangers trying to comfort a third. The train pulled into the station. Both of us rose to get off.

As I walked up the stairs and stepped out into the night air, I remembered the last point I had made in my talk that evening, how I prayed that I would always be present where I was needed. I had something now I wanted to add to that: ask for help when offering help and God sometimes sends just the right companions to your aid.

> *Be present with me, God, so I can*
> *be with You and Yours.*
> —RICK HAMLIN

Digging Deeper: ROMANS 15:1

Fri 20

And he shall spread forth his hands in the midst of them, as he that swimmeth spreadeth forth his hands to swim.... —ISAIAH 25:11 (KJV)

I don't know where I'd be without my swimming group. Well, it's not exactly swimming that we do; it's water aerobics at the local pool. They are my workout buddies and always motivate me to keep moving. Even in the winter, we traipse indoors and exchange our snow gear for swimsuits.

Our instructor, Ron, stands on the pool deck, growling out beats and barking out routines like a drill sergeant. While in the water, seventy-nine-year-old Pat, who taught school and coached sports while raising four sons, never misses a beat. She churns the water around her, never giving a thought to letting age stop her. I smile at her as I sweat my way through the routines.

Behind Pat, Jackie moves through the water with grace, her auburn dreadlocks bouncing as she jumps. She has been battling breast cancer for several years, but still finds time and courage to volunteer at a rec center where she teaches and choreographs ethnic dance.

We've shared births, deaths, promotions, retirements, divorces, and marriages. Through it all, we just keep swimming.

I dunk my head beneath the water to cool myself. I swim a few yards and then break the surface of the water and look around, grateful for these motivators, these cherished life-givers.

Lord, thank You for good friends and good health. Bless us all! —SHARON FOSTER

Digging Deeper: PROVERBS 15:30, ISAIAH 12:3

Sat 21

Seven times a day I praise You.... —PSALM 119:164 (NKJV)

A couple of months ago, my friend Kay passed away. At the end of her life, she had to have a leg amputated. But even so, praising God was forever on her lips. Later she hemorrhaged to death. At the funeral home, Kay's caregiver related how the last thing Kay said before drawing her final breath was "Thank you."

Those words made me take a trip back in time to the last day I saw Kay. We were both at a hair salon getting perms, when Kay suddenly remembered being at my house many years before and admiring my purse. "I'll never forget it," she told me. "You unloaded the contents on the spot and insisted I take it home. I just want to say thank you again, Roberta."

Several years passed, and I lost contact with Kay. So I was surprised when her brother called to say that Kay had mentioned me in her will. She wanted to be sure I was given a picture I once needlepointed for her and a sweet little diamond cocktail ring as well.

I had a jeweler mount Kay's ring on my charm bracelet. Each time I look at it, I promise God that praise will forever be on my lips and ask that the last words I utter be "Thank you."

> *To God be the glory, great things He hath done....*
> *Thank You. Thank You. Thank You.*
> —ROBERTA MESSNER

> *Digging Deeper:* 1 CHRONICLES 16:9;
> PSALMS 7:17, 16:7

Sun 22

Do everything without grumbling....
—PHILIPPIANS 2:14 (NIV)

I'm generally an upbeat, lighthearted, optimistic gal. I like sunny days, happy hearts, "yes" smiley faces, and big laughs. Which is why it was so unsettling to me that I'd slipped into a funk and that my funkiness had lasted two days before I detected that my attitude stank. I had fired off a snippy e-mail to a business associate and was inhaling to holler for the eighteenth time for Prisca to come eat her lunch—"Now!"—when a tiny hologram of me floated just above my shoulder and saw the scene unfolding with fresh eyes. She took in my words, my actions, my reactions, and then descended to whisper something in my ear: "Um, Ash? Helloooo! Who exactly have you become?"

I hung my head. This clearly was not my best me.

Remembering that God is a fan of covenants, I pledged to Him then and there: "No more grumbling, Father. Deal? You've got my word on that." I missed the mark, and yet at least there was a mark.

This is what Scripture does for me: it reminds me of the mark. It reminds me that with God's power and protection in and around me, I really can live grumble-free.

Just for today, Father: no more grumbling.
By Your power, let it be so.
—Ashley Wiersma

Digging Deeper: Ephesians 4:29, 1 Peter 4:9

Mon 23

"Therefore what God has joined together, let no one separate."
—MARK 10:9 (NIV)

My husband is looking at the computer screen again. He's not working, not looking for work. He hasn't called a friend for months, hasn't had an around-the-house project in years, hasn't gone anywhere other than church on Sunday and to deliver Stephen to an occasional homeschool activity.

Andrew is clinically depressed. His activities are walking the dog at noon, washing the dishes after supper, reading a bedtime story to our youngest, and sometimes doing a load or two of laundry. He sees a counselor. At my insistence, he works three hours a week at a low-stress volunteer job. That's pretty much what he can manage.

I want to help my spouse, but I am not sure of where the fine line lies between being supportive and enabling. Andrew's depression is like a physical presence, an unwelcome houseguest who's here for a seemingly endless stay. I'm stretched so thin. I'm tired. I'm lonely.

I remind myself that I married Andrew for better or worse and that it's okay that we're staggering through the worse part. Then I remind God that He joined us together . . . and I rely on Him to keep us that way.

Father, show me how to love, especially when love is hard. —Julia Attaway

Digging Deeper: 1 Corinthians 7:10

Tue 24

Rejoice in hope, be patient in tribulation, be constant in prayer. —Romans 12:12 (esv)

Anytime I cough, my mother instructs me to take medicine. Every time the temperature is chilly, she warns me to wear layers and button up. Even now, from hundreds of miles away, she reminds me over the phone to take care of myself. Repetition is effective in cultivating good habits, but too often it makes you forget the original intent behind the action.

My mother always told me, "Pray to God in good and bad times. He never forgets you, so you shouldn't forget Him." I have always said a prayer at night, even if only a short one, but I had never really connected with God. Prayer became another chore I completed without too much thought.

It wasn't until my mother suffered a brain aneurysm, while I was finishing my senior year at New York University, that I rediscovered my appreciation for prayer. This time my prayers felt different. I prayed to God not out of habit but to

maintain my deep connection with my mother—
and to build a stronger connection to Him.

She was in bed recovering from her illness, but
she was more worried about me. "I'm fine," she
said. "God is always by my side. And I can't wait to
see you walk down the aisle for graduation in May."

I hung up the phone, immensely thankful that
my mom was in such good spirits and that God
was right there by her side.

> *Thank You, Lord, for allowing me a line of*
> *communication with You through prayer.*
> —ERIK CRUZ

Digging Deeper: PSALM 65:1–4

Wed 25

*A cheerful heart is good
medicine....*
—PROVERBS 17:22 (NLT)

"We're sorry for the delay and expect the plane to
be at the gate shortly," the airline agent announced and then returned to his computer screen.
I took a sip of my now-cold coffee and sighed.

It had been a long, stress-filled day of
Thanksgiving travel. The waiting area where I sat
was packed with weary passengers. The dissonance
of hundreds of conversations blurred in my ears,
and the mechanics and tedium of travel filled my
mind. Looking at the sea of somber faces around

me, it was clear I was not the only one who had forgotten to smile.

Then I saw the hat. A husky, bearded man sat several rows from me, reading a book and wearing a hat shaped like a large roasted turkey, drumsticks crossed high in the air. I laughed out loud.

When our plane finally arrived, I was glad to see that man with the hat boarding too. Throughout the flight, each time I'd see the crossed turkey legs poking above his seat, I'd smile. My thoughts moved to the meal I'd soon be enjoying with my family and then to counting my blessings.

When the plane landed and I walked to baggage claim, I saw the turkey hat bobbing ahead of me, leaving a thread of smiles through the fabric of tired travelers.

Please keep our hectic holidays laced with humor and gratitude, Lord. —KIM HENRY

Digging Deeper: PROVERBS 15:30, JEREMIAH 31:25

Thu 26

"Wealth and honor come from you; you are the ruler of all things. In your hands are strength and power to exalt and give strength to all. Now, our God, we give you thanks, and praise your glorious name."
—1 CHRONICLES 29:12–13 (NIV)

My husband's family was in town for Thanksgiving, so I had carefully planned the day's festivities. I was going to pop the turkey in the oven in the morning before we headed out for the Turkey Trot, a race for the whole family. As we hopped into the cars to head downtown (seven kids, seven strollers), I felt a surge of pride. I had done it! The turkey was in the oven. The kids' snack bags were packed. We were going to get there with plenty of time to hear the starting gun go off. The perfect Thanksgiving was a given.

But then the pumpkin bread started to crumble—literally. Just as I managed to break up a squabble between my kids over who got the biggest snack, my baby proceeded to throw up. We were two miles into a five-mile race with no bathroom in sight, so I mopped him up with my bare hands.

Then, at mile four, my father-in-law called. The little knob on the turkey said it was done. Two hours later we sat down to a dry turkey, with a cranky baby and a full load of laundry in the washer.

But as my husband said a blessing over the food, I was filled with an abundance of thanks. Because although things didn't turn out quite as I had planned, my day was still rich with family, hope, and some pretty good cold turkey.

Lord, fill me with gratitude, regardless of my circumstances. Amen. —ERIN MACPHERSON

Digging Deeper: PSALM 69:30; COLOSSIANS 3:15, 4:2

Fri 27 *"Look at the birds of the air; they do not sow or reap or store away in barns, and yet your heavenly Father feeds them...."* —MATTHEW 6:26 (NIV)

During the drought this past summer, I rigged up a fine trickle from the sprayer attachment on my hose for the birds and spent hours watching them from my kitchen window. Standing motionless in the drizzle were not just the usual cardinals and chickadees, but yellow-billed cuckoos, painted buntings, brown thrashers, hermit thrushes. Moved by the parched birds' miserable demeanor—beaks open, tongues thrust out—I had taken to watering them out of pity and worry, leaving the hose on even when I left the house for most of the day.

My winter provisions of seeds and suet evolved similarly. At first, I filled the feeders only occasionally, to watch the birds gather. Now I buy seed in fifty-pound sacks. The birds, I think, would starve without my help.

So when they suddenly disappeared from the filled-up feeders this spring, I was confused. *What can they be eating?* I wondered, scanning the woods' edge for seed-eaters scratching for worms among the robins. No cardinals or finches there, and it would be months before there'd be seeds or fruit of any kind. *How will they survive without food?* I fretted.

Just then, hearing a racket in the treetops, I looked up and got my answer. Finches, waxwings, and chickadees were chowing down on tree tassels.

God always provides, I learned, not just for birds but for us as well.

Creator God, thank You for Your ever-constant provision! Let it direct our gaze toward You.
—PATTY KIRK

Digging Deeper: GENESIS 1–2, 1 KINGS 17

Sat 28

Rejoice with those who rejoice; mourn with those who mourn.
—ROMANS 12:15 (NIV)

A July evening watching the home team Minnesota Twins playing ball on television. A sudden blank screen and darkness as the power goes out. Sirens piercing the country quiet. A cluster of neighbors gathering to the oncoming flashing lights of emergency vehicles. We would find out later that a teenager had been killed in a traffic accident at the corner, knocking out power lines.

While cycling the next morning, I couldn't help but notice the sorrowful skid marks and shattered glass yet to be cleaned up or washed away. My friend pointed out the obituary to me in the paper several days later. Nick, a college student, loved to sing in church. A vase of cut flowers was placed on the corner.

I had an idea. *How about something more lasting than a card or a plucked rose?* I bought a flowering plant at the farmer's market and placed it among the other remembrances and memorials. Over the summer I visited regularly, watering and pruning. On a late, blustery September afternoon, I watched as a woman wearing dark glasses approached me. "I wondered who was doing this," she said. "I see them every day."

It was Nick's mother. Winter was coming and the flowers would soon be no more. But not their meaning. They were a comfort to a grieving mother, a reminder of God's love manifested in His children.

Lord God, Who knows even the fall of a sparrow,
surely You are always near to the brokenhearted.
—Carol Knapp

Digging Deeper: Proverbs 10:7

GIFTS OF JOY

Sun 29

*Pride goeth before destruction, and
an haughty spirit before a fall.*
—Proverbs 16:18 (kjv)

FIRST SUNDAY IN ADVENT: ATTENTIVE

I had barely walked into the auto-parts store when
the guy behind the counter said, "No."

"Excuse me?" I said.

"You want me to resurface those wheel rotors
you're carrying, right?"

I nodded, feeling a little sheepish.

"Can't," he said. "They're too thin. When they're
that thin, you can't rely on them anymore."

He was right. I tried to save a couple of bucks
by shaving the old rotors, but there's a point when
you're simply tempting fate. The rotors warp, and
the brakes can't do their job because there's not
enough *there* there.

I have tempted such fate more than once. I
have depended on things far more fragile than
worn wheels, yet have done none of the proper
maintenance. Friends and family and prayers have
pulled me through more times than I deserve, so I
start to take chances, assume they'll be there when
needed...until I'm suddenly skittering sideways

when relationships warp and I can't depend on brakes to make everything better. The laws of physics and the consequences of hubris are both eternal.

I bought new rotors. Sometimes what appears on the surface is too thin and fragile. Despite my unwarranted confidence in my own abilities, I cannot fix everything myself. I need someone to pass me the right tools, to remind me of maintenance, both scheduled and unscheduled. In short, I need Someone to give me a hand.

Lord, this Advent, remind me to attend to more than Christmas gifts and holiday worries and to focus on less temporal things. —MARK COLLINS

Digging Deeper: PROVERBS 11:2, MATTHEW 28:20

Mon 30

But just as he who called you holy is holy, so be holy in all you do. —1 PETER 1:15 (NIV)

Why did I agree to this? I berated myself as I dodged in and out of traffic. I needed to make every hour count because I still had Christmas gifts to buy, nothing was wrapped, and I had no idea what to wear to my in-laws' celebration that evening. Instead, I was meeting a friend for lunch.

Normally, I loved talking with her, but now wasn't a good time.

I pushed opened the restaurant door and spotted Bobbie seated near the back. "How are you doing?" she asked.

"Exhausted and overwhelmed," I complained.

We made small talk and then I confided, "It's not at all how I'd planned to celebrate this year. I wanted to be centered and serene—to have a holy, meaningful holiday. Instead, everything is crazy and chaotic."

Bobbie nodded in agreement, her blue eyes shining. "I imagine that very first Christmas wasn't at all like we see it portrayed on Christmas cards and in Nativity scenes. A young, unmarried woman having labor pains while riding a donkey. No available lodging, so she's directed to a dirty animal stall. And yet amid that chaos was the most blessed and holy event of all time."

My shoulders relaxed, and I sat back into the booth. "I've missed you," I said softly as a waitress handed us menus. This time with my friend was the respite I needed. My shopping wasn't finished and I still had baking to do, but I was right where I needed to be.

Lord, let me see that holy moments are everywhere, even in my chaos. —STEPHANIE THOMPSON

Digging Deeper: PSALM 25:4–5, LUKE 10:40–42

DAILY JOYS

1 _____

2 _____

3 _____

4 _____

5 _____

6 _____

7 _____

8 _____

9 _____

10 _____

11 _____

12 _____

13 _____

14 _____

15 _____

November

16 _____

17 _____

18 _____

19 _____

20 _____

21 _____

22 _____

23 _____

24 _____

25 _____

26 _____

27 _____

28 _____

29 _____

30 _____

DECEMBER

And the angel said to them, "Fear not, for behold, I bring you good news of great joy that will be for all the people."

—LUKE 2:10 (ESV)

Tue 1

For I consider that the sufferings of this present time are not worth comparing with the glory that is to be revealed to us. —ROMANS 8:18 (ESV)

From our living room window, I watched my wife, Julee, spread the ashes of Mick, her beloved and troubled older brother. He had died by his own hand more than two years earlier at the end of a long, futile struggle with drugs and alcohol, depression and loneliness, hospitals and homeless shelters. Educated, talented, and disarmingly charming, Mick couldn't charm his demons.

The county morgue had sent his ashes to us, where the simple box and cremation certificate held a small place of honor on a bookcase. I liked to think of Mick, who loved reading most, crowded in with the books. Yet Julee knew the ashes couldn't stay there. "I have to let him go," she said. "I *have* to." But it had taken a while, a struggle in itself. Love can trap us as well as free us.

She'd had the ashes blessed by the Franciscans and spent hours talking with the brothers. Today, her birthday, we were up in the Berkshire Hills. Julee said she was as ready as she would ever be.

A few years back Mick had spent Christmas with us here and said it was the happiest day of his life. "Maybe I should move here," he said half-jokingly, knowing the turmoil that act would inevitably occasion. "Don't worry," he laughed. "But some-day I'll come back."

Now Julee stood beneath an apple tree in the middle of the yard, flinging her brother into the breeze, watching the ashes drift to the ground, a light cold rain soaking them into the earth. Mick had returned to the Berkshires at last.

Lord, You are a God of inevitabilities—of life and death, joy and pain, love and loss. And in each inevitable moment You are with us still.
—EDWARD GRINNAN

Digging Deeper: ISAIAH 25:8, ROMANS 8:38–39

GOD OF JOYFUL SURPRISES

Wed 2   *Thanks be to God for his inexpressible gift!* —2 CORINTHIANS 9:15 (RSV)

THE GREATEST GIFT

My friend Muriel had to leave her beloved oceanfront condo in Hawaii and move to an assisted-living facility. Her phone calls were so distressed that I longed to do something more than commiserate.

As I put down the phone after one such conversation, my eyes lighted on a small box covered with seashells. I'd spent my months' allowance for it, a birthday gift for my mother when I was eleven. Mother kept it on her dresser wherever she lived. When she died, the box moved to my dresser, where it spoke to me of the ocean we both loved.

What if I were to send the box to Muriel for Christmas, a little piece of seashore in her new setting? But that would be like giving away part of myself. Once I'd had the idea, though, I couldn't shake it. Reluctantly, I packed it, swathed in bubble wrap like the precious jewel it was to me, and mailed it with a note giving its history.

Five days after Christmas, a long letter came from Muriel. "Thank you for the pretty box," she wrote. "It was sweet of you to think of me."

That was all. The letter went on with a fresh catalog of negatives about her new location; I was terribly let down.

It wasn't till the next day, as I took down the ornaments from the Christmas tree, that God spoke to me: *Do you know what My gift cost? Do you know that My Son's birth was for your joy?*

God of joyful surprises, forgive my paltry thanks for the greatest gift of all.
—ELIZABETH SHERRILL

Digging Deeper: 1 CORINTHIANS 13:5

Thu 3

Every good and perfect gift is from above, coming down from the Father of the heavenly lights, who does not change like shifting shadows.
—JAMES 1:17 (NIV)

In a prayer, the minister addressed God as "the Maker of all good gifts." The phrase prompted me to take a second look at the Christmas gifts I intended to give my young neighbor who stops by every day. Needs topped the list: a coat and a calculator (for math). Things she would enjoy: a kaleidoscope, a card game, peanut butter and crackers. But I felt a deeper desire to make something that would symbolize our friendship.

I know, I thought, *I'll build on our corduroy connection.* When I wore my red-ribbed jumper, she enjoyed stroking the texture, and she relished my reading her the classic picture book about a stuffed bear named Corduroy.

I shopped for fabric and unearthed a vintage teddy-bear pattern. I spent a whole day pinning, cutting, sewing, and transforming a brown corduroy remnant into the contour of a sixteen-inch bear. A personality emerged as I stuffed it with fiberfill and added black button eyes, a felt nose, an embroidered mouth, a tiny pocket.

She named the bear Jonathan. "I gave him cereal for breakfast," she said. "He keeps candy in his pocket." My folksy one-of-a-kind gift was perfect for its intended purpose: a buddy to watch over.

Poet and artist David Jones once noted that, as humans, our nature "is to make things" not only for practical necessity but as "the signs of something other"—spontaneous expressions of beauty or relationship. Sometimes, my Maker and I have a lot in common.

Maker of all good gifts, thank You for the creative spark in me that characterizes my likeness to You.
—EVELYN BENCE

Digging Deeper: GENESIS 1:27

Fri 4

What time I am afraid, I will trust in thee. In God I will praise his word, in God I have put my trust....
—PSALM 56:3–4 (KJV)

M om, what is it?"
Her voice trembled. "I don't want to upset you, but I think I had a stroke. I'm going to the hospital."

My siblings and I met at the emergency room. "Oh, look at all of the trouble I've caused," Mom said from her hospital bed. "You all look so worried. I'm all right." We sat down, crowded in the small examining room.

In moments, a technician wheeled in a large machine. "Just an ultrasound," she said. "Won't hurt a bit." She dimmed the lights and positioned a wand on Mom's chest. A monitor lit up with beautiful swirling colors. The technician looked at me. "This is your mom's heart."

My mom's heart. I felt my throat tighten the same as it had when I was pregnant and saw the miracles of my sons' hearts beating for the very first time. The array of colors danced in front of me. *Please, God,* I prayed, *please let Mom be okay.*

As the technician froze different phases of her heartbeat and measured arcs of movement, I thought about all of the love that's come out of that heart—the blessings, the laughter, the thousands of reassurances and kind words, the wisdom and guidance, all the joy she's given me—and my prayers changed from pleading to thanking. As the amplified thumps of Mom's heart echoed in the small room, all I could think was *Thank You! Thank You! Thank You!*

Heavenly Father, even in the scariest
moments, when I focus on love,
You take away my fear and
replace it with gratitude.
—SABRA CIANCANELLI

Digging Deeper: PSALMS 71:23, 120:1;
JEREMIAH 33:3

Sat 5

"For if you forgive other people when they sin against you, your heavenly Father will also forgive you."
—MATTHEW 6:14 (NIV)

I entered high school after eight years of home-schooling. I knew very few people and had just lost a leg to cancer, so I was worried about how the other students would treat me. As if to confirm my worst fears, an upperclassman deliberately tripped me as I walked down the hall on my artificial leg and then made fun of me. When I told my mom what had happened, she cried.

Years have passed, and a few weeks ago I got an unexpected message online. It was from the upperclassman. He tracked me down to say how guilty he has felt about that day and wanted to know if I would forgive him.

I wasn't sure. Would forgiving him be tantamount to condoning his actions? Wasn't bullying wrong? I talked it over with a few friends, and the advice was split.

But then I remembered that God forgives and loves me despite much greater shortcomings than those displayed by that bully. So it was not my place to withhold forgiveness. It was not my job to evaluate the merits of his apology or decide whether he deserved forgiveness. I wrote him back and told him that it was no big deal. Because really, it wasn't.

And I'm certainly not going to let a bully trip me up in my relationship with God.

Lord, grant me the grace to forgive those who trespass against me. —Joshua Sundquist

Digging Deeper: Matthew 18:21–22

GIFTS OF JOY

Sun 6

"A virgin will be with child and bear a son, and she will call His name Immanuel." —Isaiah 7:14 (NAS)

SECOND SUNDAY IN ADVENT: FINDING PEACE

There's a radio station in Pittsburgh that starts playing Christmas songs in November, and when you add those on to the Christmas songs you hear on the elevator and Christmas department store music and every other Christmas commercial, you can really start getting resentful and angry instead of hopeful and excited.

Plus the "special sale" they had on Black Friday wasn't all that special, and why had I thought Sandee would like a pair of those earrings when she has a pair just like them. But the real problem is I don't know what to get her, and I never do because gifts are a second-rate substitute to show how I really feel but can't always express.

And don't get me started on the kids. They're older now, so I don't know what to give them other than money. And then I start thinking about the money spent at Christmas and feel even more resentful, and start wondering like I do every year why we have Christmas at all, slowly withdrawing into my own self-made lonely exile.

This might explain why my truck is pulled over on the shoulder because I might be crying a little listening to the Heinz Chapel Choir sing, "O come, O come Emmanuel/and ransom captive Israel," and thinking maybe Israel isn't the only one who could use redeeming this season.

Lord, unlike You, my anger is always swift
and often unjust. Let me know peace this
season—the peace that passeth all understanding.
—MARK COLLINS

Digging Deeper: PSALM 107:8–9, EPHESIANS 1:7–14

Mon 7

He has sent me to bind up the
brokenhearted. . . .
—ISAIAH 61:1 (NIV)

I *wonder if I can keep putting these broken, fragile figures out every year,* I mused as I tenderly unwrapped the plaster Nativity pieces from the tissue paper; they'd survived three generations, often rescued from children's curious hands.

First was a shepherd carrying a lamb with part of a leg missing. It's an appropriate reminder that sheep, especially broken ones, are totally dependent on the shepherd.

Next was an angel with a broken wing and paint-chipped knees, surely from all of the kneeling and praying before going off to take messages, including one to a virgin that she would soon be with child.

Then the wise men: there used to be three, but I'm down to two. Even wise men sometimes lose their way.

Ah, Joseph. He's the most solidly intact, which seems appropriate because that's the way he stood by Mary's side.

And Mary: she's got some obvious nicks, but she still reminds me that she said "yes" to God and allowed her life to work the Christmas miracle from the inside out.

Finally I unwrap Baby Jesus. Even He has not been spared the wear and tear. His body is broken; a hand and both feet have been carefully glued back on, which is a powerful reminder about the purpose of His life.

I gently place the figures atop the bookcase where I hope they'll be safe for another season, because their appearance brings deeper reality to the meaning of Christmas for me.

> *Lord, I, too, stand by the manger,*
> *chipped and broken and wondrously grateful*
> *that Baby Jesus came to heal people like me.*
> —CAROL KUYKENDALL

Digging Deeper: MATTHEW 4:24, ACTS 9:32–35

Tue 8

David became weak and exhausted. Ishbi-benob, a giant whose speartip weighed more than twelve pounds and who was sporting a new suit of armor, closed in on David and was about to kill him. But Abishai, the son of Zeruiah, came to his rescue and killed the Philistine. After that, David's men declared, "You are not going out to battle again! . . ."
—2 SAMUEL 21:15–17 (TLB)

Giants have a way of showing up at every phase of life, even in old age. After forty-three years in the college classroom, I was tired. Constant changes in academia drained the joy out of teaching, yet I did not want to retire. I loved students and felt I was making a difference in their lives precisely *because* of my age.

"Whatever would I do in retirement?" I muttered to my wife over supper. "Retirement could be harder than teaching."

Sharon grinned mischievously. "Well, I just happen to have a long list of projects!"

I laughed out loud. "Why does that not surprise me?"

She went on: "For the first time in your life you would be free of a school schedule. We could travel, you could do more writing, you could hoe your garden till your hands bleed."

The more we talked, the smaller my giant became, until finally it was no giant at all. I retired, with no regrets at all.

The children's story of young David and Goliath is inspiring and dramatic, but the story of old David and Ishbi-benob is more realistic because not all giants can be defeated alone. Sometimes I need to talk to someone, to get a different perspective on my problem. There is no shame, only wisdom, in asking for help.

> *I thank You, God, for the wise woman*
> *You gave me as a helpmate.*
> —Daniel Schantz

Digging Deeper: Exodus 18:19;
Proverbs 11:14, 12:15

I SURRENDER ALL

Wed 9 *Arise and eat.* —1 KINGS 19:5 (ASV)

SERENITY IN THE DAY-TO-DAY

I wrote "Surrender" in my prayer journal and scribbled a message to God: "I don't know how to let go. Help me!"

As my husband left for work, he said, "You look tired. Why don't you rest?"

I just looked at him. *Rest? How?* I had obligations. Still wearing my bathrobe, I hurried upstairs to my office with a cup of coffee.

Around noon, my friend and mentor DiAnn called. She works at home too. I admire her levelheadedness, so I told her that I felt chained to a treadmill. "Oh, Julie," she said, "your body's a temple of the Holy Spirit. Take care of yourself."

Her kindness pulled at my heart. "DiAnn, what's *your* daily schedule like?" I asked.

"I get up early, have my quiet time, exercise, take a shower, and dress."

"In normal clothes?"

"Yes." She laughed. "So I can answer the door. I eat breakfast too."

"You do all of this before sitting at your computer?"

"Yes. Always." DiAnn promised to pray for me and offered another nugget of wisdom: "Don't isolate yourself. See people."

After we hung up, I took three more steps on my surrender journey. For the first time in months, I ate breakfast. I even accepted a lunch date. Then I prayed the Serenity Prayer.

God, grant me the serenity to accept the things
I cannot change, courage to change the things
I can, and wisdom to know the difference.
—JULIE GARMON

Digging Deeper: 1 CORINTHIANS 6:19, 1 JOHN 1:7

Thu 10

"I am the Alpha and the Omega," says the Lord God, who is and who was and who is to come, the Almighty.
—REVELATION 1:8 (NRSV)

Before Michael and I married, we drove to eastern Oklahoma so I could meet his grandparents. The house where they lived was outlined with Christmas lights, red ribbons wrapped around the front pillars of their porch. Greenery lay at the bottom of each window, and an evergreen wreath graced the door. In the side yard, two eight-foot timbers were fashioned into a cross, covered with white lights. When I saw it, I felt irritated. I never liked crosses during Christmas. The season was about the birth of Christ, not the crucifixion.

Mam Ma cooked a fabulous meal, and we had so much fun getting acquainted. As we were leaving, Pap Pa took my arm. "Say, gal, did you see my old rugged cross?"

I nodded and tried to hold my tongue.

"Do you know why we have a cross in the yard at Christmastime?" he asked. I got ready to set him straight about mixing holidays, but before I could speak, he continued. "The cross symbolizes the Savior. Without the sacrifice of a Savior, the birth of the Messiah is pointless. The Messiah was born for the purpose of dying in order to save us."

That next Christmas, after Michael and I married, Pap Pa built a cross for our yard. It's my favorite decoration of all.

Thank You for Your birth and death, Lord.
—STEPHANIE THOMPSON

Digging Deeper: ISAIAH 7:14, MARK 8:29, JOHN 3:16

Fri 11   *"You whom I have taken from the ends of the earth..., 'Do not fear, for I am with you....'"*
—ISAIAH 41:9–10 (NAS)

I am a grown man, but I still have my teddy bear. He sits beside my favorite reading chair that my wife gave me on the occasion of my first Father's Day, thirty years ago. Somehow my tattered teddy bear and my worn-out recliner go together.

Teddy and I met under the Christmas tree in 1957. It was my first Christmas living in the Philippine Islands. Uncle Bill and Aunt Earlene found Teddy in a toy store in North Carolina, packaged him in a sturdy cardboard box, and sent him across the vast Pacific Ocean to me. Teddy and I have been traveling together ever since.

When my father died in 1965, my family returned to Georgia. Teddy made the trip, tucked carefully in the corner of a large locker trunk. He sat in my room through high school but didn't go to college. However, when Beth and I were married, Teddy came to live with us.

Tattered and torn, Teddy needed some TLC, so my mother recently put him through the ordeal of a comprehensive restoration process. He has a new right eye, a stitched nose, and a patched ear. But he is the same teddy bear.

Teddy has become my sentimental symbol of the eternal presence of God in my life. Sometimes I hold Teddy late at night and simply recite, "Fear not, I am with thee, oh be not dismayed, for I am thy God and will still give thee aid!" (Isaiah 41:10).

Father, thank You for always being near. Amen.
—Scott Walker

Digging Deeper: Psalm 46

Sat 12

"Do not despise these small beginnings, for the Lord rejoices to see the work begin...." —Zechariah 4:10 (NLT)

"Cut it here," my wife, Margi, said.

"What? That's way too short," I replied.

"Trust me. It will be pretty."

And so our towering, hard-won Christmas tree shrank from a glorious twelve-foot giant to a pathetic three-foot shrimp.

Our home in Northern California offers a unique opportunity to trek deep into mountain forests on bumpy logging roads to cut down our own Christmas tree. Not only has this given us a family tradition, but it also gives me an excuse to fire up my chainsaw.

Permits in hand, we waded through snow, hiked over boulders, and scanned the horizon for our perfect tree. This year's tree was miles into the forest. Fresh snow frosted the branches. We felled the tree, wrestled it into the pickup, and headed down the mountain with our prize.

Once home, we set the tree in its stand. Then we discovered a huge problem. The snow that topped the branches also hid a massive bare spot. I suggested drilling holes and inserting branches. Margi had a different idea: just use the top; three measly feet.

I resisted. I didn't want a Charlie Brown tree.

Margi promised she could make it nice. And she did. It rises up from our coffee table and whispers daily the Christmas truth that sometimes God's best gifts come in the smallest packages.

Father, give me eyes to see and a heart to treasure all the gifts You bestow, great and small.
—BILL GIOVANNETTI

Digging Deeper: PROVERBS 4:18

GIFTS OF JOY

Sun 13   *Consider the lilies of the field, how they grow; they toil not, neither do they spin: And yet I say unto you, That even Solomon in all his glory was not arrayed like one of these.*
—MATTHEW 6:28–29 (KJV)

THIRD SUNDAY IN ADVENT: BEING PRESENT

Disclaimer: I love all three of my daughters. However, we have but one shower, and it would be nifty if we could agree on a single shampoo. Instead, we have nearly a dozen bottles! One is for moisturizing, one is for straight hair, one is for oily hair, one is for curly hair, and one is for (I'm not making this up) that "just-out-of-bed, messy look." I mastered that years ago.

My choice, I'm proud to say, is genius: I funnel all the old shampoo into a single pump bottle. I now have that "messy, used-a-random-mixture-of-shampoo" look. One daughter suggested that my thinning gray hair may be the product of washing with a shampoo potpourri. I suggested that my thinning gray hair was the result of having three daughters.

I know why they do this. They're searching for what will make their hair perfect, what will somehow make *them* perfect. I know they're already perfect. They're quirky, mistake-prone, sometimes kind, sometimes rude, often laughing, mostly loving . . . you know, human. Perfectly human. But they dwell on what isn't there (or on what they *think* isn't there).

We do the same at Christmas, focusing on finding the perfect gift instead of, well, on finding the Perfect Gift. We dwell instead on what isn't there, blind to what we have been given: our own stockings, the ones we're wearing, filled with wonder. Us. Our presence is the right present for this birthday, despite our Christmas-morning-just-out-of-bed look. Which, I've been told, is perfect.

Lord, let my daughters see in themselves what You see.
—Mark Collins

Digging Deeper: Isaiah 49:1

Mon 14

"So it is not the will of your Father in heaven that one of these little ones should be lost."
—Matthew 18:14 (nrsv)

Every year I help organize a women's retreat for faculty at the university where I teach. Everyone's so busy that only a fraction of us manage to go: typically either those who are single or those whose children have grown up.

My two daughters were still small the first time I attended, then in high school, now in college. And each year I've reported on my current worries about them: their meanness toward each other as small ones, their waning interest in church as teenagers, their bouts of surliness on their occasional visits home from college.

Although my colleagues eagerly pray for my girls, I always come away envious of the other mothers among them. I've met their obviously devout children over the years and read online posts about their kids' mission work, nestled in among photos of jolly grandbabies. *What have they done as mothers that I somehow overlooked?* I'd wonder as I drove home.

This time, though, as we chatted around the fire, one colleague revealed her own struggles with a daughter. "I have to remind myself that God's not just *my* Father," she said. "He's *her* Father too."

Ever since that night, I've seen my girls differently. Not as my sisters, surely, but nevertheless as children of the same fond Dad. *God's got plans for them,* I tell myself. *And if my experience is any measure, they won't be able to resist whatever it is He has in mind.*

> *Best Parent of all parents, thanks for looking out for all of us!* —PATTY KIRK

> *Digging Deeper:* JOHN 6:44–47

Tue 15

Look to the Lord and his strength; seek his face always.
—1 CHRONICLES 16:11 (NIV)

When I picked up my son from Cub Scouts, his pack leader pulled me aside. "Stephen got very upset tonight and punched Cory," he said. "I tried to find out what was wrong, but

Stephen wouldn't talk." My stomach sank, not just in the "my-kid's-*caused*-trouble" way, but with a "my-kid-*has*-trouble" ache. The anxiety disorder that plagues my family manifests itself differently in each person. My husband, Andrew, withdraws. Our son John explodes. Our daughter Maggie gets depressed. Stephen gets flustered and then goes mute.

It was one more day before my nine-year-old was able to talk about what happened. After telling a bully to stop taunting him numerous times, Stephen took a swing and hit the wrong kid. Stephen was so distraught he could barely understand what the leader was saying and couldn't talk.

I said to my son all the things moms say and prayed the things moms pray. We reviewed strategies for calming down. He wrote a note of apology. I told him I love him. I jotted down a reminder to discuss the incident with his counselor.

Late that night, I gave myself time to think and cry. Most days I do pretty well with my high-needs family: I cope, I'm resourceful, I'm resilient. Yet sometimes it feels like too much. Sometimes I wish that what's normal in my family could be more like what I think normal should be.

So I said to God all the things that hurting mothers say. I told Him I love Him. And I thought that maybe, even though life is hard now, perhaps what's normal for me is exactly what normal should be.

> *Jesus, help me seek Your peace instead of the peace I think I want.* —JULIA ATTAWAY

> *Digging Deeper:* MATTHEW 11:13, 28

Wed 16

Therefore, as God's choice, holy and loved, put on compassion, kindness, humility, gentleness, and patience.... And over all these things put on love....
—COLOSSIANS 3:12, 14 (CEB)

My favorite dress is a Christmas gift from my sister Amanda. It is black rayon with tiny flowers and vines in cream, green, pink, and red. The waist is fitted, the skirt flared, and the front buttons are bordered in antique gold. I was stunned when I opened the box because Amanda frequently wore the dress and I often admired it.

"Why are you giving me your best dress?" I asked.

"Because I want you to have it," she responded. "You give lots of talks, and this dress is perfect for you." She paused and added, "Plus, the gifts I bought for you and others flew out the back window of the van while we were driving home."

While I was sorry about that, I received the dress with joy. Between us, Amanda and I have now worn it for nearly fifteen years. I still feel special every time I put it on; I become more of my best self. I think it's because of the love and sacrifice the dress represents. When I wear it, I remember my sister's generosity, kindness, and love. Somehow a little bit of her rubs off on me.

Thank You, Jesus, for a sister who gave up her favorite dress with love. —PENNEY SCHWAB

Digging Deeper: PROVERBS 31:25–26, GALATIANS 3:27

Thu 17

For great is your love, higher than the heavens; your faithfulness reaches to the skies.
—PSALM 108:4 (NIV)

Plumes of white mist hovered over the bubbling water as I sat in our hot tub on a frigid night. The sky was intensely black, a perfect backdrop for a universe of dazzling pinpoints of light. I took a deep breath and released it slowly, wishing the soothing water would absorb the depth of loss I felt.

I missed my mother terribly. It had been about one month since she had died at the age of ninety-four. She had lived a long and vibrant life, full of appreciation for God's wonders, which she often described as "exquisite!" How she would have loved this night.

"Mother," I said out loud, "are you out there somewhere?"

Even if she is, I thought, *her brightness would be eclipsed by tonight's radiant stars.*

That thought had barely formed when the largest, most brilliant, most magnificent comet I have ever seen streaked across the sky and then fizzled out as quickly as it had come.

An intense joy filled me. I laughed out loud. I clapped. I knew without a doubt that all was well with my mother. I could almost hear her say, "Wasn't that exquisite?"

Thank You, Lord God, that out of Your goodness and Your love, You even open up the heavens to us.
—KIM HENRY

Digging Deeper: PSALM 8:3–5, 2 TIMOTHY 4:7–8

Fri 18

Even if I had the gift of faith so that I could speak to a mountain and make it move, I would still be worth nothing at all without love.
—1 CORINTHIANS 13:2 (TLB)

The year my youngest child left for college, I invented a strange hobby to keep my mind off the fact that I was an empty nester. I began to paint glass jars with puffy fabric paint . . . jelly jars, pickle jars, mayonnaise jars, spaghetti sauce jars, even large thirty-three-ounce jars that hold artichoke hearts. I gave one of them to my friend Kay, who was so thrilled she talked about it for weeks. That was the beginning.

Since then I've painted over seven thousand jars. I decorate the lids with paint, jewelry, buttons, beads, old watches, beach glass, even rocks. I've sold some jars at art shows and various events, but mostly I've given them away.

I've become a crazed and joyful gift-giver. Everywhere I go, I take a jar filled with something as a hostess gift. I've filled many with dollar bills taped together and rolled up for my grandkids. At Christmas, I give my painted jars filled with cookies, candy, homemade granola, tea, pretzels, paper clips, cotton swabs, and trinkets to everyone I know.

Sometimes when I see all the expensive gifts that are heaped on children and grandchildren these days, I am reminded that in Jesus's time the gifts they exchanged were probably very simple things: a loaf of bread baked over an open fire, apple jelly sweetened with honey, a flowering plant.

I love the idea of giving handmade gifts from my heart rather than spending money on things I can't afford. Now that I'm living on a fixed income, my hand-painted jars make even more sense.

Jesus, help me continue to give something of myself to those I love and not to fall into the trap of commercialism this holiday season.
—PATRICIA LORENZ

Digging Deeper: MATTHEW 23:19,
2 CORINTHIANS 9:15

Sat 19

For in this hope we were saved. But hope that is seen is no hope at all. Who hopes for what they already have? But if we hope for what we do not yet have, we wait for it patiently.
—ROMANS 8:24–25 (NIV)

The cardamom bread is homemade, fumbled together by hands far less experienced than the now-arthritic pair that had carefully crafted it for me so many times before. Hot from the oven, mine looks serviceable and smells like my childhood.

My china cups are mismatched—one blue, one pink, three green—from the antiques store down the road. The purple-and-white-flowered linen tablecloth was found at a garage sale. The napkins are plain white paper.

My tea party is far from the perfect ones of my childhood, but it is fueled by a loving nostalgia that I hope will overcome any inadequacies I have. Because while I'll never be able to serve tea like my grandmother used to, I pray that my efforts will be enough to show her aging heart, her waning spirit, that I love her and that I remember, even if she can't.

I hold her feeble hand; I butter her bread; I pour cream into her tea and stir gently. Then I wait. Not for appreciative words or remembrances of tea parties past, but for that glimmer of a smile, that glint in her eyes, which show a small spark of her enduring spirit.

*Lord, thank You for those
moments when I get to show this dear
one how much I love her. Help me to live as
she has, with an enduring spirit.*
—ERIN MACPHERSON

Digging Deeper: TITUS 3:7, I PETER 1:3

GIFTS OF JOY

Sun 20

Then shall the virgin rejoice in the dance, both young men and old together: for I will turn their mourning into joy, and will comfort them, and make them rejoice from their sorrow.
—JEREMIAH 31:13 (KJV)

FOURTH SUNDAY IN ADVENT:
MAKING ROOM

We live in the smallest house in the neighborhood. Actually, we may live in the smallest house in several neighborhoods. Sandee and I moved here BK (before kids) and referred to our tiny abode as "our starter home." That was twenty-five years and three kids ago. Whatever we were supposed to start is surely finished by now.

Five people in a small house is—well—intimate. I can honestly say that I learned more about my daughters' daily habits than I wanted to. I have seen my kids stand on the porch in a driving rainstorm, just to have privacy on the phone. Perhaps I uttered some blue language while working on a car in the driveway, only to have my kids—on the second floor, mind you—chastise my swearing.

Now it's Christmas and they're all home again, plus some out-of-town guests, so one or more kids will sleep on the floor or couch. You'd think this would lead to conflicts, but it's mostly (and surprisingly) peaceful. There is a lot of laughter, a lot of screaming (usually lyrics to the B-52s), a lot of what loosely would be labeled dancing.

And having survived on this small island for twenty-five years, isolated with four others in the primitive tribe, I happily join the natives in dance. Turns out, it doesn't require much space to make a family... couple of walls, really, or maybe a barn if there's no other place. I'm sure someone will sleep on the floor if that's what it takes to make room this season.

Lord, sometimes my home is crowded and my heart is not open. Let me learn how to make more room in both. —MARK COLLINS

Digging Deeper: ROMANS 12:16–18

Mon 21

"Blessed is she who has believed that the Lord will fulfill his promises to her!"
—LUKE 1:45 (NIV)

When I was five, my three older brothers and I acted out cowboy dramas. Every day, mimicking what we'd seen on TV, we magically transformed the basement of our home into the Wild West. Dressed in my Easter bonnet and carrying a small white straw purse, I was an innocent schoolmarm riding in a stagecoach to a frontier town.

Each time, just as I was about to arrive safely at my destination, my coach was stopped by three armed and masked bandits who robbed me of the contents of my purse. At first, the holdups were exciting. But as spring turned to summer and then fall, I grew weary of being the victim. When winter came, I devised a plan. I'd ask Santa for a toy gun of my own. He would rescue me!

Christmas came, and my brothers and I scrambled under the tree for our presents. There were trains and cars for my brothers and a doll and dollhouse for me! How could Santa have failed me? My mother, busy stuffing the turkey and baking pies, shook her head and said I'd get over it.

But my father understood my despair. He grabbed his coat, pulled on his boots, and trudged out into the snow. Soon he returned with not one but two toy guns. I was overjoyed.

The next day, I rode into the frontier town on the imaginary stagecoach. Just like every other day, the bandits stopped my progress. But this time when they demanded the contents of my purse, I whipped out one of my toy pistols and the bandits ran away!

Lord, thank You for a father who saw, as
You always have, what I was going
through, answered my cry, and gave me
the tools to rescue myself.
—SHARON FOSTER

Digging Deeper: JUDGES 6:12–14,
JEREMIAH 24:6

Tue 22

Give generously to them and do so without a grudging heart; then because of this the Lord your God will bless you in all your work and in everything you put your hand to.
—DEUTERONOMY 15:10 (NIV)

Three days before Christmas I'm feeling frantic, quite sure I'm never going to get done all the things that need doing. That present to my goddaughter that has to be mailed; those stocking stuffers I promised to buy; the Christmas cards that still need to be sent; the "Merry Christmas" e-mails I wanted to write; the present for my wife I have to pick up; the music I brought home from choir rehearsal that I must study before Christmas Eve— *when will I get to it?*

Then I remember this program at church where we volunteer to give Christmas to a family that's going through hard times. I haven't gotten those kids presents yet. *When am I going to do that? Just one more thing!*

I dash out at lunch, pop my goddaughter's present in the mail, buy some gloves from a street vendor for stocking stuffers, duck into another store for Carol, and finally make it to the toy store. *Now, what would a four-year-old, six-year-old, and eight-year-old boy like?* Standing in the aisle of cars and trucks,

I still feel frantic, but I'm happy-frantic instead of worried-frantic.

Christmas Eve, I'm amazed at how many presents are under the tree. In choir, the piece that had seemed impossible comes together miraculously. Before the service I check my e-mail to see a message from my goddaughter's mother: "Package just arrived." Another miracle. How did the post office do it? How did the choir do it? How did any of us do it?

Then I remember: we did it with love. That was the fuel. That's where we got the energy. Love and joy and happiness. A miracle good enough to last all year long.

I can do all good things with the energy of Your love, Lord. —RICK HAMLIN

Digging Deeper: 2 CORINTHIANS 8:7

Wed 23   *The steps of a good man are ordered by the Lord, And He delights in his way.* —PSALM 37:23 (NKJV)

It was Christmas week, and I was on my way home from shopping when I felt my car barely tap the Jeep in front of me at a red light. The lady flew out of the vehicle and hurled every manner of accusation at me. When I recounted the event to a coworker, she remarked: "I bet that woman takes your insurance company for a ride. People do that at Christmastime when they need money."

Her comment was all I could think about for days. Suddenly, every vehicle became another threat. I exercised great caution to stay several feet behind any car in front of me.

Then on Christmas Eve, I was in line at a drive-through when ahead of me I saw a Jeep similar to the one I had inadvertently tapped. Fear filled my mind. *Be careful, Roberta. It's just another opportunist who will take advantage of your insurance company.*

But was I ever in for a surprise. When I pulled up to the window, the drive-through clerk had an extrabig smile on his face. "No charge today," he said. "The car in front of you paid for your order and said to wish you a blessed Christmas."

Help me to leave past experiences where they belong, Father—in the past. —ROBERTA MESSNER

Digging Deeper: ISAIAH 43:18–19, PHILIPPIANS 3:13

GIFTS OF JOY

Thu 24   *"Thus the saying 'One sows and another reaps' is true. I sent you to reap what you have not worked for. . . ."* —JOHN 4:37–38 (NIV)

CHRISTMAS EVE: RENEWAL

The season of Advent corresponds to another season in Pittsburgh: shoveling snow.

Fun fact about driving in Pittsburgh: if you shovel out a parking space in front of your house, you get to reserve that spot by placing an object—usually a folding chair—in that space. It doesn't have to be a chair; a garbage can or an old sawhorse will do. (I've seen walkers and vacuum cleaners serve as unofficial markers.) While the *objet de snow* is there, no one but you can park in the spot. Although this practice exists in other northeastern cities, the tradition is unofficially known as "the Pittsburgh parking chair." Nice to be known for something.

Seems like a selfish gesture during the season of gift-giving, no? Right answer: no, it's not. Gifts are undeserved; a shoveled parking spot is earned. Technically speaking, parking chairs aren't legal, but local tradition dictates respect.

That's what makes Christmas gifts (and grace) so special: they're undeserved. Let's face it: we all deserve a little coal for our annual transgressions. Yet each Christmas we are forgiven and not because we've earned it. Can you think of a better birthday gift than renewal? So put a small chair in front of the crèche this year and reserve your spot. No one will take your place. No one *can* take your place.

Lord, You have invited all of us without reservation. This season, let us realize the chance for God and sinner to reconcile. —MARK COLLINS

Digging Deeper: PSALM 127:4–5

GIFTS OF JOY

Fri 25

That was the true Light, which lighteth every man that cometh into the world. —JOHN 1:9 (KJV)

CHRISTMAS: KNOWING THE LIGHT

I'm an amateur mechanic. My automotive repairs don't always conform to daylight hours, so I have mastered the flashlight-in-the-mouth look. Sometimes a trouble light just won't fit, so I cram a small penlight between my teeth and slide underneath the car.

Seems pretty primitive, right? Let me tell you: in ancient times, a guy with a miniflashlight would be worshipped as a deity. All they had in the darkness was flame and stars—lots and lots of stars.

Which makes those crazy wise men even more crazy. *Hey, let's follow that star in the East! The bright one. No, the* other *bright one!* Isn't it strange that one of them didn't say, "Um, why are we doing this again?" or "Okay, we can get there following the star, but how do we get back?"

Actually, I know the answer. I used to teach at a field camp in the Rocky Mountains. At night—especially a moonless night—you can see the entire firmament. You can see the edge of the Milky Way. You can see, it seems, forever, as if you are looking at heaven itself.

It's dark beneath a car. Without even the tiniest light, you could be turning something the wrong way. At Christmastime, even as the winter daylight fades and evening comes early, we have enough light to know which way to turn.

> *Lord, Christmas lights twinkle*
> *over our entire neighborhood.*
> *Let each be a star to guide*
> *wisdom into our homes.*
> —MARK COLLINS

Digging Deeper: JOHN 1:14–17, I JOHN 4:11

Sat 26

"The virgin shall conceive and bear a son, and they shall name him Emmanuel," which means, "God is with us." —MATTHEW 1:23 (NRSV)

Christmas was almost over, but for us it was just beginning.

It was nearly noon on Christmas Day. Kate was done leading the final service at our Episcopal church, where she's rector. There had been two services the night before, plus weeks of Advent, a pageant, choir rehearsals, liturgy planning, the pressure that always builds at Christmas.

Our children, Frances and Benjamin, had opened a few gifts that morning but most remained under the tree. My family was due to arrive from Los Angeles later, and when they did, we sat around the candlelit table. We held hands, and I said grace. Then we ate and ate. Kate's apple and cranberry pie tasted even better than last year.

I sat back in my chair, feeling a rare moment of pure happiness. I'd been just as tense as Kate the past few weeks. When her work ramps up, the burden is on me to pick up the slack, juggling kids and work. Now that was over for a while. The holiday had begun.

I closed my eyes and listened to the clink of forks on plates, the sound of laughter and kids begging for another piece of pie. *This, too, is the incarnation of God,* I thought, *people gathered in love, forgetting for a moment their imaginary castles of stress.* That's why we celebrate this day: because God came to be with us and is still here.

Give me the gift of Your presence today, Lord.
—JIM HINCH

Digging Deeper: JOHN 1:14

Sun 27

A time to keep and a time to throw away. —ECCLESIASTES 3:6 (NIV)

"Y̶ou can't get rid of that!" I told my husband as he pulled an old piano stool off a shelf in our basement, which we were converting into a workout room.

"It's beat up," he replied. "We don't use it and don't have anywhere to store it now."

The next morning on my prayer walk I was still trying to figure out a way to hang on to my garage-sale treasures when I saw a man with a huge backhoe getting ready to tear down a dilapidated farmhouse. My heart cried, *Save it!* Yet common sense said, *There's a tree growing through the porch and the roof has holes in it big enough to crawl through.* And so with warring emotions, I found a cold seat on a stone wall and watched the demise of the old home.

I winced as the backhoe claw grabbed through the broken roof and knocked down an outer wall in a splintery crumble of brittle boards and thick brown dust. The backhoe attacked an inner wall. The roof groaned and part of it gave way. Seeing what a rotten ruin the house had become made me admit, albeit reluctantly, that it was way past time to let it go.

"To every thing there is a season, and a time to every purpose under heaven," crept quietly into my mind (Ecclesiastes 3:1, KJV). Letting go of the old is part of the cleansing, healthy rhythm of life.

Dear Father, help me to make room in my life for the new things You have for me today. Amen.
—KAREN BARBER

Digging Deeper: MARK 2:21–22, LUKE 9:59–62

Mon 28

If any of you lacks wisdom, let him ask God, who gives generously to all without reproach, and it will be given him. —JAMES 1:5 (ESV)

Our daughter Charlotte gave us a Lego set for Christmas, inviting us to construct a model of the Farnsworth House, a famous glass-sided building designed by Mies van der Rohe.

My husband and I opened the box, pulled out the instructions, and got to work. We emptied out all of the tiny plastic pieces, many of them identical, with little bumps to help fit them together. We felt challenged but persevered, and clicked the floor and ceilings into place.

"We're finished," I said, putting in a final piece. "But we must have made a mistake." Five pieces of different colored plastic stared accusingly from the table.

"We didn't do it right," I told my daughter with obvious disappointment. I wanted to prove we could rise to the challenge.

"Oh, Mom," said Charlotte patiently, "there are always some pieces left over. Didn't you know that?"

I didn't. We had done our best, but I'd wanted it to be perfect. Looking at the little white house with the green steps, I was reminded that most of the time not all of the pieces of who we are and what we do fit together exactly. It was time to toss those extra pieces and move on.

Lord, help me to remember that You know
we are far from perfect, but we're
doing the best we can.
—BRIGITTE WEEKS

Digging Deeper: PSALM 119:96,
HEBREWS 7:18–20

Tue 29

"Do thyself no harm. . . ."
—ACTS 16:28 (KJV)

There's nothing darker than a moonless night in rural Africa. There are no lights to tint the sky, only vivid stars that sparkle on black velvet. In such darkness, I am following my friend Paddington down a steep, rocky path. We have stayed too long visiting a neighbor.

All is quiet until Paddington breaks the silence. "Pam, if you see a stick that moves, don't foot it."

He certainly knows how to get my full attention. "So, Paddington, what exactly would the moving stick be?" I ask.

"Black mamba," he says.

"Paddington," I take the discussion deeper, "what if there was a moving stick and I did 'foot it'?"

"Oh, Pam," he says as we break through the clearing and see the fire from the cooking hut ahead, "it would be very, very unfortunate."

Later, enjoying a bowl of sadza, I probe the subject of black mambas. They are among the world's deadliest snakes, and the Zimbabweans build their huts without chimneys to keep them out.

"We teach our children to fear the black mamba," Paddington explains, "to stay away from the places where they go."

"And if they see a black mamba?"

"Ah, we teach our children to run away as fast as they can."

Back in Nashville, Tennessee, I miss the beautiful nights and hospitable dinners served in the cooking hut in Zimbabwe, but I don't miss the possibility of "moving sticks." Of course, there are always dangers to teach our children to avoid: moving cars, deep water, disrespectful friends, cruel attitudes. As adults, there are negative influences, venomous selfishness, you name it. In all these things, Paddington's wisdom rings true: Avoid. Run in the opposite direction. Don't foot it.

Father, keep us watchful of the "moving sticks" that would do us harm. —PAM KIDD

Digging Deeper: PROVERBS 11:27, MATTHEW 10:16

Wed 30

Tribulation worketh patience; And patience, experience; and experience, hope.
—ROMANS 5:3–4 (KJV)

I want to start a college fund for my son," Bill said as he entered my office. The look on his face told me there was more, so I waited. "Sometimes I think it's the only good thing I'll ever be able to do for him," he explained, describing his nasty divorce and the ensuing separation from his son. "I feel like he doesn't want to be with me and that I should make it easy for him and just give up." Tears pooled in his eyes.

I had a lot to do and appointments were backing up, but I could feel God nudging me: *Tell your story, Brock.*

I leaned back in my chair. "I've been there, Bill, and it's not easy. My son, Harrison, wasn't even two years old when his mother and I divorced." I went on to describe the dread I felt waiting in his mom's driveway: how I'd plaster a smile on my face and walk to the door, anticipating Harrison's screams when I reached out for him.

"Luckily my sister, Keri, an expert in child behavior, had programmed a scenario in my head: *Be patient. Speak calmly. React with love.* I would drive to a nearby parking lot and tell Harrison, still screaming and kicking in his car seat, that I loved him, that I was going to get out of the car and wait until he stopped crying, and then we were going to Daddy's house to have a fun weekend. I would stand by his window with my head turned, so he wouldn't see that I was crying too. Over time his crying fits diminished, and I began to feel hopeful enough that I never gave up." I picked up a framed photo of Harrison and me standing together, holding a big fish as we smiled into the camera. Bill looked at it and then back at me; his face was awash with hope.

> *Father God, be patient with us and*
> *fill us with Your hope so that*
> *we might be patient too.*
> —BROCK KIDD

Digging Deeper: PSALM 37:7, ROMANS 12:12

Thu 31

A heart at peace gives life to the body. . . . —PROVERBS 14:30 (NIV)

It had been a long time since I had enjoyed New Year's Eve. My parents were in town to watch my sons, so I was free to go! I started sending out texts and making phone calls and ended up with a few options: a small gathering at a friend's house; Times Square with some coworkers; or a party downtown as a friend's guest.

As New Year's Eve approached, I narrowed down where I should go. My friend's small gathering sounded perfect. But that evening, instead of making myself pretty, I gave the boys a bath, read them books, and kissed them good night. My parents were already watching the pre-countdown shows, and I got hooked. I snuggled next to them with a bowl of ice cream. By 10:30 PM it was clear I wasn't going anywhere. I called my friend and told her I was staying home with my family.

The year before, I was aching to go somewhere exciting and felt trapped. But this time I was completely content to be with my parents, whom I don't often see, and to listen to my kids, who were still chatting away in their bedroom.

It wasn't the most exciting New Year's Eve, but it was exactly where I wanted to be.

Father, give me a heart that is content, and thank You for giving me all I need.
—KAREN VALENTIN

Digging Deeper: I TIMOTHY 6:6

DAILY JOYS

1 _____

2 _____

3 _____

4 _____

5 _____

6 _____

7 _____

8 _____

9 _____

10 _____

11 _____

12 _____

13 _____

14 _____

15 _____

December

16 _____

17 _____

18 _____

19 _____

20 _____

21 _____

22 _____

23 _____

24 _____

25 _____

26 _____

27 _____

28 _____

29 _____

30 _____

31 _____

It has been a year of many blessings for SAM ADRIANCE of New Haven, Connecticut. Chief among them was his marriage to Emily Siefken in Austin, Texas. "Our wedding was a perfect day because it was so true to us both," he says. "It was an intimate ceremony that focused on sharing our love with each other and our family." He also saw his brother, Ned, graduate from Davidson College and start work on Capitol Hill in Washington, DC, the same city where Sam spent his summer off from law school, working as a legal intern at the Department of Justice. Sam still frequently sees his parents, who live in New Jersey with the family dog, Nellie.

"It was a very challenging year for me and my husband, Charlie," MARCI ALBORGHETTI of New London, Connecticut, acknowledges. "I believe it was an opportunity to grow closer to God by realizing that no matter how much I want to control my life, He is in charge. I'm trying to trust Him even more." She also used the time to work on two new books, *Being the Body of Christ* and *The People of the Nativity Story*. Marci lost her dear friend and correspondent Lynn Holm, a longtime Guideposts reader, and "one of the most truly godly men I've ever known. The only comfort for all of us who knew him and were mentored by him is that he's now where he most wanted to be: with God and his wife and daughter."

ANDREW ATTAWAY of New York City writes, "As our daughter Maggie, 12, and our son Stephen, 10, continually remind us, we've had three seniors in the house this year: college senior Elizabeth, 19, our son John, 17, a senior in high school, and me, now a senior citizen. We've also got Mary, 15, diligent as a high school sophomore, joyful and radiant as a dancer. And my wife, Julia, who does more for her family and her community than I have room to tell. And, of course, there's Amsterdam, who sheds nearly as much happiness as he does hair."

"We had a Philippians 4:11 year," writes JULIA ATTAWAY of New York City. "One in which we've had to find contentment in all kinds of difficult circumstances." She notes that there's value in having to dig deep—and then deeper—to find God's presence and light. "Every now and then I still find myself praying, 'Please let some of this be over already!' But I've learned that a strong relationship with God doesn't depend on getting to the other side of a hardship. I have to, and want to, love Him at every moment, in every situation. Figuring out how to do that is ongoing work."

"One of the greatest joys of the Prayer Igniters trip to Israel that I took," says KAREN BARBER, "was having the opportunity to worship with an Arab Christian church in Nazareth, with a Messianic Jewish congregation on Mount Carmel, and with an Anglican church full of Dutch tourists in Jerusalem. What a heavenly experience when you're singing the English words of 'How Great Thou Art' while the rest of the congregation is singing in Arabic! Now that I'm back home in Alpharetta, Georgia, where Gordon and I are enjoying our children and grandchildren, it's amazing to think that our times of greatest joy get even better when we join together in worshipping God."

EVELYN BENCE of Arlington, Virginia, is particularly grateful for her extended family: siblings spread across the country who support one another through prayer and lifelong encouragements. "I also get great joy through my small church community, hosting potlucks and serving as a lay Eucharistic minister. The many aspects of hosting took on new meaning this year as

I finished the book manuscript *Room at My Table: Preparing Heart and Home for Christian Hospitality*, fifty-two personal meditations along with some favorite family recipes."

"BlueDog, my McNabb cow dog, has been my constant guardian through the entire ordeal with back surgery," writes ERIKA BENTSEN of Sprague River, Oregon. "However, I'm afraid he's become positively rotund from all the inactivity. But I have great news at last! My doctor has determined the pain is being caused by an inflamed facet joint. Through a combination of treatments, we now have the pain curbed into manageable levels. If healing continues, I hope BlueDog and I can get back into shape to begin the next exciting chapter in life that God has in store for us."

"This was the year that my husband died," says RHODA BLECKER of Bellingham, Washington. "We called hospice on Friday, just days after the doctor had told us Keith had six months to live. We were not that fortunate, and he died on Sunday. He waited until only he and I were home, and I was right beside him, singing the song we blessed each other with every Shabbos. My husband died just as he wished: in our home, in our bed. It was a blessing. And now my prayer is that when it's my time to die, Keith comes to get me so that we can be together again. As for me, one of the nuns who came the evening he died said that she thought the grace of God was all around me. And so, I believe, it is."

LISA BOGART won the 2010 Guideposts Writers Workshop, and her articles have appeared in *Guideposts* and *Angels on Earth*. She lives with her husband in San Rafael, California, and works three days a week at Piedmont Yarn in Oakland. There she gets to share her passion for yarn and handicraft with all kinds of lovely knitters. Lisa is an everyday knitter, working on many different projects for family and friends and charities. She loves the quiet alone time that knitting offers, as well as hanging out with her friends in one of three weekly knit circles.

JEFF CHU of Brooklyn, New York, spent much of the past year on the road traveling to meet with readers following the publication of his first book, *Does Jesus Really Love Me?* Spending so much time away from home has sent him back into the pages of John Bunyan's *The Pilgrim's Progress*, which remains a literary and spiritual touchstone for him. As Jeff has traveled, he has been reminded of the importance of perseverance, perspective, and the fragility of the joy that can only come from clinging to things above and unseen.

"My boys, Solomon and Henry, are growing up so fast," says SABRA CIANCANELLI of Tivoli, New York. "It seems they change a little every day, finding new interests, making friends, growing out of their clothes, even smiling differently—with their adult teeth replacing baby ones and lots of gaps in between. Henry just lost a front tooth, and this morning I saw him proudly trying out his new grin in the mirror. I'd forgotten how many transitions kids go through, and watching them adjust so naturally helps me to trust and welcome change in my own life, to see each day as an opportunity for something new and wonderful to come."

"When I was younger, it took a lot to scare me—mostly because I wasn't very bright," admits MARK COLLINS of Pittsburgh, Pennsylvania. "I played hockey without a helmet, drove like my hair was on fire, even risked get-togethers with the in-laws. Nowadays I frighten easily because nothing seems settled. I realize today how my ignorance is both broad and deep. The earth shifts beneath my feet; no wonder I find myself groping for a hand from above." Among his blessed uncertainties are seminew college graduates Faith and Hope and about-to-enter college Grace, 18. "I have been assured that prayer will take away my worry, but so far that hasn't worked because then I worry I haven't prayed enough."

ERIK CRUZ of Harrison, New Jersey, was born in New York City, moved to Puerto Rico when he was three, and settled in Colorado when he was twelve. He left the Rockies behind when he got an acceptance letter to NYU: "We are contacting you because we do not have space in New York City and would like to offer you the opportunity to enter the College of Arts and Science by spending your fall semester at our campus in Florence, Italy, and then coming to the NYC campus for your spring semester." Erik received his bachelor's degree and now works as an office manager at NYU's Center for Neural Sciences. "Every day I'm thankful to God for the wonderful parents He gave me and all the opportunities I have been granted."

"One of the greatest highlights of this past year was my trip to Cuba," says PABLO DIAZ of Carmel, New York. "I had desires to visit and never thought it would be possible in my lifetime. To my excitement, permission was granted for Guideposts Outreach Ministries to share our Spanish language booklets with Cuba's Bible Commission, planting seeds of hope. This experience did not disappoint. I enjoyed the island, its people, and its rich culture. I also feel blessed that my children, Christine and Paul, had an opportunity to travel to China while my wife, Elba, enjoyed spending time with good friends in our absence. My uncle Felix, who was a great influence on my life, was called home to be with the Lord. I will miss him, but his presence, counsel, and love will always be with me."

BRIAN DOYLE is the editor of *Portland* magazine at the University of Portland in Oregon. He is the author of many books, among them the sprawling novels *Mink River* and *The Plover*. Readers absorbed by his strange head-long spiritual essays should seek out his three essay collections: *Leaping, Grace Notes,* and *The Thorny Grace of It.* He lives with his chaotic, snarling, holy, lanky family and a dog that, no kidding, some-how survived alone as a pup in the deep woods for a year, which makes him an amazing silent terror among the squirrel population of these United States, which is suddenly in rapid decline around the city of Portland.

Although blind, JANET PEREZ ECKLES helps folks see the best of life. When she's not serving as a Spanish language interpreter, she travels across the country and visits groups to deliver keynote messages and teach the path to triumph over trials. She uses her own example of victory when she lost her sight at 31. At the time, her sons, who were 3, 5, and 7, saw in her a mom with a sense of humor and a passion to overcome. Janet lives in Orlando, in the sunshine state of Florida, warmed by the love of Gene, her husband of thirty-eight years, and by the joy of her two grandchildren.

"Beauty in the breathless," writes SHAWNELLE ELIASEN of Port Byron, Illinois. "That's what I'm asking the Lord to give me the eyes to see." She and her husband, Lonny, have five sons, and it's a wild, busy life. "Soccer. Guitar. Swim team. Basketball. Bible club. We live fast-forward most of the time." Often she and Lonny divide and conquer, passing each other on the road that winds along the river, he shuttling sons in one direction, she in the other. "We just wave and blow a kiss. It's a crazy time of life, but we're blessed with many good things."

"My son Chase's life as an operatic tenor took him from Oman to Milwaukee, Wisconsin, and then to Nome, Alaska," says SHARON FOSTER of Durham, North Carolina. "My daughter, Lanea, has been hard at work growing her nonprofit, Southeast Community Resources, which helps serve the homeless and those at risk of being homeless. Work with my daughter took us to Florida, where we had the most amazing times with my father. Then after a wonderful spring with him, we lost him. We are still grieving his passing but are reminded to rejoice in all things. So we rejoice and remind ourselves that the best is yet to come."

KATIE GANSHERT is a wife and mama who loves Jesus, grace, her family, writing, and dark chocolate. She was born and raised in Iowa, where she currently resides in the town of Bettendorf with her husband, Ryan, their young son, Brogan, and goofy black Labrador, Bubba. When Katie isn't busy plotting her next novel, she's usually filling out paperwork for their adoption and dreaming about the day they get to bring home their daughter, who's from the Republic of the Congo. Even in the midst of the long wait, God continues to show Katie that with Him joy is never lost.

"My most satisfying joys this year are about relationships," writes JULIE GARMON of Monroe, Georgia. "My husband and I still have porch parties every morning, sharing the first few minutes of the day together, rocking and talking. On Mother's Day, my son Thomas taught me to download music, so, rain or shine, I walk our gravel driveway with my MP3 player, singing and praising out loud. Jamie, our oldest child, calls daily; I listen and she listens and we laugh a lot. Daughter Katie and I volunteer together every other Tuesday night at a local pregnancy resource center. Oh, the joy in serving when it comes straight from your heart!"

"With every passing year, I'm convinced more deeply that God has blessed me better than I deserve," writes BILL GIOVANNETTI of Redding, California. "I'm blessed with a healthy family and a healthy, growing church. This year we moved into our new worship center, seating one thousand people, the culmination of years of prayers and loving sacrifice of countless folks. I am so thankful to stand in the pulpit and preach the unsearchable riches of Christ to Neighborhood Church. I'm also excited over the recent release of my fourth book, *Grace Intervention*."

This has been a year of transitory joy, says EDWARD GRINNAN, editor-in-chief and vice president of *Guideposts* magazine. Besides moving the office from midtown Manhattan to downtown, his and his wife's apartment building underwent major renovations. "I lived out of boxes at work and at home. But in the end, ridding yourself of stuff you've collected for no reason is liberating." Even so, there were discoveries to be made. "Julee and I found things we thought we'd lost forever, like her high school class ring and some funny pictures of my boss, Van Varner, having dinner at our apartment when I first started at *Guideposts*." Their dog, Millie, might not agree. "One night she was whimpering and moping and we couldn't figure out why, until we realized that the painters had moved all of her toys and bones. Change is challenging, even for an easygoing golden retriever."

RICK HAMLIN of New York City recently celebrated his thirtieth year of working on staff for *Guideposts* magazine. "We were moving offices and I had to clean out some files, so I started looking back at some of the *Daily Guideposts* devotions I'd written. I sat there reading for much longer than I expected. What a record of the past, the early days of Carol's and my marriage, the birth of the kids, their growing up, various health crises, the milestones. I couldn't help but see how God has been present through the years." Their sons, William and Tim, are in their twenties and often travel for work. "We're thrilled to see them when they're home, and yet we also enjoy the silence when they're gone."

CARLA HENDRICKS's husband, Anthony, leads the Conway campus of Mosaic Church in central Arkansas, where Carla coleads the women's ministry, teaches in children's ministry, and manages the church's social-media sites. Carla has dedicated her life to her husband and four children, Kalin, Christian, Joelle, and Jada, and is an orphan advocate. She serves the CALL, which trains foster and adoptive parents, and the Christian Alliance for Orphans, which works to inspire, equip, and connect Christians around the country to care for orphans domestically and internationally. Carla is affected personally by adoption, having adopted both Christian and Joelle.

"Each morning, cup of coffee in hand, I stand on my back deck in Elizabeth, Colorado, and watch God's glorious sunrise," says KIM HENRY. "Then I retreat to my comfy study chair for an hour or two of quiet time with Him. This is a far cry from when I fast and furiously juggled raising three children with a twenty-five-year career as a litigation attorney and corporate executive. My husband and I now live with two Australian shepherds, and I write, take walks, bike, work out, enjoy friendships, and try to find the best way I can serve God."

"It's been a year of milestones," says JIM HINCH of San Jose, California. "Frances, 6, lost two teeth, started kindergarten, and learned to read. Benjamin, 3, dispensed with the last vestiges of babyhood. Good-bye crib, diapers, and stroller! We only (sort of) miss having a very little one in the house. Mostly we're excited to move into the big-kid phase of family life. This past year Kate and I took the kids backpacking in the Sierra Nevada, on a road trip to Seattle, and on multiple trips to Los Angeles and San Francisco. They're game for everything. We do our best to be faithful, knowing God always is."

"Sometimes," says JEFF JAPINGA, who lives in Holland, Michigan, with his wife, Lynn, "life's greatest joys come not through one's own deeds but through the achievements of those people with whom you've had some influence behind the scenes. That's why it's still fun to be stopped by people wanting to talk about that four-day *Jeopardy!* winning streak our son, Mark, had in 2013. Our daughter, Annie, graduates from college this year—wow, that time went by fast! And in my work as a seminary dean, I find no greater joy than to read the names of students at commencement and remember what I've done to help each one get to that point. Of course, there's also my lifelong devotion to the Chicago Cubs. Could this finally be the year they win the World Series? Now that would really be news of great joy!"

Celebrating a year filled with joy was easy for ASHLEY KAPPEL of Birmingham, Alabama. She welcomed her darling, beloved daughter, Olivia. While Colby, her golden retriever, is still wary of the new addition, he is happy that she is now dropping scraps on the floor for him to enjoy. Ashley volunteers at the zoo, works as a food writer, and savors every moment with her sweet husband, Brian, and their daughter.

"This year we baptized our second little girl, Ella Grace," says BROCK KIDD of Nashville, Tennessee. "As my wife, Corinne, my 13-year-old son, Harrison, and our sweet Mary Katherine, almost 2, stood in the church chancel, the importance of God's presence in our lives had never been clearer. When my father stepped forward to conduct the sacraments, Mary Katherine leaned over and planted a kiss on Ella Grace's cheek, causing the congregation to laugh. *How can life get any better than this?* I thought. Career-wise, I'm fortunate to be able to say I still feel the excitement every day in the investment business as if it were my first."

"When David decided to retire from the ministry after over three decades at the same Nashville, Tennessee, church," writes PAM KIDD, "my biggest surprise was gaining a new husband! Suddenly, I had someone to sit by in church. I no longer had to go to funerals alone and got to stay long enough at weddings to eat cake. Now there's time for a second cup of coffee in the mornings and long walks at noon. Our trips to Zimbabwe, where our other family continues to embrace AIDS orphans, are less hurried. We enjoy our children, Brock and Keri, and their families more than ever, and David is always ready to pitch in with dinners, parties, and everyday chores. When I look back on that scary time of transition, I was one of little faith. After officially working for God through all those years, it's great to realize that God never, ever stops working for us."

Attending to first her mother-in-law and then her father a few months later on their final journeys in this life has prodded PATTY KIRK of Westville, Oklahoma, to seek God in unusual places—sickness and death, grief and aging. What a surprise to discover joy even in these dark alleys! Now with both daughters in college and no aging parents to take care of, Patty has more time for her own pursuits. She has expanded her vegetable garden, adding a table with an umbrella and a rabbit-proof fence; rediscovered her love of sewing and playing piano; and is at work on her first novel.

"After thirty years away, my husband, Terry, and I are moving 'home' to the Pacific Northwest to the small town in north Idaho where we met in high school," CAROL KNAPP writes. "Our picture windows overlook a pretty valley with forest and a meandering river, and Gold Cup Mountain beyond. We will be near our mothers to give care. We will have more travel time to visit grandchildren (number eighteen arrives this summer!). The campgrounds, we hope, will see our tent, the highways Terry's motorcycle, and the lakes our canoe. Terry's vision is to start DIY (Do-It-Yourself) Academy to teach teens how to use tools and fix things. I intend to inhabit space in front of our inspiring view and write great stuff!'"

CAROL KUYKENDALL of Boulder, Colorado, writes, "A 'Summer Sibling Celebration' was a highlight of my year as my sister, two brothers, and our spouses gathered in Grand Teton National Park, where we used to vacation as children. We picnicked and watched the sunset on the shore of Jackson Lake, layering a vivid new memory on top of our childhood ones. My husband, Lynn, and I also welcomed our tenth grandchild ("the final one" according to our three children and their families). They range in age from 6 months to 11 years. Special blessings for the two of us who have survived advanced cancer and currently enjoy good health! Lynn is a hospice volunteer, and I continue to teach storytelling and lead a stories ministry in our community. God has saved some of His best for last in this season of our lives."

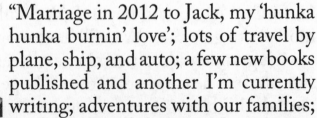

"Marriage in 2012 to Jack, my 'hunka hunka burnin' love'; lots of travel by plane, ship, and auto; a few new books published and another I'm currently writing; adventures with our families; friends who keep us laughing; daily water aerobics class in the heated pool across the street from our home; good health; and deep faith have all combined to make my sixties downright joyful," says PATRICIA LORENZ of Largo, Florida. "One of my greatest pleasures is visiting my four kids and eight grandkids in California, Wisconsin, and Ohio, and my dad and stepmom in Illinois. I thank God every day that I have all five ingredients I need for happiness: someone to love, something to do, something to hope for, faith, and laughter. Now I'm wondering if my seventies will be as blessed as my sixties. I sure hope so!"

ERIN MACPHERSON of Austin, Texas, says, "I'm starting to pay attention, to tune in, and to listen as God speaks. I hear Him in the songs of my kids. I see glimpses of Him at family dinners, on treks through the park, on afternoon bike rides. I hear His voice in the questions my children ask. And in all those things, I can't help but feel grateful for the marvelous abundance that comes from the everyday things in life. Sure, I am blessed in big ways—with three beautiful kids, a new series of books (The Christian Mama's Guide series), and a job I love—but it's often the little things that make me realize just how great God is."

ROBERTA MESSNER, who lives in a historic log cabin in Huntington, West Virginia, selected paint colors to brighten the one-hundred-plus-year-old structure she has called home sweet home for fifteen years. "I chose exuberant hues like cooking apple green, leap frog, and sun-kissed yellow," she says, and discovered that paint is the cheapest—and easiest—way to transform one's surroundings. An unexpected joy was when the owner of the paint mart discovered eight gallons of the crisp white trim paint she thought was discontinued in a back storeroom. "He let me have it at his cost, which left a little extra money to buy a wonderful hanging cupboard at the flea market." Infusing the cabin with all that color brought to mind the verse from Nehemiah 8:10 (NAS) that proclaims, "The joy of the Lord is your strength." When Roberta saw those colors on her cabin walls, her heart nearly exploded with joy.

LINDA NEUKRUG lives in Walnut Creek, California, with her two cats, Prince and Junior. Linda tries to find joy in the simple things of life like tent camping and toasted marshmallow-chocolate-and-graham-cracker s'mores roasted over a glowing fire. She has jumped into substitute teaching almost full time (Is that a contradiction?), and enjoys the unexpected experiences (and there are plenty of them when you are subbing!), like being in four or five different classrooms in a single week. A favorite quote of hers is "Life should contain something to love, some work to do, and some joy to anticipate." Linda is in the early stages of planning an RV cross-country trip for when she retires and she's aiming to find joy in the process, not just the results.

REBECCA ONDOV tells us that "over the last decade, each year has bubbled over with more joy and peace than the previous year." If you asked why, she'd share that it's correlated directly to the hour or more she invests in Bible study and prayer nearly every day. Through that time, God has led her to opportunities that have filled her life with blessings, including the collection of devotional horse books she's written (*Great Horse Stories* was released in 2014). When she's not writing, Rebecca saddles up and rides the narrow craggy Rocky Mountain trails close to her home in Hamilton, Montana, with her golden retriever, Sunrise, trotting by her side.

Originally from Indianapolis, NATALIE PERKINS now resides in New York City and is filled with joyful anticipation of her upcoming graduation from Union Theological

Seminary this May with her master of divinity degree. Prior to seminary, she enjoyed a career performing professionally and teaching. Most recently, she had the pleasure of singing and dancing in the productions of *Hairspray* with the Indianapolis and Baltimore symphony orchestras in honor of the movie's release twenty-five years ago, as well as performing for veterans with the USO Show Troupe. Along with ministering to several performance casts, Natalie ministers in churches. Her writing is featured in the Bible commentary of *Emancipation Proclamation: Forever Free,* which honors the document's 150th anniversary.

DANIEL SCHANTZ of Moberly, Missouri, and his wife, Sharon, are watching their grandchildren go out into life. Hannah, 22, is attending the University of Missouri and spent the summer studying in Spain. Silas, 19, is choosing a college. Rossetti, 17, is finishing high school, and her softball team went to state. Abram, 16, wants to be a writer and attended a writing camp. Dan and Sharon celebrated their fiftieth anniversary with a trip to London. They toured palaces and gardens and the homes of Charles Dickens and William Shakespeare, cruised the Thames River, saw the white cliffs of Dover, and worshipped in Westminster Abbey. "The trip exceeded our dreams.

It's like God took us by the hand and showed us the time of our lives. It was pure joy."

"Before one can be filled with joy, sometimes one has to empty oneself," says GAIL THORELL SCHILLING of Concord, New Hampshire, who gave up her apartment two years ago to provide house- and pet-sitting services for others in their homes. "Not only did not having my own place fund more travel, I also learned to trust God's grace in providing continuous lodging, often several places at once! As if that security wasn't joy enough, our family celebrated daughter Trina's graduation from the University of New Hampshire, in communication and speech disorders, and an immediate job offer. Within weeks, son Tom and Canay married in the Bay Area and asked me to make the cake. Now son Greg and Nikki have announced wedding plans too. My memoir, *Do Not Go Gentle. Go to Paris,* makes its debut. So much joy! I am blessed indeed."

"I'm learning that God's joy doesn't depend on circumstances," writes PENNEY SCHWAB of Copeland, Kansas. "Even though life is often chaotic and stressful, my husband, Don, and I are blessed with times of peace, laughter, and joy. I am grateful for caring, praying friends and for God's words of encouragement through the Psalms." They attended high school/college graduations for three grandsons and made frequent trips to eastern Kansas, Texas, and Colorado to see their grandchildren play basketball, ice hockey, and participate in livestock shows. Penney is the organist at her church and active in the women's group. As a lay speaker, she is privileged to be able to share Christ's love through sermons in her own and other churches several times a year.

Last year marked a kind of milestone for ELIZABETH SHERRILL of Hingham, Massachusetts, when she finally learned to love the Internet. Like most of her contemporaries, she says, she'd approached the electronic universe with trepidation. "It was only when my granddaughter Kerlin entered computer play school that I was shamed into buying my first computer." Doing research online, getting her own e-mail address, going on Facebook, Elizabeth took each step with reluctance. Then, in Germany, she opened an e-mail from her granddaughter Lindsay in Georgia. "There on my tablet was a photograph of little Taylor Ann, three hours old, taken just one hour earlier! All the frustrations, the mistakes I make wrestling with ever-changing new technology, were forgotten in the wonder of sharing this family joy four thousand miles distant but now as near as the touch of a screen." Read more from Elizabeth in her memoir *Surprised by Grace*, available on ShopGuideposts.org.

"This has truly been a joy-filled year for my family and me," says JOSHUA SUNDQUIST of Arlington, Virginia. "My dad, who has long dreamed of putting his financial skills to work for a ministry, got a job as an accountant for a large church in my area, and he, my mother, and my sister relocated nearby. I finished a draft of my next book and continue to give motivational speeches around the world. My girlfriend, Ashley, and I are still in a wonderful relationship. She persuaded me to paint my previously austere apartment and even to hang up some decorations."

"It's been a year of really appreciating family," writes MELODY BONNETTE SWANG of Mandeville, Louisiana. "Two things stand out that helped me get through the loss of my husband. First, my four children and eleven grandchildren filled my life with such love. Second was my church. Its glorious praise music and Pastor Steve's inspiring messages did so much to heal my broken heart and bind up my wounds—not to mention the caring women in my Bible study. And my family continues to grow!

Misty married a wonderful man, and we welcomed Jeff and his two children, Blake and Riley, into the fold. Kristen's husband, Paul, is head chef at a local seafood restaurant; Christopher is playing music again; and Kevin is out of the US Air Force and studying computer science. Life is good!"

"This past year, we moved from Evanston, Illinois, to Ann Arbor, Michigan," says JON SWEENEY, "which we're all enjoying immensely, although I find the abundantly stocked used bookstore much too tempting!" In addition to buying too many books, Jon's writing them. "This year I became the author of a total of more than twenty books." *The Pope Who Quit,* about the late thirteenth-century Celestine V, was recently optioned by HBO. His latest book, *When Saint Francis Saved the Church,* is available now. Jon is married and the father of three.

A former TV news reporter, syndicated newspaper columnist, radio talk show host, and public relations director, STEPHANIE THOMPSON found her favorite job opportunity at forty-one, when she became a first-time mother. "Parenting Micah has allowed me to understand God's love on a deeper level," she says. "My life these days reminds me of James 1:17, that every good gift comes from above." Stephanie and her husband, Michael, live in Edmond, Oklahoma, with their daughter, a pug named Princess, a Shih Tzu-terrier mix named Missy, and Mr. Whiskers, the stray who stayed, a long-haired tuxedo cat. Reared a city girl, Stephanie enjoys their rural residence. "We've seen deer, raccoons, opossums, armadillos, hawks, rabbits, coyotes, and even a cougar from our big picture window that looks out into the backyard. A couple of years ago, we had an up-close encounter with a baby bobcat that was treed in the oak across the street. When he began mewing frantically for his mother, we decided to go indoors."

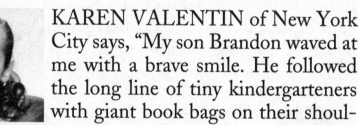

KAREN VALENTIN of New York City says, "My son Brandon waved at me with a brave smile. He followed the long line of tiny kindergarteners with giant book bags on their shoulders. It was his first day of school. As the teacher led them toward their classroom, that line felt like a severed umbilical cord. It's a season of letting go. I've had enough practice this year to see me through my little boy's first rite of passage. I've let go of anger, control, fears, excuses, expectations, finances—all those areas that I held on to with a tight grip. Letting go is unsettling, but there's a tremendous freedom in it as well. It's out of my hands. I can just watch and see what God does with it now. Brandon runs to me when I meet him at the end of the day. 'How was it?' I ask. My heart is reassured once again: 'It was great!' he says."

"This year has been a blending of the generations," says SCOTT WALKER of Macon, Georgia. "My mother is 91 and now lives with Beth and me. She is ever youthful while adjusting to inevitable physical change. She is teaching me to grow old with grace and beauty. All of our children were home for Christmas. Drew practices law in Columbia, South Carolina, and his wife, Katie Alice, is truly our new daughter. Luke and Jodi both live in Washington, DC, and enjoy young adulthood. And as for our three golden retrievers—Muffy, Bear, and Buddy—they keep me laughing and sane. They never have a bad day."

"My life in retirement continues to be involved with both the beginning and the end of life," writes BRIGITTE WEEKS of New York City. "My five grandchildren provide a lively lesson on how to manage growing up. The oldest is now 11 and the youngest 6. They cheerfully play intricate video games with friends on the other side of the Atlantic or in the same room. My work-shifts at a hospice bring me close to patients at the end of life. I am constantly struck by the calm and fortitude of those I meet. Some just want a prayer—I've committed a few to memory so as not to be struck dumb. Others are eager to chat about their diverse lives, from opera singer to housewife. And the dedication of the full-time staff is an ongoing inspiration to me."

MARION BOND WEST of Watkinsville, Georgia, writes, "Joy seemed somewhat elusive for most of the year. If possible, I would have chased her down, held on, made her mine. Forcefully. Instead, I gradually learned to sit on the side of the bathtub early each morning, still in my pajamas. I allowed my fifteen-year-old cat, Girl Friend, to drink from the dripping tub faucet as she's come to expect. Then I filled little Gracie's pink dish with cat food. Speaking softly, I told them (and perhaps myself), 'Sweet Girl Friend, no hurry. Drink all you want. Relax. Grace Face, there's nothing to be afraid of today. You're safe, little one.' They purr loudly, seemingly in rhythm. The first rays of amber light slip into the bathroom. Joy comes and sits herself down beside me. So does my Father. I smile. I love it when joy surprises me early in the morning."

"This year," writes ASHLEY WIERSMA, "I finally found my sweet spot in terms of the number of freelance projects I can say yes to, while still prizing motherhood as my primary role. And it's a gratifying place to be." In the past two years, she's completed three book projects—*Sons and Daughters,* a collaboration with Pastor Brady Boyd of New Life Church in Colorado Springs; *Unseen,* a collaboration with Pastor Jack Graham in the Dallas area; and *Empowered to Serve,* a youth-advocacy curriculum—and a video curriculum with Pastor Bill Hybels, based on his best-selling classic *Too Busy Not to Pray.* She and her husband, Perry, enjoy working from home in Monument, Colorado, and including daughter, Prisca, now 3, in the flow of their daily life.

SCRIPTURE REFERENCE INDEX

Scripture Reference Index

CONNECT WITH OURPRAYER MINISTRY

OurPrayer, Guideposts' prayer network, prays daily by name and need for each of the requests we receive.

To request prayer:

- Visit OurPrayer.org
- Post on Facebook.com/OurPrayer
- Call the prayer line (203) 778-8063 between 7:00 AM and 10:00 PM (Eastern time zone), Monday through Friday
- Write to OurPrayer, PO Box 5813, Harlan, Iowa 51593-1313
- Fax prayer requests to (203) 749-0266

To learn how you can volunteer to pray for others:

- Visit OurPrayerVolunteer.org

We also invite you to join us when we observe our annual:

- Good Friday Day of Prayer, April 3, 2015, OurPrayerGoodFriday.org
- Thanksgiving Day of Prayer, November 23, 2015, OurPrayerThanksgiving.org

A NOTE FROM THE EDITORS

We hope you enjoy *Daily Guideposts 2015*, created by the Books and Inspirational Media Division of Guideposts, a nonprofit organization that touches millions of lives every day through products and services that inspire, encourage, help you grow in your faith, and celebrate God's love in every aspect of your daily life.

Thank you for making a difference with your purchase of this book, which helps fund our many outreach programs to military personnel, prisons, hospitals, nursing homes, and educational institutions. To learn more, visit GuidepostsFoundation.org.

We also maintain many useful and uplifting online resources. Visit Guideposts.org to read true stories of hope and inspiration, access OurPrayer network, sign up for free newsletters, download free e-books, join our Facebook community at Facebook.com/DailyGuideposts, and follow our stimulating blogs. To delve more deeply into *Daily Guideposts*, visit DailyGuideposts.org/DGP2015.

You may purchase the 2016 edition of *Daily Guideposts* anytime after July 2015. To order, visit ShopGuideposts.org, call (800) 932-2145, or write to Guideposts, PO Box 5815, Harlan, Iowa 51593.